All-in-One CCIE R&S 400-101 Written Study Guide

by
Paul Adam
April 4th, 2015 (2nd Edition)

Contents at a Glance

Part 1 Network Principles
Chapter 1: Network Theory
Chapter 2: Network Implementation and operation
Chapter 3: Network Troubleshooting

Part 2 Layer 2 Technologies
Chapter 4: LAN Switching Technologies
Chapter 5: Layer 2 Multicast
Chapter 6: Layer 2 WAN Circuit Technologies

Part 3 Layer 3 Technologies
Chapter 7: Addressing Technologies
Chapter 8: Layer 2 Multicast
Chapter 9: Fundamental Routing Concepts
Chapter 10: RIPv2 (IPv4/IPv6)
Chapter 11: EIGRP (IPv4/IPv6)
Chapter 12: OSPF (v2, v3)
Chapter 13: BGP
Chapter 14: ISIS (IPv4/IPv6)

Part 4 VPN Technologies
Chapter 15: Tunneling
Chapter 16: Encryption

Part 5 Infrastructure Security
Chapter 17: Device Security
Chapter 18: Network Security

Part 6 Infrastructure Services
Chapter 19: System Management
Chapter 20: Quality of Service
Chapter 21: Network Services
Chapter 22: Network Optimization

Table of Contents

Preface
What this study guide covers
How to use this study guide
What's available on the CCIEin8Weeks website
Part 1 Network Principles
    Chapter 1: Network Theory
    Describe basic software architecture differences between IOS and IOS XE
    Table 1-1. shows functions of Cisco IOS XE Software Subpackages
    Control plane and Forwarding plane
    Table 1-2. compares classic IOS ("IOS) and IOS XE architectures
    Impact to troubleshooting and performances
    Table 1-3. shows comparison of troubleshooting differences between classic IOS ("IOS) and IOS XE
    Identify Cisco express forwarding concepts
    RIB, FIB, LFIB, Adjacency table
    Routing Information Base (RIB)
    Forwarding Information Base (FIB)
    Label Information Base (LIB)
    Adjacency Tables
    Load balancing Hash
    Per-Destination load balancing
    Per-Packet load balancing
    Polarization concept and avoidance
    Explain general network challenges
    Unicast flooding
    Asymmetric Routing
    Spanning-Tree Protocol Topology Changes
    Forwarding Table Overflow
    Out of order packets
    Impact of micro burst
    Explain IP operations
    ICMP unreachable, redirect
    IPv4 options, IPv6 extension headers
    Table 1-5. shows IP header options and their description
    Table 1-6. IPv6 Extension Headers and their Recommended Order in a Packet
    IPv4 and IPv6 fragmentation
    TTL

IP MTU
Explain TCP operations
IPv4 and IPv6 PMTU
Latency
Windowing
Bandwidth delay product
Global synchronization
Options
Options have up to three fields:
Explain UDP operations
Starvation
Latency
RTP/RTCP concepts
Exam Essentials
Chapter 2: Network Implementation and Operation
Evaluate proposed changes to a network
Changes to routing protocol parameters
Migrate parts of a network to IPv6
Routing protocol migration
Further Reading
Adding multicast support
Further Reading
Migrate spanning tree protocol
PVST+ to MST Migration
STP to RSTP (802.1w) or MSTP (802.1s)
Configuration Steps:
Further Reading
Evaluate impact of new traffic on existing QoS design
Exam Essentials
Chapter 3: Network Troubleshooting
Use IOS troubleshooting tools
Further Reading
Debug, conditional debug
Ping, traceroute with extended options
Further Reading
Embedded packet capture
Further Reading
Performance monitor
Further Reading
Apply troubleshooting methodologies
Further Reading
Interpret packet capture
Using Wireshark trace analyzer

- Further Reading
- Using IOS embedded packet capture
- Basic EPC Configuration
- Further Reading
- Exam Essentials

Part 2 Layer 2 Technologies
- Chapter 4: LAN Switching Technologies
- Implement and troubleshoot switch administration
- Managing MAC address table
- Further Reading
- Errdisable recovery
- Further Reading
- L2 MTU
- Implement and troubleshoot layer 2 protocols
- CDP, LLDP
- Further Reading
- UDLD
- Further Reading
- Implement and troubleshoot VLAN
- Access ports
- VLAN database
- Normal, extended VLAN, voice VLAN
- Table 4-1, shows various default VLANs and the respective L2 protocols
- Implement and troubleshoot trunking
- VTPv1, VTPv2, VTPv3, VTP pruning
- Table 4-2, summaries different VTP versions and their limitations
- Dot1Q
- Native VLAN
- Manual pruning
- Implement and troubleshoot EtherChannel
- Further Reading
- LACP, PAgP, manual
- Further Reading
- Layer 2, layer 3, Load-balancing
- Table 4-3, shows various platforms and the load balancing options that are available
- Further Reading
- Etherchannel misconfiguration guard
- Implement and troubleshoot spanning-tree
- Further Reading
- PVST+/RPVST+/MST
- Table 4-4, summarizes different STP versions and their limitations
- Further Reading

Switch priority, port priority, path cost, STP timers
Further Reading
Port Fast, BPDUguard, BPDUfilter
Loop Guard, Root Guard
Further Reading
Implement and troubleshoot other LAN switching technologies
SPAN, RSPAN, ERSPAN
Further Reading
Describe chassis virtualization and aggregation technologies
Multi-chassis
Further Reading
VSS concepts
Alternative to STP
Further Reading
StackWise
Table 4-5. shows rules and their respective priority order
Excluding specific platform implementation
Describe spanning-tree concepts
Further Reading
Compatibility between MST and RSTP
Further Reading
STP dispute, STP bridge assurance
Further Reading
Exam Essentials
Chapter 5. Layer 2 Multicast
Implement and troubleshoot IGMP
Further Reading
IGMPv1, IGMPv2, IGMPv3
Table 5-1. shows IGMPv2 intervals and their default values
Further Reading
IGMP Snooping
IGMP Querier
Further Reading
IGMP Filter
Further Reading
IGMP proxy
Further Reading
Explain MLD
Explain PIM Snooping
Further Reading
Exam Essentials
Chapter 6: Layer 2 WAN Circuit Technologies
Implement and troubleshoot HDLC

Implement and troubleshoot PPP
Authentication (PAP, CHAP)
PPPoE
MLPPP
Describe WAN rate-based Ethernet circuits
Further Reading
Metro and WAN Ethernet topologies
Table 6-1. shows breakdown of metro ethernet services into port or VLAN based categories
Use of rate-limited WAN Ethernet services
Ethernet Private Line (EPL)
Ethernet Virtual Private Line (EVPL)
Further Reading
Exam Essentials

Part 3 Layer 3 Technologies
    Chapter 7: Addressing Technologies
    Address types, VLSM
    Further Reading
    ARP
    Further Reading
    Identify, implement and troubleshoot IPv6 addressing and subnetting
    Unicast, multicast
    Table 7-1. shows various IPv6 address types and respective formats
    Further Reading
    EUI-64
    ND, RS/RA
    Router Solicitation
    Further Reading
    Autoconfig/SLAAC, temporary addresses (RFC 4941)
    Global prefix configuration feature
    Further Reading
    DHCP protocol operations
    DHCP Server Function
    Table 7-2. shows various DHCP messages and their intended use
    Client Function
    Further Reading
    SLAAC/DHCPv6 interaction
    Stateful, Stateless DHCPv6
    DHCPv6 prefix delegation
    Exam Essentials
    Chapter 8: Layer 3 Multicast
    Troubleshoot reverse path forwarding
    RPF failure

RPF failure with tunnel interface
Further Reading
Implement and troubleshoot IPv4 protocol independent multicast
PIM dense mode, sparse mode, sparse-dense mode
Static RP, auto-RP, BSR
Further Reading
Bidirectional PIM
Further Reading
Source-specific multicast
Further Reading
Group to RP mapping
Table 8-1. shows various mechanisms for disseminating RP information
Further Reading
Multicast boundary
Further Reading
Implement and troubleshoot multicast source discovery protocol
Intra-domain MSDP (anycast RP)
SA filter
Further Reading
Describe IPv6 multicast
IPv6 multicast addresses
Table 8-2. shows IPv6 multicast address format
PIMv6
Exam Essentials
Chapter 9: Fundamental Routing Concepts
Implement and troubleshoot static routing
Implement and troubleshoot default routing
Compare routing protocol types
Distance vector
Further Reading
Link state
Further Reading
Path vector
Implement, optimize and troubleshoot administrative distance
Implement and troubleshoot passive interface
Implement and troubleshoot VRF lite
Implement, optimize and troubleshoot filtering with any routing protocol
Implement, optimize and troubleshoot redistribution between any routing protocol
Distance Vector Protocols
Link State Protocols
Further Reading
Implement, optimize and troubleshoot manual and auto summarization with any routing protocol

Implement, optimize and troubleshoot policy-based routing
Further Reading
Identify and troubleshoot sub-optimal routing
Implement and troubleshoot bidirectional forwarding detection
Implement and troubleshoot loop prevention mechanisms
Route tagging, filtering
Implement and troubleshoot routing protocol authentication
MD5
OSPF Authentication
RIP and EIGRP
Further Reading
Key-chain
EIGRP HMAC SHA2-256 bit
Configuration Steps
Further Reading
OSPFv2 SHA1-196bit
OSPFv3 IPsec authentication
Further Reading
Exam Essentials
Chapter 10: RIPv2 (IPv4/IPv6)
Implement and troubleshoot RIPv2
Further Reading
Describe RIPv6 (RIPng)
Further Reading
Exam Essentials
Chapter 11: EIGRP (IPv4/IPv6)
Describe packet types
Packet types (hello, query, update, and such)
Further Reading
Route types (internal, external)
Implement and troubleshoot neighbor relationship
Multicast, unicast EIGRP peering
Further Reading
OTP point-to-point peering
OTP route-reflector peering
OTP multiple service providers scenario
Further Reading
Implement and troubleshoot loop free path selection
RD, FD, FC, successor, feasible successor
Further Reading
Classic metric
Wide metric
Implement and troubleshoot operations

Topology table, update, query, active, passive
Further Reading
Stuck in active
Graceful shutdown
Implement and troubleshoot EIGRP stub
Stub
Leak-map
Further Reading
Implement and troubleshoot load-balancing
Equal-cost
Unequal-cost
Add-path
Implement EIGRP (multi-address) named mode
Types of families
IPv4 address-family
IPv6 address-family
Implement, troubleshoot and optimize EIGRP convergence and scalability
Describe fast convergence requirements
Further Reading
Control query boundaries
IP FRR/fast reroute (single hop)
Summary leak-map and metric
Exam Essentials
Chapter 12: OSPF (v2 and v3)
Describe packet types
LSA types (1, 2, 3, 4, 5, 7, 9)
Table 12-1 summarizes various LSA types and their description
Table 12-2, shows various OSPF network types and traffic that are allowed
Route types (N1, N2, E1, E2)
Implement and troubleshoot neighbor relationship
Further Reading
Implement and troubleshoot OSPFv3 address-family support
Configuration Steps
Verification Steps
Further Reading
IPv4/v6 address-family
Implement and troubleshoot network types, area types and router types
Point-to-point, multipoint, broadcast, non-broadcast
Point-to-Point Sub-interfaces
Point-to-Multipoint Interfaces
Broadcast Interfaces
Table 12-3, shows the various OSPF network types and their associated default set of timers

LSA types, area type: backbone, normal, transit, stub, NSSA, totally stub
Table 12-4, shows the differences between the types of the OSPF areas.
Internal router, ABR, ASBR
Virtual link
Implement and troubleshoot path preference
Further Reading
Implement and troubleshoot operations
General operations
Further Reading
Graceful shutdown
Generic TTL Security Mechanism (GTSM)
Further Reading
Implement, troubleshoot and optimize OSPF convergence and scalability
Metrics
LSA throttling, SPF tuning, fast hello
LSA propagation control (area types, ISPF)
IP FRR/fast reroute (single and multi hop)
Further Reading
OSPFv3 prefix suppression
Further Reading
Exam Essentials
Chapter 13: BGP
Describe, implement and troubleshoot peer relationships
Peer-group, template
Further Reading
Active, passive
States, timers
Dynamic neighbors
Implement and troubleshoot IBGP and EBGP
EBGP, IBGP
4-bytes AS number
Private AS
Explain attributes and best-path selection
Further Reading
Implement, optimize and troubleshoot routing policies
Attribute manipulation
BGP Path Attributes
Next-Hop Attribute
Local Preference Attribute
Origin Attribute
AS_Path Attribute
MED Attribute
Community Attribute

Atomic Aggregate and Aggregator Attributes
Table 13-1. shows BGP attributes and the category they belong to
Conditional advertisement
Outbound route filtering
Communities, extended communities
Multi-homing
Implement and troubleshoot scalability
Route-reflector, cluster
Confederations
Further Reading
Aggregation, AS set
Implement and troubleshoot multiprotocol BGP
IPv4, IPv6, VPN address-family
Further Reading
Implement and troubleshoot AS path manipulations
Local AS, allow AS in, remove private AS
Prepend
Regexp
Table 13-2. shows various regular expressions and their description
Further Reading
Implement and troubleshoot other features
Multipath
BGP synchronization
Soft reconfiguration, route refresh
Describe BGP fast convergence features
Prefix independent convergence
Add-path
Next-hop address tracking
Exam Essentials
Chapter 14: ISIS (IPv4/IPv6)
Describe basic ISIS network
Single area, Single topology
Describe neighbor relationship
Table 14-1. describes the configuration steps to enable ISIS
Further Reading
Describe network types, levels and router types
NSAP addressing
Further Reading
Point-to-point, broadcast
Describe operations
Describe optimization features
Metrics, wide metric
Exam Essentials

Part 4 VPN Technologies
    Chapter 15: Tunneling
        Implement and troubleshoot MPLS operations
        Label stack, LSR, LSP
        Further Reading
        LDP
        Further Reading
        MPLS ping, MPLS traceroute
        Further Reading
        Implement and troubleshoot basic MPLS L3VPN
        L3VPN, CE, PE, P
        Extranet (route leaking)
        Further Reading
        Implement and troubleshoot encapsulation
        GRE
        Dynamic GRE
        LISP encapsulation principles supporting EIGRP OTP
        Further Reading
        Implement and troubleshoot DMVPN (single hub)
        NHRP
        Further Reading
        DMVPN with IPsec using pre-shared key
        QoS profile
        Pre-classify
        Further Reading
        Describe IPv6 tunneling techniques
        6in4, 6to4
        Further Reading
        ISATAP
        6RD
        Further Reading
        6VPE
        Further Reading
        Describe basic layer 2 VPN —wireline
        L2TPv3 general principles
        Further Reading
        ATOM general principles
        Further Reading
        Describe basic L2VPN — LAN services
        MPLS-VPLS general principles
        Further Reading
        OTV general principles
        Table 15-1 shows the OTV entities/roles and their description

- Further Reading
- Exam Essentials
- Chapter 16: Encryption
- Implement and troubleshoot IPsec with pre-shared key
- IPv4 site to IPv4 site
- Further Reading
- IPv6 in IPv4 tunnels
- Further Reading
- Virtual tunneling Interface (VTI)
- Further Reading
- Describe GET VPN
- Group Member
- Key Server
- Further Reading
- Exam Essentials

Part 5 Infrastructure Security
- Chapter 17: Device Security
- Implement and troubleshoot IOS AAA using local database
- Further Reading
- Implement and troubleshoot device access control
- Lines (VTY, AUX, Console)
- Further Reading
- SNMP
- Further Reading
- Management plane protection
- Further Reading
- Password encryption
- Further Reading
- Implement and troubleshoot control plane policing
- Further Reading
- Describe device security using IOS AAA with TACACS+ and RADIUS
- AAA with TACACS+ and RADIUS
- Local privilege authorization fallback
- Exam Essentials
- Chapter 18: Network Security
- Implement and troubleshoot switch security features
- VACL, PACL
- Further Reading
- Stormcontrol
- DHCP snooping
- IP source-guard
- Further Reading
- Dynamic ARP inspection

- Port-security
- Private VLAN
- Implement and troubleshoot router security features
- IPv4 access control lists (standard, extended, time-based)
- Further Reading
- IPv6 traffic filter
- Further Reading
- Unicast reverse path forwarding
- Implement and troubleshoot IPv6 first hop security
- RA guard
- Further Reading
- DHCP guard
- Binding table
- Device tracking
- ND inspection/snooping
- Source guard
- PACL
- Describe 802.1x
- 802.1x, EAP, RADIUS
- MAC authentication bypass
- Further Reading
- Exam Essentials

Part 6 Infrastructure Services
- Chapter 19: System Management
- Implement and troubleshoot device management
- Console and VTY
- Telnet, HTTP, HTTPS, SSH, SCP
- FTP, TFTP
- Implement and troubleshoot SNMP
- SNMP v2c, v3
- Implement and troubleshoot logging
- Local logging, syslog, debug, conditional debug
- Further Reading
- Timestamp
- Exam Essentials
- Chapter 20: Quality of Service
- Implement and troubleshoot end-to-end QoS
- CoS and DSCP mapping
- Further Reading
- Implement, optimize and troubleshoot QoS using MQC
- Classification
- Network based application recognition (NBAR)
- Policing, shaping

Further Reading
Congestion management (queuing)
HQoS, sub-rate ethernet link
Congestion avoidance (WRED)
Further Reading
Describe layer 2 QoS
Further Reading
Queuing, scheduling
Exam Essentials
Chapter 21. Network Services
Implement and troubleshoot first-hop redundancy protocols
HSRP, GLBP, VRRP
Further Reading
Redundancy using IPv6 RS/RA
Further Reading
Implement and troubleshoot network time protocol
Further Reading
NTP Authentication
Implement and troubleshoot IPv4 and IPv6 DHCP
DHCP client, IOS DHCP server, DHCP relay
Further Reading
DHCP options
DHCP protocol operations
Further Reading
SLAAC/DHCPv6 interaction
DHCPv6 prefix delegation
Further Reading
Implement and troubleshoot IPv4 network address translation
Static NAT, dynamic NAT, policy-based NAT, PAT
Further Reading
NAT ALG
Further Reading
Describe IPv6 network address translation
NAT64
Further Reading
NPTv6
Further Reading
Exam Essentials
Chapter 22: Network Optimization
Implement and troubleshoot IP SLA
ICMP, UDP, Jitter, VoIP
Further Reading
Implement and troubleshoot tracking object

Tracking object, tracking list
Further Reading
Tracking different entities (e.g. interfaces, routes, IPSLA, and such)
Implement and troubleshoot Netflow
Netflow v5, v9
Table 22-1. describes various NetFlow versions and their description
Further Reading
Export (configuration only)
Further Reading
Implement and troubleshoot embedded event manager
EEM policy using applet
Further Reading
Identify performance routing (PfR)
Further Reading
Basic load balancing
Further Reading
Voice optimization
Delay
Jitter
Packet Loss
Mean Opinion Score (MOS)
Further Reading
Exam Essentials

Preface

Congratulations! You have taken your first step towards passing the CCIE R&S 400-101 written exam. Given the appreciation and strong endorsement that I have received for my CCIE 400-101 V5 Study Guide (1st edition), I thought it was time to take a step further by revising it and add even more value for all of you counting on it.

This book is dedicated to *all those souls who will never settle for less than they can be, do, share, and give!*

What this study guide covers

As you may already have noticed on the "Contents at a Glance" page that this guide has been formatted around the Cisco's official CCIE 400-101 exam topics or curriculum. So as you read through parts and chapters, you know exactly where you're within your learning journey.

All contents are carefully covered in enough details however still trimmed to exactly what's necessary to pass the exam. The result of this approach is that you have 250 odd pages on your hands (as opposed to 700 to 1,400 pages long reference manuals!). Each exam topic has "Further Reading" section, which you can refer to if you are looking for more in-depth details. We have done the research for you.

How to use this study guide

This guide is for everyone who's studying for CCIE R&S written 400-101 exam, regardless if this is your first time sitting for a CCIE written exam or you're a pro who's recertifying.

I strongly suggest to take a methodical approach for exam preparation, i.e. start with a target date when you would like to sit for the actual exam and then work backwards to see what kind of study plan would work for you. I believe you can cover the entire contents within eight weeks including the practice questions (refer to website).

If you're totally in a crunch and consider yourself an advanced learner, you could try your luck by skimming through the "Exam Essentials" sections for each chapter- I guarantee you that you will be better prepared to tackle the exam with it than without it!

What's available on the CCIEin8Weeks website

CCIEin8Weeks.com carries the extras that go hand in hand with this study guide to further ensure your exam success!

Website includes:
- 7 Practice Exams (one for each section as per official curriculum), One final exam
- 4 Study Plans, to help you track your progress or help you come up with your own plan

- CCIE Exam community forum, to help you interact with others, share knowledge, find study partners etc.
- Last but not least, this study guide in printable PDF format

Part 1 Network Principles

Chapter 1: Network Theory
Chapter 2: Network Implementation and Operation
Chapter 3: Network Troubleshooting

Chapter 1: Network Theory

This chapter covers the following exam topics from Cisco's official 400-101 (v5) written exam curriculum.

- Basic software architecture differences between classic IOS and IOS XE
- Cisco Express Forwarding (CEF)
- General network challenges (such as unicast flooding, out of order packets, asymmetric routing and impact of microbursts)
- IP operations (such as ICMP unreachable/redirect, IPv4 options, IPv6 extension headers, IPv4/v6 fragmentation, TTL, IP MTU)
- TCP operations (IPv4/IPv6 PMTU, Maximum Segment Size-MSS, Latency, Windowing, BW delay product, global synchronization)
- UDP operations (TCP starvation / UDP dominance, latency, RTP/RTCP concepts)

Chapter 1: Network Theory

Describe basic software architecture differences between IOS and IOS XE

Cisco classic IOS has always had a monolithic software architecture, which means that it is both downloaded and run as a single binary image where all processes share the same memory address space. Monolithic and non-modular architecture leads to no memory protection between processes, as a result software defects in classic IOS code can potentially corrupt data used by other processes. It also has a run to completion scheduler, which means that the kernel does not preempt a running process — the process must make a kernel call before other processes can be scheduled and get a chance to run.

In all variations of classic Cisco IOS, packet routing and forwarding (switching) are distinct functions. Routing and other protocols run as IOS processes and contribute to the formation of Routing Information Base (RIB). This is processed to generate the final IP forwarding table (FIB, Forwarding Information Base), which is used by the forwarding function of the router. On router platforms with software-based forwarding (e.g., Cisco 7200 or Cisco ISR G2) most traffic handling is done at interrupt level using Cisco Express Forwarding (CEF). This helps avoid process context switching that would need to be done otherwise to forward packets. Routing functions such as OSPF or BGP run at the process level. In routers with hardware-based forwarding, such as the Cisco ASR1000 (which runs IOS XE), ASR9000 or CRS-1 or NCS series (which run IOS XR), IOS computes the FIB in software running on route processor (RP) hardware (typically x86 CPUs) and loads it into the forwarding hardware (such as an ASIC or a network processor), which performs the actual packet forwarding function.

The IOS XE is a POSIX based environment along with various open source software for the common drivers, tools and utilities needed to manage the system. In addition to the standard set of off-the-shelf drivers, IOS XE also includes a set of Cisco specific drivers and associated chassis/platform management modules.

On top of the base operating system (Linux) and drivers, IOS XE provides a comprehensive set of infrastructure modules which define how software is installed, how processes are started and sequenced, how high-availability (HA) and software upgrades are performed. The core application that runs on top of this new infrastructure is the IOS feature set in the form of IOS daemon (IOSd). By running Cisco IOS, products reap the benefits of an extensive feature set for routing and switching platforms that has been built into IOS over last two decades.

Finally, the evolved IOS architecture is specifically designed to accommodate other applications outside of IOS blob or IOSd. These applications can be upgraded or restarted independently of IOSd. If an application does require services from IOS, it can integrate with IOS through a set of client libraries called service points. These service points generically extend IOS information and services to outside applications such that these services are not replicated or managed separately. IOS XE is not a new network "OS" per se, it is rather an incarnation of classic IOS ("IOS") where role of classic IOS is reduced to an application running on top of a Linux kernel. This approach also allows building routing/switching platforms that use a variety of data plane hardware (ASICs or network processors such as Cisco's QFP or CPP) by way of the abstraction provided between control and data planes.

Each Cisco IOS XE Software subpackage provides specific functions for the Cisco ASR 1000 Series router.

Table 1-1, shows functions of Cisco IOS XE Software Subpackages

Package	Function
RPBase	Provides the operating system software for the route processor
RPControl	Controls the control plane processes that interface between Cisco IOS Software and the rest of the platform
RPAccess	Provides software required for router access • The non-K9 version of this subpackage is included only in consolidated packages that do not have cryptographic support. • The K9 version of this subpackage includes restricted components (Secure Sockets Layer [SSL] and Secure Shell [SSH]); consolidated packages with this subpackage are subject to export controls.
RPIOS	Provides the Cisco IOS Software kernel, which is where Cisco IOS Software features are stored and run; each consolidated package has a different RPIOS subpackage
ESPBase	Provides the ESP operating system and control processes and the ESP software
SIPSPA	Provides the shared port adaptor (SPA) driver and associated field-programmable device (FPD) images
SIPBase	Controls the Session Initiation Protocol (SIP) carrier card operating system and control processes

Control plane and Forwarding plane

IOS XE allows development of data plane ASICs outside the IOS instance and have them program to a set of standard APIs which in turn enforces Control Plane and Data Plane processing separation. It achieves Control Plane / Data Plane separation through the introduction of the Forwarding and Feature Manager (FFM) and its standard interface to the Forwarding Engine Driver (FED). FFM provides a set of APIs to control plane processes. FFM programs the data plane via the FED and maintains forwarding state for the entire system. The FED is the instantiation of the hardware driver for the data plane.

Table 1-2, compares classic IOS ("IOS") and IOS XE architectures

Software Architecture	Classic IOS ("IOS")	IOS XE
Monolithic	Yes	No
Control and Data Plane separation (Software)	No	Yes
Control and Data Plane separation (Hardware)	Platforms that run classic IOS do not have clear separation of control and data plane in hardware	Platforms that run IOS XE do have clear separation of control and data plane hardware
Feature parity	All IOS versions contain a singular set of IOS features (E.g. all platforms in T train contain same features such as Cisco ISR G2 and 7200)	All IOS XE versions contain software that is specific to one or a set of platforms E.g., IOS XE running on Cisco ASR 900 contains different feature set than one running on Cisco ASR1000
Example Platforms	All software based platform Cisco ISRs (3900, 2900, 1900, 8XX), 7200 (end of life)	Cisco ISR 4K Cisco ASR1000 series (1006, 1004, 1002, 1001)

Impact to troubleshooting and performances

Significant differences in software architecture lead to significant differences in how you troubleshoot the platforms that run classic IOS versus IOS XE. We can break down those differences in few larger areas.

Table 1-3, shows comparison of troubleshooting differences between classic IOS ("IOS) and IOS XE

Troubleshooting Area	Classic IOS ("IOS")	IOS XE
Methodology	All software based platforms use single set of troubleshooting approach	Different set of show/debug platform CLIs for control and data planes
Command Line Interface (CLI) - show and debug commands	All software based platforms use single set of CLIs	Show/Debug CLIs can be specific to a given platform (e.g. ASR1000 versus ISR 4451)
Files and locations	All software based platforms use single set of rules (E.g., crash dump go to internal bootflash by default) Classic IOS image naming conventions	It can be specific to a given platform (e.g. ASR1000 versus ISR 4451) ASR1000 dumps SPA driver cashdump on harddisk: by default Newer software packages naming conventions
Level of difficulty	Straightforward, upside of software-based platforms	Complex, downside or cost of modularity i.e. clear separation of control and data plane software and hardware leads to more involved troubleshooting

Identify Cisco express forwarding concepts

Cisco Express Forwarding (CEF) is advanced, layer 3 IP forwarding technology. CEF optimizes network performance and scalability where networks have large and dynamic traffic patterns, such as the Internet itself.

CEF offers the following benefits:

- Improved performance—CEF is less CPU-intensive than older fast switching. As a result, more CPU processing power can be dedicated to other layer 3 services such as quality of service (QoS) and encryption.

- Scalability—CEF offers full switching capacity at each line card or blade when distributed CEF (dCEF) mode is active.
- Resilience—CEF offers switching consistency and stability in large dynamic networks. In dynamic networks, fast-switched cache entries go through high level of churn and are frequently invalidated due to routing changes. These changes can cause traffic to be process switched using the routing table, rather than fast switched using the route cache. With CEF, Forwarding Information Base (FIB) lookup table contains all known routes that exist in the routing table, it eliminates route cache maintenance and as a result avoids sub optimal forwarding scenarios that takes place with the fast-switch or process switching.

CEF uses a FIB to make IP destination prefix-based switching decisions. The FIB is conceptually similar to a routing table or information base. It maintains a mirror image of the forwarding information contained in the IP routing table. When routing or topology changes occur in the network, the IP routing table is updated, and those changes are reflected in the FIB. The FIB maintains next hop address information based on the information in the IP routing table.

Hardware based switching platforms use Content Addressable Memory (CAM) for storing the CEF related information. These tables are finite and can fill up to exhaustion, which would cause forwarding to fall back to software. Catalyst 4500, as an example, can carry up to 128K entries in Supervisor IV/V CAMs. Once those entries are filled up, it switches to software forwarding with an error message "C4K_L3HWFORWARDING-2-FWDCAMFULL". You can verify CAM table usage by show platform hardware ip route summary command.

"show mls cef exception status" can be used on Catalyst 6500 to check on FIB TCAM usage. A switch with FIB TCAM full will repeatedly throw an error message like below:

%MLSCEF-DFC4-7-FIB_EXCEPTION: FIB TCAM exception, Some
entries will be software switched

As a result of this TCAM exception condition, connectivity is affected and might result in elevated CPU usage due to software switching.

RIB, FIB, LFIB, Adjacency table

Routing Information Base (RIB)

RIBs (Routing Information Base) maintain the network topologies and routing tables for each protocol. This would include many routes going to the same destination prefix. It is built on per routing protocol basis, so RIP and OSPF have their own copy of RIBs.

Forwarding Information Base (FIB)

FIBs are the best routes from possibly many routing protocols in the RIBs pushed down to fast forwarding lookup memory (or just DRAM for software-based platforms) for the best path(s). This is what you see in show ip route command output. There is one copy of FIB per system for centralized forwarding platforms, or one for each line card in case of distributed systems.

Label Information Base (LIB)

LIB (Label Information Base) is the software table maintained by IP/MPLS capable routers to store the details of port and the corresponding MPLS router label to be popped or pushed on incoming or outgoing MPLS packets respectively. LIB entries are populated from label-distribution protocols. LIB functions in the control plane of Cisco routers. It is used by the label distribution protocol for mapping the next hop labels.

Label forwarding information base (LFIB) is a data structure and way of managing forwarding in which destinations and incoming labels are associated with outgoing interfaces and labels. The forwarding paradigm employed by MPLS is based on the notion of label swapping. When a packet with a label is received by an Label Switching Router (LSR), the switch uses the label as an index in its LFIB to determine the outgoing interface.

Adjacency Tables

Routers or Switches in a network are considered adjacent if they can reach each other with a single hop across a link layer. In addition to the FIB, CEF uses adjacency tables to prepend Layer 2 addressing information such as MAC addresses. The adjacency table maintains Layer 2 next-hop addresses for all FIB entries.

Load balancing Hash

In a router, act of distributing packets across multiple links based on layer 3 routing information is known as load balancing. If a router discovers multiple paths to a destination, the routing table is updated with multiple entries for that destination.

Router> show ip route

[...]

I   192.168.25.0/24 [115/10] via 192.168.24.6

                [115/10] via 192.168.24.10

[115/10] via 192.168.24.14

[...]

Usually the paths have the same metric, however there are routing protocols that allow unequal cost (or metric) load balancing. A router learns about the existence of parallel paths through the routing protocols and builds its routing table accordingly.

The number of paths used is limited by the number of entries the given IP routing protocol puts in the routing table, the default in IOS is 4 entries for most routing protocols with the exception of BGP, where it is one entry (only the best path). The maximum number of paths that can be configured are 6.

Cisco IOS supports two primary modes of load balancing, i.e. per-destination and per-packet basis.

Per-Destination load balancing

In per-destination mode all packets for a given destination are forwarded along the same path. This preserves packet order however may lead to unequal usage of the links. If one host receives the majority of the traffic all packets will use one link, leaving bandwidth on other links unused. This is the default load balancing mode in IOS using universal algorithm. Original per-destination algorithm creates a 4-bit hash of the source and destination IP address and load balances based on this 16 (2^4) value hash.

Per-Packet load balancing

Per-packet load balancing guarantees equal load across all links however packets may arrive out-of-order at the destination as differential delay may exist for each link used. In particular, per-packet load balancing can result in unsatisfactory data transmission for video and voice streaming.

Router(config)#ip cef load-sharing algorithm ?
  include-ports Algorithm that includes Layer 4 ports
  original   Original algorithm
  tunnel   Algorithm for use in tunnel only environments
  universal   Algorithm for use in most environments

The following load-balancing algorithms are provided for use with Cisco Express Forwarding traffic.

- Original algorithm—The original Cisco Express Forwarding load-balancing algorithm produces distortions in load sharing across multiple routers because the same

algorithm was used on every router. Depending on your network environment, you should select either the universal algorithm (default) or the tunnel algorithm instead.
- Universal algorithm—The universal load-balancing algorithm allows each router on the network to make a different load sharing decision for each source-destination address pair, which resolves load-sharing imbalances. The router is set to perform universal load sharing by default.
- Tunnel algorithm—The tunnel algorithm is designed to balance the per-packet load when only a few source and destination pairs are involved.
- Include-ports algorithm—The include-ports algorithm allows you to use the Layer 4 source and destination ports as part of the load-balancing decision. This method benefits traffic streams running over equal cost paths that are not load shared because the majority of the traffic is between peer addresses that use different port numbers, such as Real-Time Protocol (RTP) streams.

Polarization concept and avoidance

CEF polarization occurs when traffic uses per destination load balancing and the same algorithm, which is default, is used throughout the network which causes traffic to not be load balanced after the first distribution.

As an example think of a layer 3 network with multiple layers or levels each with a possible path to the right or left. If 100Mbps of traffic was coming into a router, it would be load balanced 50/50, with 50Mbps to Router-right and 50Mbps to Router-left, but as Router-level-1-right & Router-level1-left will use the same algorithm to determine which path the traffic will take, but as the algorithm is identical it will be a 100/0 split, with 50Mbps going to Router-level2-right and Router-level2-left and no data going to other paths. Whenever there is an even number of ECMP available, traffic will not be distributed evenly.

To counter this issue, a newer algorithm called the universal algorithm was developed where a 32-bit value is added to the hashing algorithm, this value can be manually set but defaults to the highest loopback IP on the router. This is based on the concept called unique-ID/universal-ID. Hash function is known as universal-ID, a randomly generated value at the time of the router or layer 3 switch boot up that can be manually controlled. This seeds the hash function on each router with a unique ID, which ensures that the same source/destination pair hash into a different value on different routers along the path within the network. This process provides a better network-wide load-sharing and avoids the polarization issue. In order to configure a custom ID, you can use the following CLI:

Router(config)#ip cef load-sharing algorithm universal <id>

Another way to avoid polarization would be to use alternate between default (Source IP and Destination IP) and full (Source IP + Destination IP + Layer 4 ports) hashing inputs configuration at each layer of the network. Of course, this is not practical if we're talking about a large network with many layers some possibly outside the control of the given network administrator.

Explain general network challenges

Unicast flooding

Unicast flood is the unintentional behavior of a switch treating a unicast packet as a broadcast packet; a packet destined for one host is flooded or transmitted out of all the ports of a switch. The underlying cause of flooding is that destination MAC address of the packet is not in the L2 forwarding table (there is one for each VLAN) of the switch.

The primary reasons for unicast flooding behavior include asymmetric routing, STP topology changes (i.e. repeated TCNs), and MAC forwarding table overflow.

Asymmetric Routing

When communication between two hosts (or end points of any type) take different paths on their way out and another on their way in, it is called asymmetric routing. It can also cause packets to arrive out of order if packets that are part of a given flow take different paths.

Large amounts of flooded traffic might saturate low-bandwidth links causing network performance issues or complete connectivity outage to devices connected across such low-bandwidth links. An example of such situation could be a topology where there are two switches (ports in two VLANs, say A and B), two routers (doing inter-VLAN routing between A and B) and two hosts one in VLAN A and one in VLAN B. Now since the routers will proxy ARP for respective hosts as they are default gateways, switches will never be able to learn actual end hosts MAC addresses (router will rewrite them every single time to their own). Switch A and B will continue to flood traffic since they are unaware of the actual host A and host B MAC addresses.

The solution approach is normally to bring the router's ARP timeout and the switch's' forwarding table-aging time close to each other. This will cause the ARP packets to be broadcast, relearning must occur before the L2 forwarding table entry ages out.

Spanning-Tree Protocol Topology Changes

TCNs are triggered by a port that is transitioning to or from the forwarding state. After the TCN, even if the particular destination MAC address has aged out, flooding should not happen for long in most cases since the address will be relearned. The issue might arise when TCNs are occurring repeatedly within short period of time. The switches will constantly be fast-aging their forwarding tables so flooding will be nearly constant.

Typically, a TCN is rare occurrence in a well-configured network. As said before, when the port on a switch goes up or down, there is eventually a TCN once the STP state of the port is changing to or from forwarding. However, when a port is flapping, repetitive TCNs and flooding occurs.

The solution approach would be to configure ports with the STP portfast feature and avoid TCNs when going to or from the forwarding state. Configuration of portfast on all end-device ports (such as printers, PCs, servers, and so on) should limit TCNs to a low amount.

Forwarding Table Overflow

As mentioned before, another possible but not so common cause of flooding can be overflow of the switch forwarding table. In this case, new addresses cannot be learned and packets destined to such addresses are flooded until some space becomes available in the forwarding table. New addresses will then be learned. Since most modern switches have large enough forwarding tables to accommodate MAC addresses for most designs, L2 table overflows are uncommon.

Out of order packets

Using per-packet load balancing to share the traffic load across available paths to a given destination can lead to out-of-order packets for a given data flow.

Impact of micro burst

Micro-bursting is a phenomenon where rapid bursts of data packets are sent in quick succession, leading to periods of full line-rate transmission that can overflow packet buffers of the network stack, both in network endpoints and routers and switches inside the network.

Symptoms of micro bursts will manifest in the form of ignores and/or overruns (also shown as accumulated in "input error" counter within show interface output). This is indicative of receive ring and corresponding packet buffer being overwhelmed due to data bursts coming in over extremely short period of time (microseconds). You will never see a sustained data traffic within show interface's "input rate" counter as they are averaging bits per second (bps) over 5 minutes by default (way too long to account for microbursts). You can understand microbursts from a scenario where a 3-lane highway merging into a single lane at rush hour – the capacity burst cannot exceed the total available bandwidth (i.e. single lane), but it can saturate it for a period of time.

In order to troubleshoot microbursts, you need a packet sniffer that can capture traffic over a long period of time and allow you to analyze it in the form of a graph which displays the saturation points (packet rate during microbursts versus total available bandwidth). You can eventually trace it to the source causing the bursts (e.g. stock trading applications). You can implement larger packet buffers to avoid or mitigate microbursts.

Explain IP operations

ICMP unreachable, redirect

If a router or a layer 3 switch receives a non-broadcast packet destined for itself that uses an unknown protocol, it sends an ICMP protocol unreachable message back to the source. Similarly, if the software receives a packet that it is unable to deliver to the ultimate destination because it knows of no route to the destination address, it will send an ICMP host unreachable message to the source. This feature is enabled by default.

You can disable it by using the following CLI:

Router(config-if)# no ip unreachables

IPv4 options, IPv6 extension headers

The possible options that can be put in the IPv4 header are as follows:

Table 1-5, shows IP header options and their description

Field	Size (bits)	Description
Copied	1	Set to 1 if the options need to be copied into all fragments of a fragmented packet.
Option Class	2	A general options category. 0 is for "control" options, and 2 is for "debugging and measurement". 1, and 3 are reserved.
Option Number	5	Specifies an option
Option Length	8	Indicates the size of the entire option (including this field). This field may not exist for simple options
Option Data	Variable	Option-specific data. This field may not exist for simple options

IPv6 uses two distinct types of headers:

- Main/Regular IPv6 Header
- IPv6 Extension Headers

The main IPv6 header is equivalent to the basic IPv4 one despite some field differences that are the result of lessons learned from operating IPv4.

Table 1-6, IPv6 Extension Headers and their Recommended Order in a Packet

Order	Header Type	Next Header Code
1	Basic IPv6 Header	-
2	Hop-by-Hop Options	0
3	Destination Options (with Routing Options)	60
4	Routing Header	43
5	Fragment Header	44
6	Authentication Header	51
7	Encapsulation Security Payload Header	50
8	Destination Options	60
9	Mobility Header	135
	No next header	59
Upper Layer	TCP	6
Upper Layer	UDP	17
Upper Layer	ICMPv6	58

Extension headers are an intrinsic part of the IPv6 protocol and they support some basic functions and certain services. The following is a list of situations where EHs are commonly used:

- Hop-by-Hop EH is used for the support of Jumbo-grams or, with the Router Alert option, it is an integral part in the operation of Multicast Listener Discovery (MLD). Router Alert is an integral part in the operations of IPv6 Multicast through MLD) and RSVP for IPv6.

- Destination EH is used in IPv6 Mobility as well as support of certain applications.
- Routing EH is used in IPv6 Mobility and in Source Routing. It may be necessary to disable ipv6 source routing using ipv6 source-route command on routers to protect against DDoS.
- Fragmentation EH is critical in support of communication using fragmented packets (in IPv6, the traffic source must do fragmentation-routers do not perform fragmentation of the packets they forward)
- Mobility EH is used in support of Mobile IPv6 service
- Authentication EH is similar in format and use to the IPv4 authentication header
- Encapsulating Security Payload EH is similar in format and use to the IPv4 ESP header. All information following the Encapsulating Security Header (ESH) is encrypted and obfuscated and for that reason, it is invisible to intermediary network devices.

IPv4 and IPv6 fragmentation

IP implements datagram fragmentation, breaking it into smaller pieces, so that packets can pass through a link with a smaller maximum transmission unit (MTU) than the original datagram size. The Identification field, and Fragment offset field along with Don't Fragment (DF) and More Fragment (MF) flags in the IP protocol header are used for fragmentation and reassembly of IP datagrams.

The details of the fragmentation mechanism, as well as the overall architectural approach to packet fragmentation, are different between IPv4 and IPv6. In IPv4, routers perform fragmentation, whereas in IPv6, routers do not fragment, but drop the packets that are larger than the MTU. While the header formats are different for IPv4 and IPv6, analogous fields are used for fragmentation, so the algorithm can be reused for fragmentation and reassembly.

In IPv4, hosts must make a best-effort attempt to reassemble fragmented IP datagrams with a total reassembled size of up to 576 bytes - equal to the minimum MTU for IPv4. They may also attempt to reassemble fragmented IP datagrams larger than 576 bytes. In IPv6, this minimum MTU is increased to 1,280 bytes larger than the minimum MTU for IPv4. IPv6 fragment header and identification header are 64 bits and 32 bits long respectively.

TTL

Time to live (TTL) or hop limit is a mechanism that limits the lifespan or lifetime of data in a network. TTL prevents a data packet from circulating indefinitely. If the TTL field reaches zero before the datagram arrives at its destination, then the datagram is discarded and an ICMP error datagram (11 - Time Exceeded) is sent back to the sender.

IP MTU

IPv4 allows fragmentation: dividing the datagram into pieces, each small enough to pass over the single link that is being fragmented for, using the MTU parameter configured for that interface. This fragmentation process takes place at the IP layer (OSI layer 3) and marks packets it fragments as such, so that the IP layer of the destination host knows it should reassemble the packets into the original datagram. This method implies a number of possible drawbacks:

- All fragments of a packet must arrive for the packet to be considered received. If the network drops any fragment, the entire packet is lost.
- When the size of most or all packets exceed the MTU of a particular link that has to carry those packets, almost everything has to be fragmented. In certain cases the overhead this causes can be considered unreasonable or unnecessary. For example, various tunneling situations cross the MTU by very little as they add just a header's worth of data. The addition is small, but each packet now has to be sent in two fragments, the second of which carries very little payload. The same amount of payload is being moved, but every intermediate router has to do double the work in terms of header parsing and routing decisions.
- As it is normal to maximize the payload in every fragment, any further fragmentation that turns out to be necessary will increase the overhead even more.
- There is no simple method to discover the MTU of links beyond a node's direct peers.
- The Internet Protocol requires that hosts must be able to process IP datagrams of at least 576 bytes (for IPv4) or 1,280 bytes (for IPv6). However, this does not preclude Data Link Layers with an MTU smaller than IP's minimum MTU from conveying IP data. For example, according to IPv6's specification, if a particular Data Link Layer physically cannot deliver an IP datagram of 1,280 bytes in a single frame, then the link layer must provide its own fragmentation and reassembly mechanism, separate from IP's own fragmentation mechanism, to ensure that a 1280-byte IP datagram can be delivered, intact, to the IP layer.

Explain TCP operations

IPv4 and IPv6 PMTU

TCP Maximum Segment Size (MSS) defines the maximum amount of data that a host is willing to accept in a single TCP/IP datagram, it takes care of fragmentation at the two endpoints of a TCP connection, however it doesn't handle the case where there is a smaller MTU link in the middle between these two endpoints. PMTUD was developed to avoid fragmentation in the path between the endpoints. It is used to dynamically determine the lowest MTU along the path from a packet's source to its destination. PMTUD is only supported by TCP. If PMTUD is enabled on a host, and it almost always is, all TCP/IP packets from the host will have the DF bit set.

When a host sends a full MSS data packet with the DF bit set, PMTUD works by reducing the send MSS value for the connection if it receives information that the packet would require fragmentation. A host usually "remembers" the MTU value for a destination by creating a "host" (/32) entry in its routing table with this MTU value.

If a router tries to forward an IP datagram, with the DF bit set, onto a link that has a lower MTU than the size of the packet, the router will drop the packet and return an Internet Control Message Protocol (ICMP) "Destination Unreachable" message to the source of this IP datagram, with the code indicating "fragmentation needed and DF set" (type 3, code 4). When the source station receives the ICMP message, it will lower the send MSS, and when TCP retransmits the segment, it will use the smaller segment size.

There are three things that can break PMTUD, two of which are uncommon and one of which is common.
- A router can drop a packet and not send an ICMP message.
- A router can generate and send an ICMP message but the ICMP message gets blocked by a router or firewall between this router and the sender. (Common)
- A router can generate and send an ICMP message, but the sender ignores the message.
- When path MTU discovery fails, it results in application slowdowns and timeouts since intermediary devices may be doing both fragmentation and reassembly.

Latency
Maximum achievable throughput for a single TCP connection is determined by different factors. One trivial limitation is the maximum bandwidth of the slowest link in the path. But there are also others, less obvious limits for TCP throughput. Bit errors can create a limitation for the connection as well as round-trip time.

Windowing
Flow control allows us to deal with a situation when a sending computer tries to transmit information at a faster rate than the destination computer can receive and process it. This can happen if the receiving computers have a heavy traffic load in comparison to the sending computer, or if the receiving computer has less processing power than the sending computer.

Sliding-window flow control is best utilized when the buffer size is limited and pre-established. During a typical communication between a sender and a receiver the receiver allocates buffer space for n frames (n is the buffer size in frames). The sender can send and the receiver can accept n frames without having to wait for an acknowledgement. The receiver acknowledges a frame by sending an acknowledgement that includes the sequence number of the next frame expected. This acknowledgement announces that the receiver is ready to receive n frames, beginning with the number specified. Both the sender and receiver maintain what is called a window. The size of the window is less than or equal to the buffer size.

Sliding window flow control has a far better performance than stop-and-wait flow control. For example in a wireless environment data rates are low and noise level is very high, so waiting for an acknowledgement for every packet that is transferred is not very feasible. Therefore, transferring data as a bulk would yield a better performance in terms of higher throughput.

Bandwidth delay product

Bandwidth-delay product refers to the product (or multiplication) of a data link's capacity (in bits per second) and its end-to-end delay (in seconds). The result, an amount of data measured in bits (or bytes), is equivalent to the maximum amount of data on the network circuit at any given time, i.e., data that has been transmitted but not yet acknowledged.

In wide area networks (WANs), where the end-to-end delay-bandwidth product becomes a significant factor, TCP uses the network buffers to sustain a steady-state throughput that matches the available network capacity. TCP receive window size can become limiting factor for links with larger bandwidth and smaller delay.

Global synchronization

Global synchronization happens when multiple TCP hosts reduce their transmission rates in response to packet dropping, then increase their transmission rates once again when the congestion is reduced.

WRED avoids the globalization problems that occur when tail drop is used as the congestion avoidance mechanism on the router.

Options

A TCP segment consists of a segment header and a data section. The TCP header contains 10 mandatory fields, and an optional extension field.

Options have up to three fields:
- Option-Kind (1 byte)
- Option-Length (1 byte)
- Option-Data (variable)

The ACL IP Options Selective Drop feature allows a router to filter IP options packets, thereby mitigating the effects of these packets on a router and downstream routers, and perform the following actions:
- Drop all IP options packets that it receives and prevent options from going deeper into the network.
- Ignore IP options packets destined for the router and treat them as if they had no IP options.

The following example shows how to configure the router (and downstream routers) to drop all options packets that enter the network:

Router(config)# ip options drop

show ip traffic command can be used to verify the actual IP options drop statistics.

Explain UDP operations

Starvation

When TCP flows are combined with UDP flows within a single class and the class experiences congestion, TCP flows continually lower their transmission rates due to congestion control, potentially giving up their bandwidth to UDP flows that are oblivious to drops. This effect is called TCP starvation or UDP dominance.

Even if WRED is enabled on the class, the same behavior would be observed because WRED (for the most part) manages congestion only on TCP-based flows.

Latency

UDP is faster (lower latency, better use of network pipe) than TCP (with the exception of applications that only confine to small writes). UDP is preferred if you're transmitting some sort of real time data or just blasting packets over the network that don't need reliable delivery.

RTP/RTCP concepts

Real-time Transport Control Protocol (RTCP) is a sister protocol of the Real-time Transport Protocol (RTP). RTCP provides out-of-band control information for an RTP flow. It partners RTP in the delivery and packaging of multimedia data, but does not transport any data itself. It is used periodically to transmit control packets to participants in a streaming multimedia session. The primary function of RTCP is to provide feedback on the quality of service being provided by RTP. RTCP transports statistics for a media connection and information such as transmitted octet and packet counts, packet loss, packet delay variation, and round-trip delay time. An application may use this information to control quality of service parameters, perhaps by limiting flow, or using a different codec.

Exam Essentials

- IOS XE allows development of data plane ASICs outside the IOS instance and have them program to a set of standard APIs which in turn enforces Control Plane and Data Plane processing separation. It accomplishes Control Plane / Data Plane separation through the introduction of the Forwarding and Feature Manager (FFM) and its standard interface to the Forwarding Engine Driver (FED)
- Hardware based switching platforms use Content Addressable Memory (CAM) for storing the CEF related information. These tables are finite and can fill up to exhaustion, which would cause forwarding to fall back to software. Once those entries are filled up it switches to software forwarding with an error message similar to "C4K_L3HWFORWARDING-2-FWDCAMFULL" (catalyst 4500)
- The number of load balanced paths used is limited by the number of entries the routing protocol puts in the routing table, the default in IOS is 4 entries for most IP routing protocols with the exception of BGP, where it is one entry. The maximum number that can be configured is 6 different paths.
- CEF polarization occurs when traffic uses per destination load balancing and the same algorithm is used throughout the network which causes traffic to not be load balanced after the first distribution. You can use universal algorithm to avoid polarization where a 32 bit value is added to the hashing algorithm
- Configuration of portfast on all end-device ports (such as printers, PCs, servers, and so on) should limit TCNs to a low amount
- The primary reasons for unicast flooding behavior include asymmetric routing, STP topology changes (as evident with repeated TCNs), and MAC forwarding table overflow.
- Using per-packet load balancing to share the traffic load across available paths to a given destination can cause out-of-sequence packets in a particular data flow. This can result in unsatisfactory data transmission for video and voice streaming traffic.
- Micro-bursting is a behavior where rapid bursts of data packets are sent in quick succession, leading to periods of full line-rate transmission that can overflow packet buffers of the network stack, both in network endpoints and routers and switches inside the network.
- If the TTL field reaches zero before the datagram arrives at its destination, then the datagram is discarded and an ICMP error datagram (11 - Time Exceeded) is sent back to the sender
- PMTUD is only supported by TCP

- Global synchronization of TCP hosts, for example, can occur because packets are dropped all at once. Global synchronization manifests when multiple TCP hosts reduce their transmission rates in response to packet dropping, then increase their transmission rates once again when the congestion is reduced.
- When TCP flows are combined with UDP flows within a single class and the class experiences congestion, TCP flows continually lower their transmission rates due to congestion control, potentially giving up their bandwidth to UDP flows that are oblivious to drops. This effect is called TCP starvation or UDP dominance
- FIB and LFIB are data plane related tables
- "ip forward-protocol spanning-tree" command is supported over Advanced Research Projects Agency (ARPA)-encapsulated Ethernet, FDDI, and High-Level Data Link Control (HDLC) encapsulated serials, but is not supported on Token Rings. As long as the Token Rings and the non-HDLC serials are not part of the bridge group being used for UDP flooding, turbo flooding will behave normally.
- IPv4 option type field is 8-bit long and is divided into three sub-fields namely Copied (1-bit), Option Class (2-bit) and Option number (5-bit)

Chapter 2: Network Implementation and Operations

This chapter covers the following exam topics from Cisco's official 400-101 (v5) written exam curriculum.

- Evaluate proposed changes to a network (changes to routing protocol, migration, adding multicast support, impact of new traffic on existing QoS design

Chapter 2: Network Implementation and Operation

Evaluate proposed changes to a network

The objective of the change management process is to minimize service downtime by ensuring that requests for changes are recorded and then evaluated, authorized, prioritized, planned, tested, implemented, documented and reviewed in a controlled and consistent manner.

Changes to routing protocol parameters

Cisco IOS allows you to change just about any routing protocol parameter so you can tune them to your specific needs. You can change administrative distance, metric, tags, maximum paths and authentication etc.

Migrate parts of a network to IPv6

There are both pre-deployment and deployment phases when it comes to migrating from IPv4 to IPv6. The specifics would really depend on the network that is being migrated however we can note down some broader areas that would need planning in each phase.

Pre-Deployment:
- Establish the network starting point
- Network assessment
- Defining early IPv6 security guidelines and requirements

Deployment:
- Transport considerations for integration
- Campus IPv6 migration options
- WAN IPv6 migration options
- Advanced IPv6 services options

Routing protocol migration

There are two common approaches for migrating between routing protocols.

1. Use administrative distance (AD) to migrate the routing protocols
2. Use redistribution and a moving boundary

When using migration by AD method, two routing protocols are run at the same time. This approach assumes sufficient resources such as memory, CPU, and bandwidth are in place. The first step in migration by AD is to turn on the new protocol, but make sure that it has a higher AD than the older routing protocol so it is not preferred. This step enables the protocol and allows adjacencies or neighbors and routing databases to be formed but does not actually rely on the new routing protocol for routing decisions. When the new protocol is fully deployed, various checks can be done with show commands to confirm that everything is working as desired. During the final cutover, the AD is shifted for one of the two protocols so that the new routing protocol will now have a lower AD hence preferred.

With migration by redistribution method, the migration is completed as a series of smaller steps. In each step, part of the network is converted to the new routing protocol. In a big network, the AD approach might be used to support this conversion. In a smaller network, an immediate cutover might suffice. To provide full connectivity during migration by redistribution, the boundary routers between the two parts of the network would have to bi-directionally redistribute between the two routing protocols. Filtering via tags would be one effective way to manage this situation.

Further Reading
http://goo.gl/odC3wl

Adding multicast support

Traditional IP communication allows a host to send packets to a single host (unicast transmission) or to all hosts (broadcast transmission). IP multicast provides a third scheme, allowing a host to send packets to a group of hosts. These hosts are known as group members. Packets delivered to group members are identified by a single multicast group address. Multicast packets are delivered to a group using best-effort with UDP transport, just like IP/UDP unicast packets. The multicast environment consists of senders and receivers. Any host, regardless of whether it is a member of a group or not, can send to a group. However, only the members of a group receive the data.

A multicast address is chosen for the receivers in a multicast group. Senders use that address as the destination address of a datagram to reach all members of the group. Membership in a multicast group is dynamic; hosts can join and leave at any time. There is no restriction on the location or number of members in a multicast group, and a host can be a member of more than one multicast group at a time.

The Cisco IOS supports the following protocols to implement IP multicast routing:
- IGMP is used between hosts on a LAN and the routers on that LAN to track the multicast groups of which hosts are members.

- Protocol Independent Multicast (PIM) is used between routers so that they can track which multicast packets to forward to each other and to their directly connected LANs.
- Distance Vector Multicast Routing Protocol (DVMRP) is used on the MBONE (the multicast backbone of the Internet). The Cisco IOS software supports PIM-to-DVMRP interaction.
- Cisco Group Management Protocol (CGMP) is used on routers connected to Catalyst switches to perform tasks similar to those performed by IGMP.

Further Reading

http://goo.gl/I5YVck

Migrate spanning tree protocol

The Spanning Tree Protocol (STP) is a network protocol that ensures a loop-free topology for any bridged Ethernet local area network. The basic function of STP is to prevent bridge loops and the broadcast radiation that results from them. Spanning tree also allows a network design to include spare (redundant) links to provide automatic backup paths if an active link fails, without the danger of layer-2 loops, or the need for manual enabling/disabling of these backup links. Spanning Tree Protocol (STP) was originally, standardized as IEEE 802.1D most recently in 802.1d-1998, but deprecated as of 802.1d-2004 in favor of Rapid Spanning Tree Protocol (RSTP). RSTP creates a spanning tree within a network of connected layer-2 bridges (typically Ethernet switches), and disables those links that are not part of the spanning tree, leaving a single active path between any two network nodes. While STP can take up to 50 seconds to respond to a topology change, RSTP is typically able to respond to changes within 3 x Hello times (default hello interval is 2 seconds) or even within a few milliseconds of a physical link failure.

In 2001, the IEEE introduced Rapid Spanning Tree Protocol (RSTP) as 802.1w. Cisco's proprietary versions of Spanning Tree Protocol, Per-VLAN Spanning Tree (PVST) and Per-VLAN Spanning Tree Plus (PVST+), create a separate spanning tree for each VLAN.

Rapid Per-VLAN Spanning Tree (RPVST) creates a spanning tree for each VLAN, just like PVST/PVST+. Multiple Spanning Tree Protocol (MSTP) is similar to Cisco's Multiple Instances Spanning Tree Protocol (MISTP), and is an evolution of the Spanning Tree Protocol and the Rapid Spanning Tree Protocol.

PVST+ to MST Migration

It is difficult to convert all the switches in the enterprise network to MST at the same time. Because of the backward compatibility, you can convert it step by step. It is recommended to implement the changes in the scheduled maintenance window because the spanning tree reconfiguration can disrupt the traffic flow.

When you enable MST, it also enables RSTP. The spanning tree uplinkfast and backbonefast features are PVST+ features, and it is disabled when you enable MST because those features are built within RSTP, and MST relies on RSTP. When you migrate from PVST to RPVST, port status cycles through block and learning before moving to forwarding.

STP to RSTP (802.1w) or MSTP (802.1s)

The IEEE has pretty much incorporated most of the Cisco's RSTP and MISTP concepts into two standards, namely 802.1w (RSTP) and 802.1s (MST).

Configuration Steps:
- Identify point-to-point and edge ports, ensuring all switch-to-switch links, on which a rapid transition is desired, are full-duplex.
- Figure out how many instances are needed in the switched network (an instance translates to a logical topology)
- Decide what VLANs to map onto those instances, and carefully select a root and a back-up root for each instance.
- Choose a configuration name and a revision number that will be common to all switches in the network.
- Migrate the core first. Change the STP type to MST, and work your way down to the access switches. MST can interact with legacy bridges running PVST+ on a per-port basis, so it is not a problem to mix both types of bridges as long as interactions are clearly understood.

Further Reading
http://goo.gl/YTBXqV
http://goo.gl/6pbdi3

Evaluate impact of new traffic on existing QoS design

There can at least be two major scenarios that you need to keep in mind when introducing new traffic to an existing QoS design or implementation.

- New traffic could just go to default-class which may be totally undesired
- New traffic ends up matching an existing class causing a mix of transport types in a given class.

For example, if new traffic is UDP and existing traffic is TCP, it could lead to TCP starvation (also known as UDP dominance).

Exam Essentials

There are two common approaches for migrating between routing protocols, namely using administrative distance (AD) and using redistribution with a moving boundary

Spanning Tree Protocol (STP) was originally, standardized as IEEE 802.1D most recently in 802.1d-1998, but deprecated as of 802.1d-2004 in favor of Rapid Spanning Tree Protocol (RSTP)
- IEEE introduced Rapid Spanning Tree Protocol (RSTP) as 802.1w
- When you migrate from PVST to RPVST, port status cycles through block and learning before moving to forwarding
- When you enable MST, it also enables RSTP

Chapter 3: Network Troubleshooting

This chapter covers the following exam topics from Cisco's official 400-101 (v5) written exam curriculum.

- IOS troubleshooting tools (debug/conditional debug, ping/traceroute, embedded packet capture, performance monitor)
- Troubleshooting methodologies (root cause diagnosis, designing valid solutions according constraints, verify and monitor resolution)

Chapter 3: Network Troubleshooting

Use IOS troubleshooting tools

There are two categories of troubleshooting tools that are out there. One that help you troubleshoot IOS related issues but they are web based (E.g. Cisco Output Interpreter), the others are built-in tools that are part of Cisco IOS itself and help a router or switch administrator troubleshoot a network. Example of IOS based tools are ping, traceroute, and show and debug CLIs.

Further Reading

http://goo.gl/AJ6yJm

Debug, conditional debug

When the conditionally triggered debugging feature is enabled, the router generates debugging messages matching a given condition. For example, you may only want to see debugging messages for one interface or subinterface. You can also turn on debugging for all interfaces that meet specified conditions.

Normally, the router will generate debugging messages for every interface, resulting in a large number of message that consume system resources and can make it difficult to find the specific information you need. By limiting the number of debugging messages, you can receive messages related to only the ports you want to troubleshoot.

You can use conditional debug as follows:
router# debug condition interface <interface>

You can verify conditional debug configuration using show debug or show debug condition.

Ping, traceroute with extended options

When a normal ping command is sent from a router or a layer-3 switch, the source address of the ping is the IP address of the interface that the packet uses to exit the router. If an extended ping command is used, the source IP address can be changed to any IP address on the router. The extended ping is used to perform a more advanced check of host reachability and network connectivity. The extended ping command works only at the privileged EXEC command line.

The extended traceroute command is a variation of the traceroute command. An extended traceroute command can be used to see what path packets take in order to get to a destination. This is helpful for when you troubleshoot routing loops, or for when you determine where packets are getting lost (if a route is missing, or if packets are being blocked by an Access Control List (ACL) or firewall). You can use the extended ping command in order to determine the type of connectivity problem, and then use the extended traceroute command in order to narrow down where the problem occurs.

Further Reading

http://goo.gl/EMJ4zN

Embedded packet capture

The Cisco IOS Embedded Packet Capture (EPC) is a software feature consisting of infrastructure to allow for packet data to be captured at various points in the packet forwarding path. The network administrator may define the capture buffer size and type (circular, or linear) and the maximum number of bytes of each packet to capture. The packet capture rate can be throttled using further administrative controls in order to ensure that it doesn't overwhelm the router. For example, options allow for filtering the packets to be captured using an ACL or by specifying a maximum packet capture rate and/or by specifying a sampling interval. You can optimize the configuration to capture more packets by adjusting the sampling interval or capture rate and increasing the buffer size.

Further Reading

http://goo.gl/wcpK4j

Performance monitor

Cisco performance monitor enables you to monitor the flow of packets in your network and become aware of any issues that might impact the flow before it starts to significantly impact the performance of the application in question. Performance monitoring is especially important for video traffic because high quality interactive video traffic is highly sensitive to network conditions (such as packet drops). Even minor issues that may not affect other applications can have dramatic effects on video quality.

Further Reading

http://goo.gl/UReuBR

Apply troubleshooting methodologies

The most important part of troubleshooting any problem is to divide the tasks of problem resolution into a systematic process of elimination. Cisco has broken this process into eight steps:

1. Define the problem.
2. Gather detailed information.
3. Consider probable cause for the failure.
4. Devise a plan to solve the problem.
5. Implement the plan.
6. Observe the results of the implementation.
7. Repeat the process if the plan does not resolve the problem.
8. Document the changes made to address the problem.

Further Reading

http://goo.gl/uknaXX

Interpret packet capture

Using Wireshark trace analyzer

Beginning with Cisco IOS Release XE 3.3.0SG, the Catalyst 4500 series switch supports Wireshark, a packet analyzer program, also known as Ethereal, which supports multiple protocols and presents information in a text-based user interface.

The key concepts around IOS XE based wireshark are:

- Capture points (a capture point is the central policy definition of the Wireshark feature)
- Attachment points (it refers to Interfaces and traffic directions)
- Filters (filters are attributes of a capture point that identify and limit the subset of traffic traveling through the attachment point of a capture point, which is copied and passed to Wireshark)
- Actions
- Storing captured packets to memory buffers

Further Reading
http://goo.gl/n67IEF

Using IOS embedded packet capture
When IOS EPC is enabled, the router captures the packets sent and received. The packets are stored within a buffer in DRAM and are thus not persistent through a reload or reboot. Once the data is captured, it can be examined in a summary or detailed view on the router. In addition, the data can be exported as a packet capture (PCAP) file to allow for further examination. IOS EPC cannot be used to capture multicast packets on egress.

Basic EPC Configuration
1. Define a 'capture buffer', which is a temporary buffer that the captured packets are stored within. There are various options that can be selected when the buffer is defined; such as size, maximum packet size, and circular/linear:

monitor capture buffer BUF size 2048 max-size 1518 linear

2. A filter can also be applied to limit the capture to desired traffic. Define an Access Control List (ACL) within config mode and apply the filter to the buffer:

ip access-list extended BUF-FILTER
   permit ip host 192.168.1.1 host 172.16.1.1
   permit ip host 172.16.1.1 host 192.168.1.1
monitor capture buffer BUF filter access-list BUF-FILTER

3. Define a 'capture point', which defines the location where the capture occurs. The capture point also defines whether the capture occurs for IPv4 or IPv6 and in which switching path (process versus cef):

monitor capture point ip cef POINT fastEthernet 0 both

4. Attach the buffer to the capture point:

monitor capture point associate POINT BUF

5. Start the capture:

monitor capture point start POINT

The capture is now active and would allow collection of the necessary data as per configuration.

Further Reading
http://goo.gl/RwVTZ3

Exam Essentials
- You can verify conditional debug configuration using show debug or show debug condition commands
- You can use the extended ping command in order to determine the type of connectivity problem, and then use the extended traceroute command in order to narrow down where the problem occurs

Part 2 Layer 2 Technologies

Chapter 4: LAN Switching Technologies
Chapter 5: Layer 2 Multicast
Chapter 6: Layer 2 WAN Circuit Technologies

Chapter 4: LAN Switching Technologies

This chapter covers the following exam topics from Cisco's official 400-101 (v5) written exam curriculum.

- Implement and troubleshoot switching administration (managing MAC address table, errdisable recovery, L2 MTU)
- Implement and troubleshoot layer 2 protocols (CDP/LLDP, UDLD)
- Implement and troubleshoot trunking (VTP v1/v2/v3, dot1Q, native VLAN, manual pruning)
- Implement and troubleshoot EtherChannel (LACP, PAgP, manual)
- Implement and troubleshoot spanning-tree (PVST+/RPVST+/MST, switching/port priorities, path cost, portfast, BPDUguard, BPDUfilter, loopguard, rootguard)
- Implement and troubleshoot other LAN switching technologies (SPAN, RSPAN, ERSPAN)
- Cisco chassis virtualization and aggregation technologies (Multi-chassis, VSS concepts, alternative to STP, StackWise)
- Spanning-tree concepts (compatibility between MST and RSTP, STP dispute, STP bridge assurance)

Chapter 4: LAN Switching Technologies

Implement and troubleshoot switch administration

Managing MAC address table

By default, MAC address learning is enabled on all interfaces and VLANs and MAC address aging is set to 300 seconds on a Cisco switch. You can control MAC address learning on an interface or VLAN to manage the available MAC address table space. Before you disable MAC address learning, be sure that you are familiar with the overall environment which includes network topology and the router system configuration. Disabling MAC address learning on an interface or VLAN could cause flooding in the network. You can disable MAC address learning on a single VLAN ID from 1 to 4094 (for example, no mac address-table learning vlan 229) or a range of VLAN IDs, separated by a hyphen or comma (for example, no mac address-table learning vlan 1-100, 16).

You can display the MAC address table by using one or more of the privileged EXEC commands.

show mac address-table address - Displays MAC address table information for the specified MAC address.

show mac address-table aging-time - Displays the aging time in all VLANs or the specified VLAN

Further Reading

http://goo.gl/BS6kzc

Errdisable recovery

If the configuration shows a port as enabled, but software on the switch detects an error situation on the port, the software shuts down that port. In other words, the port is automatically disabled by the switch operating system software because of an error condition that is encountered on the port.

When a port is error disabled, it is effectively shut down and no traffic is sent or received on that port. The port LED is set to the amber and if you issue the show interfaces command, the port status shows err-disabled. Here is an example of what an error-disabled port looks like from the command-line interface (CLI) of the switch:

Switch#show interfaces gigabitethernet 5/1 status

```
Port    Name        Status           Vlan   Duplex  Speed Type
Gi4/1               err-disabled 100 full   1000    1000BaseSX
```

Or, if the interface has been disabled because of an error condition, you can see messages that are similar to these in both the console and the syslog:

%SPANTREE-SP-2-BLOCK_BPDUGUARD:
   Received BPDU on port GigabitEthernet4/1 with BPDU Guard enabled. Disabling port.

%PM-SP-4-ERR_DISABLE:
   bpduguard error detected on Gi4/1, putting Gi4/1 in err-disable state

In order to recover a port from the errdisable state, first identify and correct the underlying cause, and then re-enable the port. If you re-enable the port before you fix the actual problem, the ports could just become error disabled again. After you fix the root problem, the ports are still disabled if you have not configured errdisable recovery on the switch. In this case, you must re-enable the ports manually. Issue the shutdown command and then the no shutdown interface mode command on the associated interface in order to manually re-enable the ports.

Major reasons for errdisable are:

- EthernetChannel misconfiguration
- Duplex mismatch
- BPDU port guard
- UDLD
- Link-flap error
- Loopback error
- Port security violation
- L2tp guard
- Incorrect SFP cable
- 802.1X security violation

Further Reading

http://goo.gl/tKJuV8

L2 MTU

There are 3 types of MTU that can be configured on a switch:

- Layer-2 MTU that affects 10 and 100 Mbps interfaces of a switch. Configured by system MTU {bytes} command in global config mode
- Layer-2 MTU that affects 1000 Mbps and higher speed interfaces of a switch. Configured by system MTU jumbo {bytes} command in global configuration mode
- Layer-3 MTU that affects SVIs and routed interfaces of a switch with IP addresses on them and originating or transit IP traffic that uses these interfaces as GW for routing between networks. Configured by system mtu routing {bytes} command in global config mode

Implement and troubleshoot layer 2 protocols

CDP, LLDP

Cisco Discovery Protocol (CDP) is a Cisco proprietary data link layer protocol. It is used to share information about other directly connected Cisco equipment, such as the operating system version and IP address. All CDP packets include a VLAN ID. If you configure CDP on a Layer 2 access port, the CDP packets sent from that access port include the access port VLAN ID. If you configure CDP on a Layer 2 trunk port, the CDP packets sent from that trunk port include the lowest configured VLAN ID allowed on that trunk port.

Link Layer Discovery Protocol (LLDP) is a vendor-neutral link layer protocol developed by IEEE. It is used by network devices for advertising their identity, capabilities, and neighbors on a local area network, principally wired Ethernet. The topology of an LLDP-enabled network can be discovered by *crawling* the hosts and querying this database. There are three TLVs that are used during the discovery process namely management address, port description and system name.

Further Reading

http://goo.gl/b88Pn1

UDLD

Unidirectional Link Detection (UDLD) protocol can help to prevent forwarding loops and black holing of traffic in switched networks.

UDLD is a L2 protocol that works with the L1 mechanisms to determine the physical status of a link. At layer 1, auto-negotiation takes care of physical signaling and fault detection (FLP or fast link pulses are sent during auto-negotiation for copper Ethernet links). UDLD performs tasks that auto-negotiation cannot perform, such as detecting the identities of neighbors and shutting down misconnected ports. When you enable both auto-negotiation and UDLD, layer 1 and Layer 2 detections work together to prevent physical and logical unidirectional connections and the malfunctioning of other protocols.

UDLD works by exchanging protocol packets between the neighboring devices. In order for UDLD to work, both devices on the link must support UDLD and have it enabled on respective ports. Each switch port configured for UDLD sends protocol packets that contain the port's own device/port ID, and the neighbor's device/port IDs seen by UDLD on that port. Neighboring ports should see their own device/port ID (echo) in the packets received from the other side. If the port does not see its own device/port ID in the incoming UDLD packets for a specific duration of time, the link is considered unidirectional.

It is recommended to keep $T_{detection} < T_{reconvergence}$ by choosing an appropriate message interval which ensures that UDLD is detected before STP forward delay expires.

Further Reading

http://goo.gl/I3qMoF

Implement and troubleshoot VLAN

Access ports

Ethernet interfaces can be configured either as access ports or a trunk ports. An access port can have only one VLAN configured on the interface hence it can carry traffic for only one VLAN.

VLAN database

When the switch is in VTP server or transparent mode, you can configure VLANs in the VLAN database mode. When you configure VLANs in VLAN database mode, the VLAN configuration is saved in the vlan.dat file, not the running-config or startup-config files. To display the VLAN configuration, enter the show running-config vlan CLI.

User-configurable VLANs have unique IDs from 1 to 4094. Database mode supports configuration of IDs from 1 to 1001, but not the extended addresses from 1006 to 4094. To create a VLAN, enter the vlan command with an unused ID. To verify whether a particular ID is in use, enter the show vlan id ID command. To modify a VLAN, enter the vlan command for an existing VLAN.

Normal, extended VLAN, voice VLAN

Normal-range VLANs are VLANs with VLAN IDs 1 to 1005. If the switch is in VTP server or transparent mode, you can add, modify or remove configurations for VLANs 2 to 1001 in the VLAN database. When a switch is in VTP transparent mode (VTP disabled), you can create extended-range VLANs (in the range 1006 to 4094).

A voice VLAN port is an access port attached to a Cisco IP Phone, configured to use one VLAN for voice traffic and another VLAN for data traffic from a device such as a PC attached to the phone.

The following table shows the default VLAN for various L2 protocols as available in "show vlan" command output.

Table 4-1, shows various default VLANs and the respective L2 protocols

Default VLAN #	Protocol
1001	ethernet
1002	fddi-default
1003	token-ring-default
1004	fddi-net-default
1005	trnet-default

Implement and troubleshoot trunking

A trunk is a point-to-point link between one or more Ethernet switch ports and another network device, such as a router or a switch. Trunks carry the traffic of multiple VLANs over a single link thus allowing you to extend VLANs across an entire network.

Two trunking encapsulations are available, depending on the hardware:
- Inter-Switch Link Protocol (ISL)—ISL is a Cisco-proprietary trunking encapsulation
- IEEE 802.1Q—802.1Q is an industry-standard trunking encapsulation

The Dynamic Trunking Protocol (DTP) manages trunk negotiation. DTP supports auto-negotiation of both ISL and 802.1Q trunks. In 802.1Q trunking, all VLAN packets are tagged on the trunk link, except the native VLAN. The native VLAN packets are sent untagged on the trunk link. This way, you can determine to which VLAN a frame belongs when you receive a frame with no tag. Native VLAN should be the same on both switches configured for trunking.

By default, VLAN 1 is the native VLAN on all switches.
- In CatOS, the native VLAN can be changed by issuing the set vlan vlan-id mod/port command, where mod/port is the trunk port.
- In Cisco IOS Software, the native VLAN can be changed by issuing the switchport trunk native vlan vlan-id interface command which is configured on the trunk port.

On Catalyst switches running CatOS, use these commands to verify trunking:
- show port capabilities module/port
- show port module/port
- show trunk module/port
- show vtp domain

On Catalyst 6000 switches running Cisco IOS Software, use the following commands to verify trunking:
- show interfaces interface-type module/port trunk
- show vlan

In order to troubleshoot trunking, make sure that:
- cable is connected and the correct type of cable is used
- trunk is enabled on both interfaces
- encapsulation at both ends using same protocol (802.1Q or ISL)
- to verify that there are no restrictions on the either side of the trunk that are preventing a VLAN traffic

VTPv1, VTPv2, VTPv3, VTP pruning

Table 4-2, summaries different VTP versions and their limitations

VTP Versions	V1	V2	V3
Extended-range VLANs	No, 1 to 1000 only	No, 1 to 1000 only	Yes (1 to 4094)

Primary/Secondary Server concept	No	No	Yes
Transparent Role		a network device will forward received VTP advertisements from its trunking LAN ports	a network device is specific to an instance
Hidden Authentication Password Support	No, plaintext	No, plaintext	Yes (using vtp password)
VLAN database information propagation	Restrictions	Restrictions	You can propagate any database information across the VTP domain. A separate instance of the protocol is running for each application that uses VTP.

When a VTP3 device detects a VTPv2 update on a given trunk port, it will send both VTPv2 and VTP3 packets.

Dot1Q

802.1Q tunneling enables service providers to use a single VLAN to support customers with multiple VLANs, while preserving customer VLAN IDs and keeping traffic in different customer VLANs segregated. A port configured to support 802.1Q tunneling is called a tunnel port. When you configure tunneling, you assign a tunnel port to a VLAN that you dedicate to tunneling, which then becomes a tunnel VLAN. To keep customer traffic segregated, each customer requires a separate tunnel VLAN, but that one tunnel VLAN supports all of the customer's VLANs.

Native VLAN

A frame in the VLAN-aware portion of the network that does not contain a VLAN tag is assumed to be flowing on the native (or default) VLAN. By default, the switch forwards untagged traffic in the native VLAN configured for the port. The native VLAN is VLAN 1 by default.

Manual pruning

With a VLAN disallowed from the trunk, the downstream client switches would not have the VLAN available, hence it would have to be manually added back to the trunk.

Implement and troubleshoot EtherChannel

EtherChannel is the Cisco term for the technology that enables the bonding of physical Ethernet links into a single logical link.

EtherChannel is a port link aggregation technology or port-channel architecture used primarily on Cisco switches. It allows the grouping of several physical Ethernet links to create one logical Ethernet link for the purpose of providing fault-tolerance and high-speed links between switches, routers, and servers. On different Cisco switches, it is possible to create logical connections that are made-up of different physical interface. It is necessary that these interfaces have the same speed. Most Cisco switches support max 64 EtherChannels. These interfaces do not have to be contiguous or even on the same module. Each channel must be made up of min 2, max 8 interfaces. The best is to use 2, 4, or 8 interfaces as that will lead to perfect load-balancing.

EtherChannel can either be configured manually, or can be dynamically negotiated via one of two protocols:

- Port Aggregation Protocol (PAgP) —Cisco's proprietary aggregating protocol.
- Link Aggregation Control Protocol (LACP) —The IEEE standardized aggregation protocol, otherwise known as 802.3ad.

Switch> enable
Switch# configure terminal
Switch(config)# interface range fasttethernet0/1-2
Switch(config-if-range)# switchport mode access
Switch(config-if-range)# switchport access vlan 10
Switch(config-if-range)# channel-group 1 mode desirable * use active to configure LACP

Show commands:
- show interfaces port-channel [channel-group-number]
- show etherchannel [channel-group-number] summary

Verify commands:
- test etherchannel load-balance interface port-channel [#] ip [src] [dst]

Configuration errors usually occur because of mismatched parameters on the ports involved (i.e. different speeds, duplex, or different spanning tree port values, etc.). You can also generate errors within the configuration if you set the channel on one side to on and wait too long before you configure the channel on the other side. This causes spanning tree loops, which generates an error, and shuts down the port.

When an error is encountered while you configure EtherChannel, be sure to check the status of the ports after you correct the EtherChannel error situation. If the port status is errdisable, that means the port has been shut down by the software and will not come up again until you enter the set port enable command. The two ports can form an EtherChannel so long as they are either in active/active, active/passive and auto/desirable.

Further Reading

http://goo.gl/JzMW15

LACP, PAgP, manual

The LACP (802.3ad) for Gigabit Interfaces allows bundling individual Gigabit Ethernet links into a single logical link that provides the aggregate bandwidth of up to 4 physical links. If you configure more than eight links for an EtherChannel group, the software automatically decides which of the hot-standby ports to make active based on the LACP priority. The software assigns to every link between systems that operate LACP a unique priority made up of these elements (in priority order):

1. LACP system priority
2. System ID (a combination of the LACP system priority and the switch MAC address)
3. LACP port priority
4. Port number

All LAN ports on a port channel must be the same speed and must all be configured as either Layer 2 or Layer 3 LAN ports. If a segment within a port channel fails, traffic previously carried over the failed link switches to the remaining segments within the port channel. Inbound broadcast and multicast packets on one segment in a port channel are blocked from returning on any other segment of the port channel.

PAgP packets are sent between Fast EtherChannel-capable ports to negotiate the forming of a channel. When PAgP identifies matched Ethernet links, it groups the links into an EtherChannel. The EtherChannel is then added to the spanning tree as a single bridge port.

Further Reading

http://goo.gl/Zwmrqw
http://goo.gl/CknQS2

Layer 2, layer 3, Load-balancing

Depending on the load balancing method selected, it can use a combination of layer 2, layer 3 and even layer 4 information to determine the path for a given frame.

Table 4-3, shows various platforms and the load balancing options that are available

Platform	Address Used in XOR	Source-Based?	Destination-Based?	Source-Destination-Based?	Load Balancing Method—Configurable/Fixed?
6500/6000	Layer 2, Layer 3 addresses, Layer 4 information, or MPLS information [2]	Yes	Yes	Yes	Configurable
5500/5000	Layer 2 address only	—	—	Yes	Cannot change the method
4500/4000	Layer 2, Layer 3 addresses, or Layer 4 information	Yes	Yes	Yes	Configurable
2900XL/3500XL	Layer 2 address only	Yes	Yes	—	Configurable
3750/3560	Layer 2 or Layer 3 address only	Yes	Yes	Yes	Configurable
2950/2955/3550	Layer 2 address only	Yes	Yes	—	Configurable

Further Reading

http://goo.gl/1xHppN

Etherchannel misconfiguration guard

EtherChannel is supposed to be point-to-point and the feature is adding a consistency check based on the source mac address of the BPDU received. If you keep receiving BPDUs from several source mac addresses, this feature will assume that you have a bundling problem and shut down the port.

You can enable EtherChannel guard to detect an EtherChannel misconfiguration if your switch is running PVST+, rapid PVST+, or MSTP. Actual command to turn this feature on is spanning-tree etherchannel guard misconfig.

Implement and troubleshoot spanning-tree

Spanning Tree Protocol (STP) is a layer-2 protocol that runs on bridges and switches. The specification for STP is IEEE 802.1D. The main purpose of STP is to ensure that you do not create loops when you have redundant paths in your network.

Before you configure STP, select a switch to be the root of the spanning tree. After you decide on the root switch, set the appropriate variables to designate the switch as the root switch. The only variable that you must set is the "bridge priority". If the switch has a bridge priority that is lower than all the other switches, the other switches automatically select the switch as the root switch.

STP calculates the path cost based on the media speed (bandwidth) of the links between switches and the port cost of each port forwarding frame. Spanning tree selects the root port based on the path cost. The port with the lowest path cost to the root bridge becomes the root port. The root port is always in the forwarding state. If the speed/duplex of the port is changed, spanning tree recalculates the path cost automatically. A change in the path cost can change the spanning tree topology.

show spantree vlan_id —Shows the current state of the spanning tree for this VLAN ID, from the perspective of the switch on which you issue the command.

- show spantree summary —Provides a summary of connected spanning tree ports by VLAN.
- show spantree statistics —Shows spanning tree statistical information.
- show spantree backbonefast —Displays whether the spanning tree BackboneFast Convergence feature is enabled.
- show spantree blockedports —Displays only the blocked ports.
- show spantree portstate —Determines the current spanning tree state of a Token Ring port within a spanning tree.
- show spantree portvlancost —Shows the path cost for the VLANs on a port.
- show spantree uplinkfast —Shows the UplinkFast settings.

Further Reading
http://goo.gl/IFvKD5

PVST+/RPVST+/MST

Table 4-4, summarizes different STP versions and their limitations

Comparison	STP	PVST	PVST+	RSTP	RPVST+	MST
Algorithm	Legacy ST	Legacy ST	Legacy ST	Rapid ST	Rapid ST	Rapid ST
Defined as	802.1D (1998)	Cisco Proprietary	Cisco Proprietary	802.1w 802.1D (2004)		Cisco 802.1s
Instances	1	Per-VLAN	Per-VLAN	1	Per-VLAN	Configurable
Trunking	N/A	ISL	ISL 802.1Q	N/A	ISL 802.1Q	ISL 802.1Q

You can use show spanning-tree detail command to look at various interface level statistics including portfast and root port status. This list shows how PVST+ interoperates with IEEE 802.1Q or IEEE 802.1D, if the Native VLAN on an IEEE 802.1Q trunk is VLAN 1:
- VLAN 1 STP BPDUs are sent to the IEEE STP MAC address (0180.c200.0000), untagged.
- VLAN 1 STP BPDUs are also sent to the PVST+ MAC address, untagged.
- Non-VLAN 1 STP BPDUs are sent to the PVST+ MAC address (also called the Shared Spanning Tree Protocol [SSTP] MAC address, 0100.0ccc.cccd), tagged with a corresponding IEEE 802.1Q VLAN tag.

Root bridge, root port, and designated port are elected during listening mode.

Further Reading
http://goo.gl/YPN5WM
http://goo.gl/nGyOfw

Switch priority, port priority, path cost, STP timers

All Bridges (Switches) are assigned a numerical value called bridge priority. The Bridge (Switch) priority value is used to find the Bridge (Switch) ID.

The Switch ID is made from two values:

- The Switch Priority, which is a numerical value defined by IEEE 802.1D, which is equal to 32,768 by default.
- The MAC Address of the Switch. If all the Switches in your Local Area Network (LAN) are configured with the default Switch Priority (32,768), the Switch MAC address will become the decisive factor in electing the Root Bridge (Switch).The Bridge (Switch) with the lowest MAC Address is then elected as Root Bridge (Switch).

> If you want one particular switch to be the Root Bridge (Switch), change the priority to a lower value than 32,768.

> If you want to affect how to the local switch elects the root port change the cost on the links. Cost is cumulative throughout the STP domain. The higher cost is the less preferred.
> If you want to affect how downstream switch elects its root port change the priority. This is only local significance between the two directly connected switches. Highest priority is less preferred. Going away from the root of the tree use priority whereas, when going towards the root of the tree use cost.
>
> There are several STP timers, as described below:
> - hello—The hello time is the time between each bridge protocol data unit (BPDU) that is sent on a port. This time is equal to 2 seconds (sec) by default, but you can tune the time to be between 1 and 10 sec.
> - forward delay—The forward delay is the time that is spent in the listening and learning state. This time is equal to 15 sec by default, but you can tune the time to be between 4 and 30 sec.
> - max age—The max age timer controls the maximum length of time that passes before a bridge port saves its configuration BPDU information. This time is 20 sec by default, but you can tune the time to be between 6 and 40 sec.
>
> Among all these parameters, the only ones which you can tune are:
> - hello
> - max age
> - forward delay
> - diameter

Further Reading

http://goo.gl/HFQ4ha

Port Fast, BPDUguard, BPDUfilter

If you connect an end-host with a single NIC card or an IP phone to a switch port, the connection cannot create a physical loop. These connections are considered leaf nodes. There is no reason to make the workstation wait 30 seconds (15 seconds listening and 15 seconds learning) while the switch checks for loops if the workstation cannot cause a loop. Cisco added the PortFast or fast-start feature. With this feature, the STP for this port assumes that the port is not part of a loop and immediately moves to the forwarding state and does not go through the blocking, listening, discarding, or learning states. You should never use the PortFast feature on switch ports (e.g. root or designated) that connect to other switches, hubs, or routers.

The STP PortFast BPDU guard enhancement allows network designers to enforce the STP domain borders and keep the active topology predictable. The devices behind the ports that have STP PortFast enabled are not able to influence the STP topology. At the reception of BPDUs, the BPDU guard operation disables the port that has PortFast configured. The BPDU guard transitions the port into errdisable state, and a message appears on the console. This message is an example:

%SPANTREE-2-RX_PORTFAST:Received BPDU on PortFast enable port.
Disabling 2/1
%PAGP-5-PORTFROMSTP:Port 2/1 left bridge port 2/1

BPDU filtering allows you to avoid transmitting BPDU on PortFast-enabled ports that are connected to an end system. When you enable PortFast on the switch, spanning tree immediately places ports in the forwarding state, instead of cycling through the listening, learning, and forwarding states. By default, spanning tree sends BPDUs from all ports regardless of whether PortFast is enabled. BDPU filtering is on a per-switch basis; after you enable BPDU filtering, it applies to all PortFast-enabled ports on the switch effectively disabling STP for those ports.

Loop Guard, Root Guard

The STP loop guard feature provides additional protection against Layer 2 forwarding loops (STP loops). An STP loop is created when an STP blocking port in a redundant topology erroneously transitions to the forwarding state. This usually happens because one of the ports of a physically redundant topology (not necessarily the STP blocking port) no longer receives STP BPDUs. In its operation, STP relies on continuous reception or transmission of BPDUs based on the port role. The designated port transmits BPDUs, and the non-designated port receives BPDUs.

When one of the ports in a physically redundant topology no longer receives BPDUs, the STP conceives that the topology is loop free. Eventually, the blocking port from the alternate or backup port becomes designated and moves to a forwarding state. This situation creates a loop.

The loop guard feature makes additional checks. If BPDUs are not received on a non-designated port, and loop guard is enabled, that port is moved into the STP loop-inconsistent blocking state, instead of the listening / discarding / learning / forwarding states. Without the loop guard feature, the port assumes the designated port role. The port moves to the STP forwarding state and creates a loop.

The root guard is mutually exclusive with the loop guard. The root guard is enabled on designated ports by default, and it does not allow the port to become non-designated. The loop guard works on non-designated ports and does not allow the port to become designated through the expiration of max_age. The root guard cannot be enabled on the same port as the loop guard. When the loop guard is configured on the port, it disables the root guard configured on the same port.

Further Reading

http://goo.gl/D3Qdhc

Implement and troubleshoot other LAN switching technologies

SPAN, RSPAN, ERSPAN

SPAN copies traffic from one or more ports, one or more EtherChannels, or one or more VLANs, and sends the copied traffic to one or more destinations for analysis by a network analyzer such as a SwitchProbe device or other Remote Monitoring (RMON) probe. Up to 64 SPAN ports per switch are supported.

RSPAN supports source ports, source VLANs, and destinations on different switches, which provides remote monitoring of multiple switches across your network. RSPAN uses a Layer 2 VLAN to carry SPAN traffic between switches. RSPAN consists of an RSPAN source session, an RSPAN VLAN, and an RSPAN destination session. You separately configure RSPAN source sessions and destination sessions on different switches. To configure an RSPAN source session on one switch, you associate a set of source ports or VLANs with an RSPAN VLAN. To configure an RSPAN destination session on another switch, you associate the destinations with the RSPAN VLAN. Traffic from a non-source VLANs is discarded when it arrives on a source VLAN. Every individual destination port requires a unique SPAN session.

Simply put, ERSPAN is RSPAN over GRE. ERSPAN supports source ports, source VLANs, and destinations on different switches, which provides remote monitoring of multiple switches across your network. ERSPAN uses a GRE tunnel to carry traffic between switches. ERSPAN consists of an ERSPAN source session, routable ERSPAN GRE-encapsulated traffic, and an ERSPAN destination session. You separately configure ERSPAN source sessions and destination sessions on different switches. To configure an ERSPAN source session on one switch, you associate a set of source ports or VLANs with a destination IP address, ERSPAN ID number, and optionally with a VRF name. To configure an ERSPAN destination session on another switch, you associate the destinations with the source IP address, ERSPAN ID number, and optionally with a VRF name.

Further Reading
http://goo.gl/pZeB9V

Describe chassis virtualization and aggregation technologies

Multi-chassis
A VSS combines a pair of Catalyst 6500 series switches into a single logical network element. The VSS manages the redundant links, which externally act as a single port channel. The VSS simplifies network configuration and operation by reducing the number of Layer 3 routing neighbors and by providing a loop-free Layer 2 topology.

Further Reading
http://goo.gl/4ruwHl

VSS concepts
The VSS incorporates the following key concepts:
- VSS Active and VSS Standby Chassis
- Virtual Switch Link
- Multi-chassis EtherChannel

When you create or restart a VSS, the peer chassis negotiate their roles. One chassis becomes the VSS active chassis, and the other chassis becomes the VSS standby. The VSS active chassis controls the VSS and runs the Layer 2 and Layer 3 control protocols for the switching modules on both chassis. The VSS active chassis also provides management functions for the VSS, such as module online insertion and removal (OIR) and the console interface. The VSS active and VSS standby chassis perform packet forwarding for ingress data traffic on their locally hosted interfaces. However, the VSS standby chassis sends all control traffic to the VSS active chassis for processing. HSRP is not required to run VSS.

For the two chassis of the VSS to act as one network element, they need to share control information and data traffic. The virtual switch link (VSL) is a special link that carries control and data traffic between the two chassis of a VSS. The VSL is implemented as an EtherChannel with up to eight links. The VSL gives control traffic higher priority than data traffic so that control messages are never discarded. Data traffic is load balanced among the VSL links by the EtherChannel load-balancing algorithm. VSS standby chassis monitors the active chassis by way of VSL link.

An EtherChannel (also known as a port channel) is a collection of two or more physical links that combine to form one logical link. Layer 2 protocols operate on the EtherChannel as a single logical entity. A Multi-chassis EtherChannel (MEC) is a port channel that spans the two chassis of a VSS. The access switch views the MEC as a standard port channel.

Alternative to STP

Cisco offers two alternatives to running STP which are using TRILL and FabricPath. Virtual PortChannel (vPC) also simplifies and addresses STP's shortcomings.

Further Reading

http://goo.gl/n9xANw

StackWise

Cisco StackWise technology provides a new method for collectively utilizing the capabilities of a stack of switches. Individual switches intelligently join to create a single switching unit with a 32-Gbps switching stack interconnect. Configuration and routing information is shared by every switch in the stack, creating a single switching unit. Switches can be added to and deleted from a working switch stack without affecting performance.

Below are the rules as to how stack master election process works.

Table 4-5, shows rules and their respective priority order

Priority	Rule

1	The switch that is currently the stack master
2	The switch that is currently the stack master
3	The switch that uses the non-default interface-level configuration
4	The switch with the higher Hardware/Software priority. These switch software versions are listed from highest to lowest priority: 1. Cryptographic IP services image software 2. Noncryptographic IP services image software 3. Cryptographic IP base image software 4. Noncryptographic IP base image software
5	The switch with the longest system up-time
6	The switch with the lowest MAC address

Excluding specific platform implementation

Describe spanning-tree concepts

The basic function of STP is to provide a loop free switched network; this is done by creating a topology of all participating STP switches. The best loop free path through the switched network is then determined from this topology information. The initial step taken by each STP is to elect a root switch; the root switch is used as a central point in a switched network to determine the best route through the switched network. Initially, all switches act as if they are the root switch and do this until they receive traffic from another superior switch (as determined by switch priority); this is referred to as a root switch election.

Another thing that must be understood is that multiple root switches can exist in the network depending on what STP mode is being used. By default, on Cisco switching equipment, each VLAN has its own STP instance and a root switch is elected for each VLAN; this mode is called Per VLAN Spanning Tree Plus (PVST+). If implementing RSTP, Rapid PVST+ is used.

Once the root switch is elected, each of the ports is given a role depending on its place within the STP topology; the available port roles when using 802.1D spanning tree are shown below:
- Root—The port given this role is the selected best path to reach the root switch
- Designated—The port given this role is selected with the best path to a specific switched segment; there is only one designated port per switched segment.

- Alternate—The port given this role is selected as a backup to the root port; if the root port should have a problem, this port would take over the root port role.
- Backup—The port given this role is selected as a back to the designated port; if the designated port should have a problem this port would take over the designated port role.

Once the best path is calculated and each of the ports has been given a role, all ports with the alternate or backup STP roles will be blocked to prevent loops.

Further Reading
http://goo.gl/N3Flst

Compatibility between MST and RSTP
Both RSTP and MSTP improve the operation of the spanning tree while maintaining backward compatibility with equipment that is based on the (original) 802.1D spanning tree, with existing Cisco per-VLAN spanning tree (PVST), and with the existing Cisco-proprietary Multiple Instance STP (MISTP). By default, RSTP uses topology change TC flag. It also doesn't use separate TCN BPDU when interoperating with another switching running 802.1D.

Further Reading
http://goo.gl/vz9oVP

STP dispute, STP bridge assurance
When a designated port detects a conflict, it keeps its role, but reverts to a discarding state because disrupting connectivity in case of inconsistency is preferable to starting a bridging loop. The 802.1w-standard BPDUs include the role and state of the sending port. With this information, switch A can detect that switch B does not react to the superior BPDUs that it sends and that switch B is the designated, not root port. As a result, switch A blocks (or keeps blocking) its port, which prevents the bridging loop.

You can use Bridge Assurance to protect against certain problems that can cause bridging loops in the network. Specifically, you can use Bridge Assurance to protect against a unidirectional link failure and a device that continues to forward data traffic when it is no longer running the spanning tree algorithm. Bridge Assurance is enabled by default and can only be disabled globally. In addition to that, Bridge Assurance can only be enabled on spanning tree network ports that are point-to-point links. Both ends of the link must have

Bridge Assurance enabled. With Bridge Assurance enabled, BPDUs are sent out on all operational network ports in both directions, including alternate and backup ports, for each hello time period. If the port does not receive a BPDU for a specified period, the port moves into the blocking state and is not used in the root port calculation. Once that port receives a BPDU, it resumes the normal spanning tree transitions.

Further Reading

http://goo.gl/Pk1sVL

Exam Essentials

- By default, MAC address learning is enabled on all interfaces and VLANs on the switch and MAC address aging is set to 300 seconds
- When a port is error disabled, it is effectively shut down and no traffic is sent or received on that port
- In order to recover a port from the errdisable state, first identify and correct the root problem, and then re-enable the port. If you re-enable the port before you fix the root problem, the ports just become error disabled again.
- UDLD is a Layer 2 (L2) protocol that works with the Layer 1 (L1) mechanisms to determine the physical status of a link
- In 802.1Q trunking, all VLAN packets are tagged on the trunk link, except the native VLAN
- EtherChannel is the Cisco term for the technology that enables the bonding of up to eight physical Ethernet links into a single logical link.
- You can enable EtherChannel guard to detect an EtherChannel misconfiguration if your switch is running PVST+, rapid PVST+, or MSTP
- The Switch Priority, which is a numerical value defined by IEEE 802.1D, which is equal to 32,768 by default. If you want one particular switch to be the Root Bridge (Switch), change the priority to a lower value than 32,768.
- With portfast enabled, STP for the port assumes that the port is not part of a loop and immediately moves to the forwarding state and does not go through the blocking, listening, discarding, or learning states. You should never use the PortFast feature on switch ports (e.g. root or designated) that connect to other switches, hubs, or routers
- The STP loop guard feature provides additional protection against Layer 2 forwarding loops (STP loops)
- The root guard is mutually exclusive with the loop guard feature. The root guard is enabled on designated ports by default, and it does not allow the port to become non-designated. It effectively protects the core of a STP domain.
- ERSPAN is RSPAN over GRE. ERSPAN supports source ports, source VLANs, and destinations on different switches, which provides remote monitoring of multiple switches across your network

- Cisco offers two alternatives to running STP which are using TRILL and FabricPath
- Cisco StackWise technology provides an innovative new method for collectively utilizing the capabilities of a stack of switches
- By default, on Cisco switching equipment, each VLAN has its own STP instance and a root switch is elected for each VLAN; this mode is called Per VLAN Spanning Tree Plus (PVST+)
- By default, RSTP uses topology change TC flag. It also doesn't use separate TCN BPDU when interoperating with another switching running 802.1D
- With Bridge Assurance enabled, BPDUs are sent out on all operational network ports in both directions, including alternate and backup ports, for each hello time period
- The role of the TC mechanism is to correct L2 forwarding tables after the forwarding topology has changed. This is necessary to avoid a connectivity outage because, after a TC, some MAC addresses previously accessible through particular ports might become accessible through different ports. TC shortens the forwarding table aging time on all switches in the VLAN where the TC occurs; thus, if the address is not relearned, it will age-out and flooding will occur to ensure packets reach the destination MAC address.

Chapter 5: Layer 2 Multicast

This chapter covers the following exam topics from Cisco's official 400-101 (v5) written exam curriculum.

- Implement and troubleshoot IGMP (IGM v1/v2/v3, snooping, querier, filter, proxy)
- MLD
- PIM snooping

Chapter 5: Layer 2 Multicast

Implement and troubleshoot IGMP

IGMP specifies how a host can register with a router in order to receive specific multicast traffic. IGMP is an IETF standard, where IGMPv1 is defined in RFC 1112, IGMPv2 in RFC 2236 and IGMPv3 in RFC 3376.

When you troubleshoot multicast networks, it is good to consider the signaling protocol used in the network and packet flows (source and receiver). The signaling protocol is used to setup and tear down the multicast sessions (such as PIM dense mode, PIM sparse mode, and DVMRP), and packet flow is the actual sending, replicating, and receiving of the multicast packets between the source and receiver, based on the forwarding table created by the signaling process.

Further Reading

http://goo.gl/o1yChS

IGMPv1, IGMPv2, IGMPv3

IGMP Version 1 (IGMPv1) messages are transmitted in IP datagrams and contain the following fields:
- Version: 1
- Type: There are two types of IGMP messages, Membership Query and Membership Report.
- Checksum
- GDA

Membership reports are issued by hosts that want to receive a specific multicast Group Destination Address (GDA). Membership queries are issued by routers at regular intervals to check whether there is still a host interested in the GDA in that segment. Host membership reports are issued either unsolicited (when the host wants to receive GDA traffic first) or in response to a membership query.

They are sent with the following fields:
- L2 Information
- Source MAC: Host MAC address
- Destination MAC: Destination MAC for the GDA
- L3 Information

- Source IP: IP address of the host
- Destination IP: GDA
- IGMP Packet
- IGMP data contains, furthermore, the GDA and some other fields.

Host membership queries are sent by the router to the all-multicast address: 224.0.0.1. These queries use 0.0.0.0 in the IGMP GDA field. A host for each group must respond to that query, or the router stops forwarding the traffic for that GDA to that segment (after three attempts). The router keeps a multicast routing entry for each source, and links it to a list of outgoing interfaces (interface from where the IGMP report came). After three IGMP query attempts with no answer, this interface is erased from the outgoing interface list for all entries linked to that GDA.

In IGMP Version 2 (IGMPv2), the version field has been removed, and the type field can now accept different values. The types are shown below.
- Membership Query
- IGMPv1 Membership Report
- Version 2 Membership Report
- Leave Group

Descriptions of the most important new features added in IGMPv2 are listed below.
- IGMP Leave Message: when a host wants to leave a group, it should send a Leave Group IGMP message to destination 224.0.0.2 (instead of leaving silently like in IGMPv1).
- A router can now send a group-specific query by sending a Membership Query to the group GDA instead of sending it to 0.0.0.0.

IGMPv2 has the following default values for each timer or interval.

Table 5-1, shows IGMPv2 intervals and their default values

Interval Type	Default Value
Query interval	125 seconds
Query Max response interval	10 seconds
Other Querier Present interval	255 seconds
Last Member Query Interval	2 seconds
Last Member Query Response interval	1 second
Group Membership interval	260 seconds

In IGMP Version 3 (IGMPv3), there is a type field that can have the following values:
- Membership query
- Version 3 Membership Report

An implementation of IGMPv3 must also support the following three message types, for interoperation with previous versions of IGMP:
- Version 1 Membership Report
- Version 2 Membership Report
- Version 2 Leave Group

IGMPv3 adds support for source filtering, that is, the ability for a system to report interest in receiving packets from specific source addresses, or from all but specific source addresses sent to a specific multicast address. This feature is also called Source Specific Multicast (SSM).
In order for a computer to support SSM, it must support IGMPv3.

You can use the following command to see all IGMP default timers.
Switch#show ip igmp interface fastEthernet 0/1
FastEthernet0/1 is up, line protocol is up
 Internet address is 12.21.22.15/8
 IGMP is enabled on interface
 Current IGMP host version is 2
 Current IGMP router version is 2
 IGMP query interval is 60 seconds
 IGMP querier timeout is 120 seconds
 IGMP max query response time is 10 seconds
 Last member query count is 2
 Last member query response interval is 1000 ms
 Inbound IGMP access group is not set

In a network using PIM stub routing, the only allowable route for IP traffic to the user is through a switch that is configured with PIM stub routing. PIM passive interfaces are connected to Layer 2 access domains, such as VLANs, or to interfaces that are connected to other Layer 2 devices. Only directly connected multicast (IGMP) receivers and sources are allowed in the Layer 2 access domains. The PIM passive interfaces do not send or process any received PIM control packets

Further Reading

http://goo.gl/UDQbL2

IGMP Snooping

IGMP snooping is a feature that allows the switch to snoop or listen in on the IGMP conversation between hosts and routers. When a switch hears an IGMP report from a host for a given multicast group, the switch adds the host's port number to the GDA list for that group. And, when the switch hears an IGMP Leave, it removes the host's port from the CAM table entry.

IGMP Querier

When there is no multicast router in the VLAN to originate the queries, you must configure an IGMP snooping querier to send membership queries. When an IGMP snooping querier is enabled, it sends out periodic IGMP queries that trigger IGMP report messages from hosts that want to receive IP multicast traffic. IGMP snooping listens to these IGMP reports to establish appropriate forwarding.

Further Reading

http://goo.gl/CeI9I5

IGMP Filter

IGMP filtering allows users to configure filters on a Switch Virtual Interface (SVI), a per-port, or a per-port per-VLAN basis to control the propagation of IGMP traffic through the network. IGMP filtering provides the capability to manage IGMP snooping, which in turn controls the forwarding of multicast traffic. When an IGMP packet is received, IGMP filtering uses the filters configured by the user to determine whether the IGMP packet should be discarded or allowed to be processed by the existing IGMP snooping code. With a IGMP version 1 or version 2 packet, the entire packet is discarded. With a IGMPv3 packet, the packet is rewritten to remove message elements that were denied by the filters.

IGMP traffic filters control the access of a port to multicast traffic. Access can be restricted based on the following:
- Which multicast groups or channels can be joined on a port. Channels are joined by IGMPv3 hosts that specify both the group and the source of the multicast traffic.
- Maximum number of groups or channels allowed on a specific port or interface (regardless of the number of hosts requesting service).
- IGMP protocol versions (for example, disallow all IGMPv1 messages).

When you enter an IGMP filtering command, a user policy is applied to a Layer 3 SVI interface, a Layer 2 port, or a particular VLAN on a Layer 2 trunk port. The Layer 2 port may be an access port or a trunk port. The IGMP filtering features will work only if IGMP snooping is enabled (either on the interface or globally).

Further Reading

http://goo.gl/R2VIxA

IGMP proxy

An IGMP proxy enables hosts in a unidirectional link routing (UDLR) environment that are not directly connected to a downstream router to join a multicast group sourced from an upstream network.

Further Reading

http://goo.gl/4h58WP

Explain MLD

MLD is an IPv6 protocol that a host uses to request multicast data for a particular group. Using the information obtained through MLD, the device maintains a list of multicast group or channel memberships on a per-interface basis. The devices that receive MLD packets send the multicast data that they receive for requested groups or channels out the network segment of the known receivers. MLD messages have a hop-limit of 1.

MLDv1 is derived from IGMPv2, and MLDv2 is derived from IGMPv3. IGMP uses IP Protocol 2 message types, while MLD uses IP Protocol 58 message types, which is a subset of the ICMPv6 messages.

The MLD process is started automatically on the device. You cannot enable MLD manually on an interface. MLD is automatically enabled when you perform one of the following configuration tasks on an interface:

- Enable PIM6
- Statically bind a local multicast group
- Enable link-local group reports

MLD snooping allows the switch to examine MLD packets and make forwarding decisions based on their content as opposed to just flooding. You can configure the switch to use MLD snooping in subnets that receive MLD queries from either MLD or the MLD snooping querier.

MLD snooping constraints IPv6 multicast traffic at Layer 2 by configuring Layer 2 LAN ports dynamically to forward IPv6 multicast traffic only to those ports that want to receive it.

Explain PIM Snooping

In networks where a Layer 2 switch interconnects several routers, the switch floods IP multicast packets on all multicast router ports by default, even if there are no multicast receivers downstream. With PIM snooping enabled, the switch restricts multicast packets for each IP multicast group to only those multicast router ports that have downstream receivers joined to that group. When you enable PIM snooping, the switch learns which multicast router ports need to receive the multicast traffic within a specific VLAN by listening to the PIM hello messages, PIM join and prune messages, and bidirectional PIM designated forwarder-election messages.

show ipv6 snooping command provides information about an interface on which both the Neighbor Discovery Inspection and RA Guard features are configured.

Further Reading

http://goo.gl/TLIVK6

Exam Essentials

- IGMPv3 adds support for source filtering, that is, the ability for a system to report interest in receiving packets from specific source addresses, or from all but specific source addresses sent to a specific multicast address. This feature is also known as Source Specific Multicast (SSM)
- IGMP filtering allows users to configure filters on a switch virtual interface (SVI), a per-port, or a per-port per-VLAN basis to control the propagation of IGMP traffic through the network
- When you enter an IGMP filtering command, a user policy is applied to a Layer 3 SVI interface, a Layer 2 port, or a particular VLAN on a Layer 2 trunk port
- MLD is an IPv6 protocol that a host uses to request multicast data for a particular group
- show ipv6 snooping command provides information about an interface on which both the Neighbor Discovery Inspection and RA Guard features are configured.

Chapter 6: Layer 2 WAN Circuit Technologies

This chapter covers the following exam topics from Cisco's official 400-101 (v5) written exam curriculum.

- Implement and troubleshoot HDLC
- Implement and troubleshoot PPP (PAP/CHAP, PPPoE, MLPPP)
- WAN rate-based Ethernet circuits (metro, WAN Ethernet topologies, rate-limited WAN Ethernet services)

Chapter 6: Layer 2 WAN Circuit Technologies

Implement and troubleshoot HDLC

HDLC is a bit-oriented synchronous data link layer protocol however doesn't use retransmission. It supports various layer 3 protocols in addition to IP. SLARP protocol is used to send keepalives. After missing three keepalives in a row, serial interface is declared as DOWN.

Implement and troubleshoot PPP

Authentication (PAP, CHAP)

The Challenge Handshake Authentication Protocol (CHAP) verifies the identity of the peer by means of a three-way handshake.

These are the general steps performed during CHAP protocol exchange:
1. After the Link Control Protocol (LCP) phase is complete, and CHAP is negotiated between both devices, the authenticator sends a challenge message to the peer.
2. The peer responds with a value calculated through a one-way hash function Message Digest 5 (MD5).
3. The authenticator checks the response against its own calculation of the expected hash value. If the values match, the authentication is successful. Otherwise, the connection is terminated.
4. By default, authenticator uses its own hostname to identify to peer.

This authentication method depends on a "secret" known only to the authenticator and the peer. The secret is never sent over the link. Although the authentication is only one-way, you can negotiate CHAP in both directions, with the help of the same secret set for mutual authentication.

PPPoE

PPPoE combines Ethernet and PPP to provide an authenticated method of assigning IP addresses to client systems. PPPoE clients are typically personal computers connected to an ISP over a remote broadband connection, such as DSL or cable service. ISPs deploy PPPoE because it supports high-speed broadband access using their existing remote access infrastructure and because it is easier for customers to use. PPPoE provides a standard method of employing the authentication methods of the Point-to-Point Protocol (PPP) over an Ethernet network. When used by ISPs, PPPoE allows authenticated assignment of IP addresses. In this type of implementation, the PPPoE client and server are interconnected by Layer 2 bridging protocols running over a DSL or other broadband connection.

PPPoE is composed of two main phases:
- Active Discovery Phase—In this phase, the PPPoE client locates a PPPoE server, called an access concentrator. During this phase, a Session ID is assigned and the PPPoE layer is established.
- PPP Session Phase—In this phase, PPP options are negotiated and authentication is performed. Once the link setup is completed, PPPoE functions as a Layer 2 encapsulation method, allowing data to be transferred over the PPP link within PPPoE headers.

MLPPP

The Multilink Point-to-Point (MLPPP) feature provides load balancing functionality over multiple WAN links, while providing multi-vendor interoperability, packet fragmentation and proper sequencing, and load calculation on both inbound and outbound traffic.

Describe WAN rate-based Ethernet circuits

A metropolitan-area Ethernet, Ethernet MAN, or metro Ethernet network is a metropolitan area network (MAN) that is based on Ethernet standards. It is commonly used to connect subscribers to a larger service network or the Internet. Businesses can also use Ethernet-based MAN to connect their own offices to each other.

Ethernet on the MAN can be used as pure Ethernet, Ethernet over SDH, Ethernet over MPLS, or Ethernet over DWDM. Pure Ethernet-based deployments are cheaper but less reliable and scalable and thus are usually limited to small scale deployments. SDH-based deployments are useful when there is an existing SDH infrastructure already in place, its main shortcoming being the loss of flexibility in bandwidth management due to the rigid hierarchy imposed by the SDH network. MPLS-based deployments are costly but highly reliable and scalable and are typically used by large service providers.

Further Reading

http://goo.gl/QAkTHJ

Metro and WAN Ethernet topologies

Familiar network domains are likely to exist regardless of the transport technology chosen to implement Metropolitan area networks: Access, aggregation/distribution, and core
Access devices normally exist at a customer's premises, unit, or wireless base station. This is the network that connects customer equipment, and may include ONT and/or Residential gateway, or office router.

- Aggregation occurs on a distribution network such as an ODN segment. Often Passive Optical Network, microwave or Digital Subscriber Line technologies are employed, but some using point-to-point Ethernet over "home-run" direct fibre. This part of the network includes nodes such as Multi Tenanted Unit switches, Optical line terminals in an outside plant or central office cabinet, Ethernet in the First Mile equipment, or provider bridges.
- A MAN may include the transport technologies MPLS, PBB-TE and T-MPLS, each with its own resiliency and management solutions.
- A core network often uses IP-MPLS to connect different MANs together.

Much of the functionality of Ethernet MANs such as virtual private lines or virtual private networks is implemented by the use of Ethernet VLAN tags that allow differentiation of each part of the network. Logical differentiation of the physical network helps to identify the rights that the traffic has and to ease the management of host access rights with respect to other users and networks.

Metro Ethernet flavors come in both port-based and vlan-based options.

Table 6-1, shows breakdown of metro ethernet services into port or VLAN based categories

Metro Ethernet Services	Port or VLAN-based
Ethernet Private Tree	Port-based
Ethernet Private LAN	Port-based
Ethernet Private Line	Port-based
Ethernet Virtual Private Line	VLAN-based
Ethernet Virtual Private LAN	VLAN-based

Use of rate-limited WAN Ethernet services

The Native Ethernet service is comprised of Layer 2 end to end native Ethernet signaling over the Metro Ethernet network where available. There is no transition of packets to any other WAN protocol and no VLAN encapsulation required. The use of native Ethernet services is mostly available for metropolitan connectivity. As the distance between offices increases, the use of a WAN transport such as SONET must be used. Traffic shaping or rate limiting of packets to the CIR should be done at the customer edge Ethernet interface to make sure packets are not dropped by the service provider.

Ethernet Private Line (EPL)

The Ethernet Private Line service is used to deploy private line WAN connectivity across the Metro network. Typically the Ethernet service will forward packets to a long haul SONET network where Ethernet packets are encapsulated in SONET frames.

The Ethernet packets are stripped off (de-encapsulated) at the SONET Provider Edge (PE) equipment and forwarded to the local Metro service provider network. The Ethernet private line is similar to any WAN link where VLAN information isn't sent between routers. The service provider does the rate limiting of traffic based on the CIR selected by the customer. The CIR is the guaranteed data rate service level agreement with the ISP. Traffic shaping or rate limiting of packets should be done at the Customer Edge (CE) on the CPE Ethernet interface to make sure packets are not dropped by the service provider.

Ethernet Virtual Private Line (EVPL)

The Ethernet virtual private line service is deployed for trunking of multiple VLANs across a Metro network (i.e. multiplexing multiple point to point EVCs). The 802.1q encapsulation protocol is the new standard that works with Cisco and other vendor equipment. The customer edge device uses 802.1q protocol to tag each Ethernet packet with VLAN membership before forwarding it across the virtual point to point Metrolink. QoS is applied at the Customer Edge (CE) Ethernet interface using per VLAN or per Class per VLAN traffic shaping.

Further Reading

http://goo.gl/Ffsq5o

Exam Essentials

- HDLC is a bit-oriented synchronous data link layer protocol
- CHAP authentication method depends on a "secret" known only to the authenticator and the peer. CHAP secret is never sent over wire
- The Ethernet virtual private line service is deployed for trunking of multiple VLANs across a Metro network (i.e. multiplexing multiple point-to-point EVCs). Rate limiting is also supported per EVC.
- The PPP Endpoint Discriminator Option represents identification of the system transmitting the packet. This option advises a system that the peer on this link could be the same as the peer on another existing link (RFC 1990)
- Clock rates are configured on DCE interfaces
- Use of MST, PAgP, and LACP is supported on EVCs
- Initial CHAP challenge packet includes both name of the challenger and packet type ID

Part 3 Layer 3 Technologies

Chapter 7: Addressing Technologies
Chapter 8: Layer 3 Multicast
Chapter 9: Fundamental Routing Concepts
Chapter 10: RIPv2 (IPv4/IPv6)
Chapter 11: EIGRP (IPv4/IPv6)
Chapter 12: OSPF (v2, v3)
Chapter 13: BGP
Chapter 14: ISIS (IPv4/IPv6)

Chapter 7: Addressing Technologies

This chapter covers the following exam topics from Cisco's official 400-101 (v5) written exam curriculum.

- Addressing technologies (IPv4 addressing/subnetting, IPv6 address types, VLSM, ARP)
- Implement and troubleshoot IPv6 addressing (unicast/multicast, EUI-64, ND, RS/RA, Autoconfig/SLAAC, temporary addresses, global prefix configuration feature, DHCP protocol operations, SLAAC/DHCPv6 interaction, stateful/stateless DHCPv6, DHCPv6 prefix delegation)

Chapter 7: Addressing Technologies

Address types, VLSM

There are three types of IPv4 addresses, namely:

- Host address
- Network or Subnetwork address
- Broadcast address

Within each type, there are five classes that addresses can be carved out from. Those classes are known as A, B, C, D, and E. There is no limit to the number of secondary addresses that can be configured on a Cisco router's interface.

::ffff:0:0/96 prefix is designated as an *IPv4-mapped IPv6 address*. With a few exceptions, this address type allows the transparent use of the Transport Layer protocols over IPv4 through the IPv6 networking.

Further Reading

http://goo.gl/IC9Neg
http://goo.gl/sDQ2dh

ARP

The Address Resolution Protocol (ARP) was developed to enable communications on an internetwork. Layer 3 devices need ARP to map IP network addresses to MAC hardware addresses so that IP packets can be sent across networks. Before a device sends a datagram to another device, it looks in its ARP cache to see if there is a MAC address and corresponding IP address for the destination device. If there is no entry, the source device sends a broadcast message to every device on the network. Each device compares the IP address to its own. Only the device with the matching IP address replies to the sending device with a packet containing the MAC address for the device (except in the case of "proxy ARP" where a router can reply to ARP request on behalf of another host). The source device adds the destination device MAC address to its ARP table for future reference, creates a data-link header and trailer that encapsulates the packet, and proceeds to transfer the data.

High CPU utilization in the ARP input process occurs if the router has to originate an excessive number of ARP requests. The router uses ARP for all hosts, not just those on the local subnet, and ARP requests are sent out as broadcasts, which causes more CPU utilization on every host in the network. ARP requests for the same IP address are rate-limited to one request every two seconds, so an excessive number of ARP requests would have to originate for different IP addresses. This can happen if an IP route has been configured pointing to a broadcast interface (as opposed to next-hop). A most common example is a default route such as:

ip route 0.0.0.0 0.0.0.0 Fastethernet0/0

In this case, the router generates an ARP request for each IP address that is not reachable through more specific routes, which practically means that the router generates an ARP request for almost every address on the Internet.

Further Reading

http://goo.gl/HCQDf6

Identify, implement and troubleshoot IPv6 addressing and subnetting

Unicast, multicast

IPv6 addresses are represented as a series of 16-bit hexadecimal fields separated by colons (:) in the format: x:x:x:x:x:x:x:x.

Following are two examples of IPv6 addresses:
2001:DB8:7654:3210:FEDC:BA98:7654:3210
2001:DB8:0:0:8:800:200C:417A

It is common for IPv6 addresses to contain successive hexadecimal fields of zeros. To make IPv6 addresses less cumbersome, two colons (::) may be used to compress successive hexadecimal fields of zeros at the beginning, middle, or end of an IPv6 address (the colons represent successive hexadecimal fields of zeros).

A double colon may be used as part of the ipv6-address argument when consecutive 16-bit values are denoted as zero. You can configure multiple IPv6 addresses per interfaces, but only one link-local address.

Table 7-1, shows various IPv6 address types and respective formats

IPv6 Address Type	Preferred Format	Compressed Format
Unicast	2001:0:0:0:DB8:800:200C:417B	2001::DB8:800:200C:417B

Multicast	FF09:0:0:0:0:0:0:101	FF09::101
Loopback	0:0:0:0:0:0:0:1	::1
Unspecified	0:0:0:0:0:0:0:0	::

An IPv6 address must be configured on an interface for the interface to forward IPv6 traffic. Configuring a global IPv6 address on an interface automatically configures a link-local address and activates IPv6 for that interface. Additionally, the configured interface automatically joins the following required multicast groups for that link:
- Solicited-node multicast group FF02:0:0:0:0:1:FF00::/104 for each unicast and anycast address assigned to the interface
- All-nodes link-local multicast group FF02::1
- All-routers link-local multicast group FF02::2

IPv6 redistribution ignores the "local" routes in the IPv6 routing table (the /128 host routes for a router's own interface IPv6 addresses) whereas IPv4 has no such concept.

Further Reading

http://goo.gl/YzuS9y

EUI-64

Extended Unique Identifier (EUI) allows a host to assign itself a unique 64-bit IPv6 interface identifier (EUI-64). This feature is a key benefit over IPv4 as it eliminates the need of manual configuration or DHCP unlike IPv4. The IPv6 EUI-64 format address is obtained through the 48-bit MAC address. The Mac address is first separated into two 24-bits, with one being Organizationally Unique Identifier (OUI) and the other being NIC specific. The 16-bit 0xFFFE is then inserted between these two 24-bits to form the 64-bit EUI address. IEEE has chosen FFFE as a reserved value which can only appear in EUI-64 generated from the an EUI-48 MAC address.

ND, RS/RA

The IPv6 neighbor discovery process uses ICMP messages and solicited-node multicast addresses to determine the link-layer address of a neighbor on the same network (local link), verify the reachability of a neighbor, and track neighboring devices.

The IPv6 static cache entry for neighbor discovery feature allows static entries to be made in the IPv6 neighbor cache. Static routing requires an administrator to manually enter IPv6 addresses, subnet masks, gateways, and corresponding MAC addresses for each interface of each device into a table. Static routing enables more control but requires more work to maintain the table. The table must be updated each time routes are added or changed.

By definition, a router is a node that forwards IP packets not explicitly addressed to it. IPv6 routers are compliant with this definition but, in addition, they regularly advertise information on the links to which they are connected—provided they are configured to do so. These advertisements are ICMPv6 Router Advertisement (RA) messages, sent to the multicast group FF02::1. All the systems on a link must belong to this group, and nodes configured for auto-configuration, among other things, analyze the option(s) of those messages. They might contain any routing prefix(es) for this segment.

ND messages facilitate requesting address of the target link layer and provide their own address to the target as well.

Router Solicitation

Upon reception of one of those RA messages and according to local algorithm policy, an auto-configuring node not already configured with the corresponding global address will prepend the advertised prefix to the unique identifier built previously.

However, the advertisement frequency, which is usually about ten seconds or more, may seem too long for the end user. In order to reduce this potential wait time, nodes can send Router Solicitation (RS) messages to all the routers on the link. Nodes that have not configured an address yet use the unspecified address "::". In response, the routers must answer immediately with a RA message containing a global prefix. This router solicitation corresponds to ICMPv6 messages of type RS, sent to the all-router multicast group FF02::2. All routers on the link must join this group.

Thus, a node soliciting on-link routers in such a way is able to extract a prefix and build its global address. The method of using an advertised prefix is possible only for end nodes. IPv6 routers are usually manually configured as a stateless automatic configuration requires the advertisement of a prefix. This prefix is sent by a router. The router sending the prefix must be fully configured to do so.

Further Reading

http://goo.gl/XN7mVv

Autoconfig/SLAAC, temporary addresses (RFC 4941)

Dynamic Host Configuration Protocol (DHCP) has allowed systems to obtain an IPv4 address as well as other information such as the default router or Domain Name System (DNS) server. A similar protocol called DHCPv6 has been published for IPv6, the next version of the IP protocol. However, IPv6 also has a stateless auto-configuration protocol unlike IPv4.

Stateless address configuration means that the client picks their own address based on the prefix being advertised on their connected interface. All Cisco devices have the ability to participate in Stateless Autoconfiguration (SLAAC). By default, SLAAC does not provide anything to the client outside of an IPv6 address and a default gateway. Additional configuration on the server is necessary before the same information can be provided to the client as Stateful DHCP. Moreover, it is important to note that SLAAC most commonly uses eui-64 format for address assignment. This means that IPv6 addresses will be built from a combination of the Layer 3 subnet prefix and the MAC address of the client. The requirement for SLAAC is that the LAN segment must use a /64 mask.

Cisco routers support both stateful and stateless DHCP. Stateless DHCP does not track IPv6 address bindings per client. It, rather, uses DHCP to hand out domain-names, DNS servers and other relevant client information.

Global prefix configuration feature

The upper 64 bits of an IPv6 address are composed from a global routing prefix plus a subnet ID. A general prefix (for example, /48) holds a short prefix, based on which a number of longer, more-specific prefixes (for example, /64) can be defined. When the general prefix is changed, all of the more-specific prefixes based on it will change, too. This function greatly simplifies network renumbering and allows for automated prefix definition. For example, a general prefix might be 48 bits long ("/48") and the more specific prefixes generated from it might be 64 bits long ("/64"). In the following example, the leftmost 48 bits of all the specific prefixes will be the same, and they are the same as the general prefix itself. The next 16 bits are all different.

General prefix: 2001:DB8:2222::/48
Specific prefix: 2001:DB8:2222:0000::/64
Specific prefix: 2001:DB8:2222:0001::/64
Specific prefix: 2001:DB8:2222:4321::/64
Specific prefix: 2001:DB8:2222:7744::/64

General prefixes can be defined in several ways:
- Manually
- Based on a 6to4 interface

- Dynamically, from a prefix received by a DHCP for IPv6 prefix delegation client

Further Reading

http://goo.gl/1eDvIF

DHCP protocol operations

DHCP Server Function

The DHCPv6 server can provide those configuration parameters that do not require the server to maintain any dynamic state for individual clients, such as DNS server addresses and domain search list options. The DHCPv6 server may be configured to perform prefix delegation.

All the configuration parameters for clients are independently configured into DHCPv6 configuration pools, which are stored in NVRAM. A configuration pool can be associated with a particular DHCPv6 server on an interface when it is started. Prefixes to be delegated to clients may be specified either as a list of pre-assigned prefixes for a particular client or as IPv6 local prefix pools that are also stored in NVRAM. The list of manually configured prefixes or IPv6 local prefix pools can be referenced and used by DHCPv6 configuration pools.

The DHCPv6 server maintains an automatic binding table in memory to track the assignment of some configuration parameters, such as prefixes between the server and its clients. The automatic bindings can be stored permanently in the database agent, which can be, for example, a remote TFTP server or local NVRAM file system.

Table 7-2, shows various DHCP messages and their intended use

Reference	Message	Use
0x01	DHCPDISCOVER	The client is looking for available DHCP servers. It is sent as broadcast
0x02	DHCPOFFER	The server response to the client DHCPDISCOVER.
0x03	DHCPREQUEST	The client broadcasts to the server, requesting offered parameters from one server specifically, as defined in the packet.

0x04	DHCPDECLINE	The client-to-server communication, indicating that the network address is already in use.
0x05	DHCPACK	The server-to-client communication with configuration parameters, including committed network address.
0x06	DHCPNAK	The server-to-client communication, refusing the request for configuration parameter.
0x07	DHCPRELEASE	The client-to-server communication, relinquishing network address and canceling remaining lease.
0x08	DHCPINFORM	The client-to-server communication, asking for only local configuration parameters that the client already has externally configured as an address.

Client Function

The DHCPv6 client function can be enabled on individual IPv6-enabled interfaces. The DHCPv6 client can request and accept those configuration parameters that do not require a server to maintain any dynamic state for individual clients, such as DNS server addresses and domain search list options. The DHCPv6 client will configure the local Cisco IOS stack with the received information. The DHCPv6 client can also request the delegation of prefixes. The prefixes acquired from a delegating router will be stored in a local IPv6 general prefix pool. The prefixes in the general prefix pool can then be referred to from other applications; for example, the general prefix pools can be used to number router downstream interfaces.

Further Reading

http://goo.gl/gtdkzE

SLAAC/DHCPv6 interaction

Stateless Address Autoconfiguration (SLAAC) is one of the most convenient methods to assign Internet addresses to IPv6 nodes. This method does not require any human intervention at all. If one wants to use IPv6 SLAAC on an IPv6 node, it is important that this IPv6 node is connected to a network with at least one IPv6 router connected. This router is configured by the network administrator and sends out Router Advertisement announcements onto the link. These announcements can allow the on-link connected IPv6 nodes to configure themselves with IPv6 address and routing parameters, as specified in RFC 2462, without further human intervention.

Stateful, Stateless DHCPv6

DHCPv6 enables DHCP servers to pass configuration parameters, such as IPv6 network addresses, to IPv6 nodes. It offers the capability of automatic allocation of reusable network addresses and additional configuration flexibility. This protocol is a stateful counterpart to "IPv6 Stateless Address Autoconfiguration" (RFC 2462), and can be used separately, or in addition to the stateless autoconfiguration to obtain configuration parameters.

Stateless DHCPv6 is a combination of "stateless Address Autoconfiguration" and DHCPv6. When using stateless-DHCPv6, a device will use Stateless Address Auto-Configuration (SLAAC) to assign one or more IPv6 addresses to an interface, while it utilizes DHCPv6 to receive "additional parameters" which may not be available through SLAAC. For example, additional parameters could include information such as DNS or NTP server addresses, and are provided in a stateless manner by DHCPv6. Using stateless DHCPv6 means that the DHCPv6 server does not need to keep track of any state of assigned IPv6 addresses, and there is no need for state refreshment as result. On network media supporting a large number of hosts associated to a single DHCPv6 server, this could mean a significant reduction in DHCPv6 messages due to the reduced need for address state refreshments. From Cisco IOS 12.4(15)T onwards the client can also receive timing information, in addition to the "additional parameters" through DHCPv6. This timing information provides an indication to a host when it should refresh its DHCPv6 configuration data.

DHCPv6 prefix delegation

DHCPv6 Prefix Delegation (DHCPv6-PD) is an extension to DHCPv6. Classical DHCPv6 is typically focused on parameter assignment from a DHCPv6 server to an IPv6 host running a DHCPv6 protocol stack. A practical example would be the stateful address assignment of "2001:db8::1" from a DHCPv6 server to a DHCPv6 client. DHCPv6-PD however is aimed at assigning complete subnets and other network and interface parameters from a DHCPv6-PD server to a DHCPv6-PD client. This means that instead of a single address assignment, DHCPv6-PD will assign a set of IPv6 "subnets". An example could be the assignment of "2001:db8::/60" from a DHCPv6-PD server to a DHCPv6-PD client. This will allow the DHCPv6-PD client (often a CPE device) to segment the received address IPv6 address space, and assign it dynamically to its IPv6 enabled interfaces.

Exam Essentials

- High CPU utilization in the Address Resolution Protocol (ARP) Input process occurs if the router has to originate an excessive number of ARP requests
- When you have a static route with an exit interface, router generates an ARP request for each IP address that is not reachable through more specific routes, which practically means that the router generates an ARP request for almost every address on the Internet
- Extended Unique Identifier (EUI), as per RFC 2373, allows a host to assign itself a unique 64-Bit IP Version 6 interface identifier (EUI-64)
- The IPv6 neighbor discovery process uses Internet Control Message Protocol (ICMP) messages and solicited-node multicast addresses to determine the link-layer address of a neighbor on the same network (local link), verify the reachability of a neighbor, and track neighboring devices
- Cisco IOS routers support both stateful DHCP and stateless DHCP. Stateless DHCP does not track IPv6 address bindings per client. It, rather, uses DHCP to hand out domain-names, DNS servers and other relevant client information
- Stateless Address Autoconfiguration (SLAAC) is one of the most convenient methods to assign Internet addresses to IPv6 nodes
- DHCPv6 Prefix Delegation (DHCPv6-PD) is an extension to DHCPv6

Chapter 8: Layer 3 Multicast

This chapter covers the following exam topics from Cisco's official 400-101 (v5) written exam curriculum.

- Troubleshoot reverse path forwarding (RPF failure, RPF failure with tunnel interface)
- Implement and troubleshoot IPv4 PIM (PIM dense/sparse/sparse-dense, static RP/auto RP/BSR, bi-dir PIM, source-specific multicast, group to RP mapping, multicast boundary)
- Implement and troubleshoot multicast source discovery protocol (intra-domain MSDP/anycast RP, SA filter)
- IPv6 multicast (addressing, PIMv6)

Chapter 8: Layer 3 Multicast

Troubleshoot reverse path forwarding

RPF failure

The Unicast RPF feature helps to mitigate problems that are caused by the introduction of malformed or spoofed IP source addresses into a network by discarding IP packets that lack a verifiable IP source address. These drops are accounted as packets that have failed RPF check.

RPF failure with tunnel interface

You can use show ip mroute count command to see RPF failures. A sample output of this command and its increasing counters for RPF failure are shown in the output below:

Router#show ip mroute count
IP Multicast Statistics
3 routes using 1642 bytes of memory
2 groups, 0.50 average sources per group
Forwarding Counts: Pkt Count/Pkts per second/Avg Pkt Size/Kilobits per second
Other counts: Total/RPF failed/Other drops(OIF-null, rate-limit etc)

Group: 224.0.1.40, Source count: 0, Packets forwarded: 0, Packets received: 0

Group: 239.1.1.20, Source count: 1, Packets forwarded: 11, Packets received: 50
  Source: 10.1.1.1/32, Forwarding: 11/0/100/0, Other: 30/19/0

You can also use show ip rpf source command to verify if RPF information is correct.

Further Reading

http://goo.gl/DeCxIj

Implement and troubleshoot IPv4 protocol independent multicast

PIM dense mode, sparse mode, sparse-dense mode

PIM can operate in dense mode (DM), sparse mode (SM), or in sparse-dense mode (PIM DM-SM), which handles both sparse groups and dense groups at the same time.

PIM DM builds source-based multicast distribution trees. In dense mode, a PIM DM router or multilayer switch assumes that all other routers or multilayer switches forward multicast packets for a group. If a PIM DM device receives a multicast packet and has no directly connected members or PIM neighbors present, a prune message is sent back to the source to stop unwanted multicast traffic. Subsequent multicast packets are not flooded to this router or switch on this pruned branch because branches without receivers are pruned from the distribution tree, leaving only branches that contain receivers. When a new receiver on a previously pruned branch of the tree joins a multicast group, the PIM DM device detects the new receiver and immediately sends a graft message up the distribution tree toward the source. When the upstream PIM DM device receives the graft message, it immediately puts the interface on which the graft was received into the forwarding state so that the multicast traffic begins flowing to the receiver.

PIM-SM uses shared trees and shortest-path-trees (SPTs) to distribute multicast traffic to multicast receivers in the network. In PIM-SM, a router or multilayer switch assumes that other routers or switches do not forward multicast packets for a group, unless there is an explicit request for the traffic (join message). When a host joins a multicast group using IGMP, its directly connected PIM-SM device sends PIM join messages toward the root, also known as the RP. This join message travels router-by-router toward the root, constructing a branch of the shared tree as it goes. The RP keeps track of multicast receivers. It also registers sources through register messages received from the source's first-hop router (designated router [DR]) to complete the shared tree path from the source to the receiver. When using a shared tree, sources must send their traffic to the RP so that the traffic reaches all receivers. Prune messages are sent up the distribution tree to prune multicast group traffic. This action permits branches of the shared tree or SPT that were created with explicit join messages to be torn down when they are no longer needed.

When the number of PIM-enabled interfaces exceeds the hardware capacity and PIM-SM is enabled with the SPT threshold is set to infinity, the switch does not create (S,G) entries in the multicast routing table for some directly connected interfaces if they are not already in the table. The switch might not correctly forward traffic from these interfaces.

Static RP, auto-RP, BSR

A rendezvous point (RP) is required only in networks running PIM sparse mode (PIM-SM). An RP acts as the meeting place (rendezvous) for sources and receivers of multicast data. In a PIM-SM network, sources must send their traffic to the RP. This traffic is then forwarded to receivers down a shared distribution tree. By default, when the first hop router of the receiver learns about the source, it will send a join message directly to the source, creating a source-based distribution tree from the source to the receiver. This source tree does not include the RP unless the RP is located within the shortest path between the source and receiver.

Following the introduction of PIM-SM v1, Cisco implemented a version of PIM-SM with the Auto-RP feature. Auto-RP automates the distribution of group-to-RP mappings in a PIM network. To make Auto-RP work, a router must be designated as an RP mapping agent, which receives the RP announcement messages from the RPs and arbitrates conflicts. The RP mapping agent then sends the consistent group-to-RP mappings to all other routers by dense mode flooding. Thus, all routers automatically discover which RP to use for the groups they support. The Internet Assigned Numbers Authority (IANA) has assigned two group addresses, 224.0.1.39 and 224.0.1.40, for Auto-RP. One advantage of Auto-RP is that any change to the RP designation must be configured only on the routers that are RPs and not on the leaf routers. Another advantage of Auto-RP is that it offers the ability to scope the RP address within a domain. Scoping can be achieved by defining the time-to-live (TTL) value allowed for the Auto-RP advertisements.

Another RP selection model called bootstrap router (BSR) was introduced after Auto-RP in PIM-SM v2. BSR performs similarly to Auto-RP in that it uses candidate routers for the RP function and for relaying the RP information for a group. RP information is distributed through BSR messages, which are carried within PIM messages. PIM messages are link-local multicast messages that travel from PIM router to PIM router. Because of this single hop method of disseminating RP information, TTL scoping cannot be used with BSR. A BSR performs similarly as an RP, except that it does not run the risk of reverting to dense mode operation, and it does not offer the ability to scope within a domain. Each method for configuring an RP has its own strengths, weaknesses, and level of complexity.

Further Reading
http://goo.gl/QXkxze

Bidirectional PIM

Bidir-PIM is a variant of the Protocol Independent Multicast (PIM) suite of routing protocols for IP multicast and is an extension of the existing PIM sparse mode (PIM-SM) feature. Bidir-PIM resolves some limitations of PIM-SM for groups with a large number of sources.

Membership to a bidirectional group is signaled via explicit join messages. Traffic from sources is unconditionally sent up the shared tree toward the RP and passed down the tree toward the receivers on each branch of the tree. Bidir-PIM is designed to be used for many-to-many applications within individual PIM domains. Multicast groups in bidirectional mode can scale to an arbitrary number of sources without incurring overhead due to the number of sources.

Bidir-PIM is derived from the mechanisms of PIM-SM and shares many shortest-path tree (SPT) operations. Bidir-PIM also has unconditional forwarding of source traffic toward the RP upstream on the shared tree, but no registering process for sources as in PIM-SM. These modifications are necessary and sufficient to allow forwarding of traffic in all routers solely based on the (*, G) multicast routing entries. This feature eliminates any source-specific state and allows scaling capability to an arbitrary number of sources.

Further Reading

http://goo.gl/YIDaKE

Source-specific multicast

The Source Specific Multicast (SSM) feature is an extension of IP multicast where datagram traffic is forwarded to receivers from only those multicast sources to which the receivers have explicitly joined. For multicast groups configured for SSM, only source-specific multicast distribution trees (no shared trees) are created.

PIM-SSM is the routing protocol that supports the implementation of SSM and is derived from PIM sparse mode (PIM-SM). IGMPv3 supports source filtering, which is required for SSM. To run SSM with IGMPv3, SSM must be supported in the Cisco IOS router, the host where the application is running, and the application itself. IGMP v3lite and URD are two Cisco-developed transition solutions that enable the immediate development and deployment of SSM services, without the need to wait for the availability of full IGMPv3 support in host operating systems and SSM receiver applications. IGMP v3lite is a solution for application developers that allows immediate development of SSM receiver applications switching to IGMPv3 as soon as it becomes available. URD is a solution for content providers and content aggregators that enables them to deploy receiver applications that are not yet SSM enabled (through support for IGMPv3). IGMPv3, IGMP v3lite, and URD interoperate with each other, so that both IGMP v3lite and URD can easily be used as transitional solutions toward full IGMPv3 support in hosts.

Further Reading

http://goo.gl/kcKUsm

Group to RP mapping

There are various mechanisms for disseminating RP information across a multicast network. Each mechanism has different pros and cons.

Table 8-1, shows various mechanisms for disseminating RP information

Comparison	Static RP	BSR	Auto-RP	Embedded RP
Must be configured on every router	Yes	No (except on candidate-BSRs and candidate-RPs)	No (except on candidate RPs and mapping agents)	No (except RP routers)
Supports IPv4 addresses	Yes	Yes	Yes	No
Supports IPv6 addresses	Yes	Yes	No	Yes
RP redundancy	No (unless used with Anycast RP)	Yes	Yes	No

Further Reading

http://goo.gl/Tu2IQp

Multicast boundary

You can set up an administratively scoped boundary on an interface for multicast group addresses. A standard access list defines the range of addresses affected. When a boundary is set up, no multicast data packets are allowed to flow across the boundary from either direction. The boundary allows the same multicast group address to be reused in different administrative domains.

The Internet Assigned Numbers Authority (IANA) has designated the multicast address range 239.0.0.0 to 239.255.255.255 as the administratively scoped addresses. This range of addresses can be reused in domains administered by different organizations. They would be considered local and not globally unique.

You can configure the filter-autorp keyword to examine and filter Auto-RP discovery and announcement messages at the administratively scoped boundary. Any Auto-RP group range announcements from the Auto-RP packets that are denied by the boundary access control list (ACL) are removed. An Auto-RP group range announcement is permitted and passed by the boundary only if all addresses in the Auto-RP group range are permitted by the boundary ACL. If any address is not permitted, the entire group range is filtered and removed from the Auto-RP message before the Auto-RP message is forwarded.

Further Reading

http://goo.gl/1wwdKF

Implement and troubleshoot multicast source discovery protocol

Intra-domain MSDP (anycast RP)

PIM-SM is the multicast forwarding protocol used in the intra-domain multicast scenarios. Anycast RP is a useful application of MSDP. This technique is used for configuring a multicast sparse mode network to provide for fault tolerance and load sharing within a single multicast domain.

Two or more RPs are configured with the same IP address (for example, 20.0.0.1) on loopback interfaces. The loopback address should be configured with a 32-bit mask. All the downstream routers are configured so that they know that 20.0.0.1 is the IP address of their local RP. IP routing automatically selects the topologically closest RP for each source and receiver. Because some sources use only one RP and some receivers a different RP, a method is needed for the RPs to exchange information about active sources. This information exchange is done with MSDP. All the RPs are configured to be MSDP peers of each other. Each RP will know about the active sources in the area of the other RP. If any of the RPs were to fail, IP routing would converge and one of the RPs would become the active RP in both areas.

SA filter

MSDP-SA messages contain Source, Group (S,G) information for rendezvous points (RPs) (also known as MSDP peers) in PIM sparse-mode (PIM-SM) domains. This mechanism allows RPs to learn about multicast sources in remote PIM-SM domains so that they can join those sources if there are local receivers in their own domain. You can also use MSDP between multiple RPs in a single PIM-SM domain to establish MSDP mesh-groups. With a default configuration, MSDP exchanges SA messages without filtering them for specific source or group addresses.

Typically, there are a number of (S,G) states in a PIM-SM domain that should stay within the PIM-SM domain, but, due to default filtering, they get passed in SA messages to MSDP peers. Examples of this include domain local applications that use global IP multicast addresses, and sources that use local IP addresses (such as 10.x.y.z). In the native IP multicast Internet, this default leads to excessive (S,G) information being shared.

Further Reading

http://goo.gl/LpQpra

Describe IPv6 multicast

IPv6 multicast addresses

IPv4 multicast addresses are defined by the leading address bits of 1110, originating from the classful network design of the early Internet when this group of addresses was designated as Class D. The Classless Inter-Domain Routing (CIDR) prefix of this group is 224.0.0.0/4. The group includes the addresses from 224.0.0.0 to 239.255.255.255. Multicast addresses in IPv6 have the prefix FF00::/8. IPv6 multicast addresses are generally formed from four bit groups, outlined as follows:

Table 8-2, shows IPv6 multicast address format

Bits	8	4	4	112
Field	prefix	flags	scope	group ID

PIMv6

The anycast RP solution in IPv6 PIM allows an IPv6 network to support anycast services for the PIM-SM RP. It allows anycast RP to be used inside a domain that runs PIM only. Anycast RP can be used in IPv4 as well as IPv6, but it does not depend on the Multicast Source Discovery Protocol (MSDP), which runs only on IPv4. This feature is useful when inter-domain connection is not required. Anycast RP is a mechanism that ISP-based backbones use to get fast convergence when a PIM RP device fails. To allow receivers and sources to rendezvous to the closest RP, the packets from a source need to get to all RPs to find joined receivers

A unicast IP address is chosen as the RP address. This address is either statically configured or distributed using a dynamic protocol to all PIM devices throughout the domain. A set of devices in the domain is chosen to act as RPs for this RP address; these devices are called the anycast RP set. Each device in the anycast RP set is configured with a loopback interface using the RP address. Each device in the anycast RP set also needs a separate physical IP address to be used for communication between the RPs.

The RP address, or a prefix that covers the RP address, is injected into the unicast routing system inside of the domain. Each device in the anycast RP set is configured with the addresses of all other devices in the anycast RP set, and this configuration must be consistent in all RPs in the set.

Exam Essentials

- The Unicast RPF feature helps to mitigate problems that are caused by the introduction of malformed or forged (spoofed) IP source addresses into a network by discarding IP packets that lack a verifiable IP source address
- The anycast RP solution in IPv6 PIM allows an IPv6 network to support anycast services for the PIM-SM RP
- DVMRP uses source trees and RPF check.
- You can use "ip pim autorp listener" command with interfaces configured for PIM sparse mode operation in order to establish a network configuration where Auto-RP operates in PIM dense mode and multicast traffic can operate in sparse mode, bidirectional mode, or source specific multicast (SSM) mode.
- When set, the R-bit indicates that the sender is a router. The R-bit is used by Neighbor Unreachability Detection to detect a router that changes to a host.

Chapter 9: Fundamental Routing Concepts

This chapter covers the following exam topics from Cisco's official 400-101 (v5) written exam curriculum.

- Implement and troubleshoot static routing
- Implement and troubleshoot default routing
- Routing protocol types (distance vector, link state, path vector)
- Implement, optimize, and troubleshoot administrative distance
- Implement and troubleshoot passive interface
- Implement and troubleshoot VRF lite
- Implement, optimize, and troubleshoot filtering with any routing protocol
- Implement, optimize, and troubleshoot redistribution between routing protocol
- Implement and troubleshoot loop prevention mechanisms (route tagging, filtering, split horizon, route poisoning)
- Implement and troubleshoot routing protocol authentication (MD5, key-chain, EIGRP HMAC SHA2-256bit, OSPFv2 SHA1-196bit, OSPFv3 IPsec authentication)

Chapter 9: Fundamental Routing Concepts

Implement and troubleshoot static routing

A router can learn about remote networks in one of two ways:
- Remote networks are manually entered into the route table using static routes.
- Remote routes are dynamically learned using a dynamic routing protocol.

Static routing provides some advantages over dynamic routing, including:
- Static routes are not advertised over the network, resulting in better security.
- Static routes use less bandwidth than dynamic routing protocols, as routers do not exchange routes.
- No CPU cycles are used to calculate and communicate routes.
- The path a static route uses to send data is known.

Static routing has the following disadvantages:
- Initial configuration and maintenance is time-consuming.
- Configuration can be error-prone, especially in large networks.
- Administrator intervention is required to maintain changing route information.
- Does not scale well with growing networks; maintenance becomes cumbersome.
- Requires complete knowledge of the whole network for proper implementation.

Implement and troubleshoot default routing

Administrator can configure a single default route to represent a path to any network that does not have a more specific match with another route in the routing table. Default routes are used to send traffic to any destination beyond the next upstream router.

Compare routing protocol types

Distance vector

The name distance vector is derived from the fact that routes are advertised as vectors of (distance, direction), where distance is defined in terms of a metric and direction is defined in terms of the next-hop router. For example, "Destination A is a distance of 7 hops away, in the direction of next-hop router Y." As that statement implies, each router learns routes from its neighboring routers' perspectives and then advertises the routes from its own perspective. Because each router depends on its neighbors for information, which the neighbors in turn may have learned from their neighbors, and so on, distance vector routing is sometimes also referred to as "routing by rumor."

Further Reading
http://goo.gl/3JKYqJ

Link state
Link state routing protocols are like a roadmap. They have a complete picture of the network. The reason is that unlike the routing-by-rumor approach of distance vector, link state routers have firsthand information from all their peer routers. Each router originates information about itself, its directly connected links, and the state of those links. This information is passed around from router to router, each router making a copy of it, but never changing it. The ultimate objective is that every router has identical information about the internetwork, and each router independently calculates its own best paths.

Further Reading
http://goo.gl/2BLSil

Path vector
A path vector protocol is a routing protocol which maintains the path information that gets updated dynamically. Updates which have looped through the network and returned to the same node are easily detected and discarded. This algorithm is sometimes used in Bellman–Ford routing algorithms to avoid "Count to Infinity" problems. BGP is an example of a path vector protocol.

Implement, optimize and troubleshoot administrative distance
Most routing protocols have metric structures and algorithms that are not compatible with other protocols. In a network with multiple routing protocols, the exchange of route information and the capability to select the best path across the multiple protocols are critical.

Administrative distance is the feature that routers use in order to select the best path when there are two or more different routes to the same destination from two different routing protocols. Administrative distance defines the reliability of a routing protocol. Each routing protocol is prioritized in order of most to least reliable (believable) with the help of an administrative distance value.

Administrative distance is the first criterion that a router uses to determine which routing protocol to use if two protocols provide route information for the same destination. Administrative distance is a measure of the trustworthiness of the source of the routing information. Administrative distance has only local significance, and is not advertised in routing updates. The smaller the administrative distance value, the more reliable the protocol. For example, if a Cisco router receives a route to a certain network from both Open Shortest Path First (OSPF) (default administrative distance - 110) and Interior Gateway Routing Protocol (IGRP) (default administrative distance - 100), the router chooses IGRP because IGRP is more reliable. This means the router adds the IGRP version of the route to the routing table.

Implement and troubleshoot passive interface

With most routing protocols, the passive-interface command restricts outgoing advertisements only. But, when used with Enhanced Interior Gateway Routing Protocol (EIGRP), the effect is slightly different. Passive-interface command in EIGRP suppresses the exchange of hello packets between two routers, which results in the loss of their neighbor relationship. This stops not only routing updates from being advertised, but it also suppresses incoming routing updates. OSPF doesn't send hellos and doesn't form neighborships over interfaces configured with passive-interface command.

Implement and troubleshoot VRF lite

VPN Routing and Forwarding (VRF) instances, are most commonly associated with MPLS. In service provider networks, MPLS encapsulation is used to isolate individual customer traffic and an independent routing table (VRF) is maintained for each customer. Most often, MP-BGP is employed to facilitate complex redistribution schemes to import and export routes to and from VRFs to provide Internet connectivity.

However, VRF configuration isn't at all dependent on MPLS (the two components just work well together). In Cisco terminology, deployment of VRFs without MPLS is known as VRF lite.

Implement, optimize and troubleshoot filtering with any routing protocol

Route filtering works by regulating the routes that are entered into or advertised out of the route table, they have different effects on link state routing protocols than they do on distance vector protocols. A router running a distance vector protocol advertises routes based on what is in its route table. As a result, a route filter influences which routes the router advertises to its neighbors.

On the other hand, routers running link state protocols determine their routes based on information in their link state database, rather than on the advertised route entries of its neighbors. Route filters have no effect on links state advertisements or on the link state database. For this reason, the information in this document only applies to distance vector IP Routing Protocols such as Routing Information Protocol (RIP), RIP version 2, Interior Gateway Routing Protocol (IGRP), and Enhanced IGRP (EIGRP).

In order to control the advertising and processing of routes in routing updates, use the distribute-list command. There are two distribute-list commands: distribute-list in and distribute-list out. They are similar in syntax, but the options available to each and their behavior are very different.

The syntax for the distribute-list in command is:
distribute-list access-list-number in [interface-name]

where access-list-number is the standard IP access-list against which the contents of the incoming routing update are matched. The [interface-name] argument is optional and specifies the interface on which the update is expected. It is important to note that the access-list referred to in access-list-number is applied to the contents of the update, not to the source or destination of the routing update packets.

The router decides whether or not to include the contents in its routing table based on the access-lists. For example:
access-list 1 permit 1.0.0.0 0.255.255.255
router rip
distribute-list 1 in

The syntax for the distribute-list out command is:
distribute-list access-list-number out [interface-name|routing process|autonomous-system-number]

where access-list-number is the standard IP access-list against which the contents of the outgoing routing updates are matched. The [interface-name] argument is optional, and specifies on which interface the update is going out. The [routing process|autonomous-system-number] arguments are used when redistribution from another routing process or autonomous system number has been specified. The list is applied to any routes imported from the specified process into the current one.

Note that checking the distribute list is only one of the many checks that are done against a distance vector route before a router includes it in the routing table or in an update. Checks are also made for desirability, policies, split horizon, and other factors.

Implement, optimize and troubleshoot redistribution between any routing protocol

The use of a routing protocol to advertise routes that are learned by some other means, such as by another routing protocol, static routes, or directly connected routes, is called redistribution. While running a single routing protocol throughout your entire IP internetwork is desirable, multi-protocol routing is common for a number of reasons, such as company mergers, multiple departments managed by multiple network administrators, and multi-vendor environments. Running different routing protocols is often part of a network design. In any case, having a multiple protocol environment makes redistribution a necessity.

Differences in routing protocol characteristics, such as metrics, administrative distance, classful and classless capabilities can affect redistribution. Consideration must be given to these differences for redistribution to succeed.

Distance Vector Protocols

When you redistribute one protocol into another, remember that the metrics of each protocol play an important role. Each protocol uses different metrics. For example, the Routing Information Protocol (RIP) metric is based on hop count, but Interior Gateway Routing Protocol (IGRP) and Enhanced Interior Gateway Routing Protocol (EIGRP) use a composite metric based on bandwidth, delay, reliability, load, and maximum transmission unit (MTU), where bandwidth and delay are the only parameters used by default. When routes are redistributed, you must define a metric that is understandable to the receiving protocol. There are two methods to define metrics when redistributing routes.

The redistribution of IGRP/EIGRP into another IGRP/EIGRP process does not require any metric conversion, so there is no need to define metrics or use the default-metric command during redistribution. A redistributed static route takes precedence over the summary route because the static route has an administrative distance of 1 whereas EIGRP summary route has an administrative distance of 5. This happens when a static route is redistributed with the use of redistribute static command under the EIGRP process and the EIGRP process has a default route.

This output below shows a RIP router redistributing static, IGRP, EIGRP, OSPF, and IS-IS routes.

router rip
network 132.110.0.0
redistribute static
redistribute igrp 10
redistribute eigrp 10
redistribute ospf 10
redistribute isis
default-metric 10

The RIP metric is composed of hop count, and the maximum value is 15. Anything above 15 is considered infinite; as an example you can use 16 to describe an infinite metric in RIP. When redistributing a protocol into RIP, Cisco recommends that you use a low metric, such as 1. A high metric, such as 10, limits RIP even further. If you define a metric of 10 for redistributed routes, these routes can only be advertised to routers up to 5 hops away, at which point the metric (hop count) exceeds 15.

Link State Protocols

It is possible to run more than one OSPF process on the same router. However, running more than one process of the same protocol is rarely needed, and consumes router's memory and CPU cycles. You do not need to define metric or use the default-metric command when redistributing one OSPF process into another.

This output shows an IS-IS router redistributing static, RIP, IGRP, EIGRP, and OSPF routes.

router isis
network 49.1234.1111.1111.1111.00
redistribute static
redistribute rip metric 20
redistribute igrp 1 metric 20
redistribute eigrp 1 metric 20
redistribute ospf 1 metric 20

The IS-IS metric must be between 1 and 63. There is no default-metric option in IS-IS—you should define a metric for each protocol, as shown in the example above. If no metric is specified for the routes being redistributed into IS-IS, a metric value of 0 is used by default.

Further Reading
http://goo.gl/8x1r0p

Implement, optimize and troubleshoot manual and auto summarization with any routing protocol

Routing protocols summarize or aggregate routes based on shared network numbers within the network. Classless routing protocols (such as RIPv2, OSPF, IS-IS, and EIGRP) support route summarization based on subnet addresses, including VLSM addressing. Classful routing protocols (RIPv1 and IGRP) automatically summarize routes on the classful network boundary and do not support summarization on any other bit boundaries. Classless routing protocols (RIPv2, OSPF, ISIS, EIGRP) support summarization on any bit boundary.

Route summarization reduces memory use on routers and routing protocol network traffic, because it results in fewer entries in the routing table (on the routers that receive the summarized routes). For summarization to work correctly, the following requirements must be met:
- Multiple IP addresses must share the same highest-order bits.
- Routing protocols must base their routing decisions on a 32-bit IP address and a prefix length that can be up to 32 bits.
- Routing updates must carry the prefix length (the subnet mask) along with the 32-bit IP address.

Implement, optimize and troubleshoot policy-based routing

PBR gives you a flexible means of routing packets by allowing you to configure a defined policy for traffic flows, lessening reliance on routes derived from routing protocols. To this end, PBR gives you more control over routing by extending and complementing the existing mechanisms provided by routing protocols. PBR allows you to set the IP precedence. It also allows you to specify a path for given type of traffic.

You can set up PBR as a way to route packets based on configured policies. For example, you can implement routing policies to allow or deny paths based on the identity of a particular end system, an application protocol, or the size of packets.

PBR allows you to perform the following tasks:
- Classify traffic based on extended access list criteria. Access lists, then, establish the match criteria.
- Set IP Precedence bits, giving the network the ability to enable differentiated classes of service.

- Route packets to specific traffic-engineered paths; you might need to route them to allow a specific QoS through the network.

Policies can be based on IP addresses, port numbers, protocols, or size of packets.

Further Reading

http://goo.gl/WVR3pY

Identify and troubleshoot sub-optimal routing

When you are redistributing between two routing protocol e.g. OSPF/EIGRP, if you don't configure filters or administrative distance modification then suboptimal routing may occur.

As an example, redistributing between different OSPF processes in multiple points on the network, it is possible to get into situations of suboptimal routing or even worse, a routing loop. When enabling multiple OSPF processes on a router, from the software perspective, the processes are independent. OSPF protocol, inside one OSPF process, always prefers the Internal route over the External route. However, OSPF does not do any OSPF route selection between processes (for instance, OSPF metrics and route types are not taken into account, when deciding the route of which process should be installed into the routing table).

There is no interaction between different OSPF processes, and the tie-breaker is the administrative distance. Thus, since both OSPF processes have a default administrative distance of 110, the first process trying to install that route makes it into the routing table. Therefore, administrative distance for routes from different OSPF processes must be configured, so that routes of certain OSPF processes are preferred over routes of another process by human intention, and not as a matter of chance.

Implement and troubleshoot bidirectional forwarding detection

BFD provides a low-overhead, short-duration method of detecting failures in the forwarding path between two adjacent routers, including the interfaces, data links, and forwarding planes. BFD is a detection protocol that you enable at the interface and routing protocol levels. Cisco supports the BFD asynchronous mode, which depends on the sending of BFD control packets between two systems to activate and maintain BFD neighbor sessions between routers.

Therefore, in order for a BFD session to be created, you must configure BFD on both systems (or BFD peers). Once BFD has been enabled on the interfaces and at the router level for the appropriate routing protocols, a BFD session is created, BFD timers are negotiated, and the BFD peers will begin to send BFD control packets to each other at the negotiated interval.

BFD provides fast BFD peer failure detection times independently of all media types, encapsulations, topologies, and routing protocols BGP, EIGRP, IS-IS, and OSPF. By sending rapid failure detection notices to the routing protocols in the local router to initiate the routing table recalculation process, BFD contributes to greatly reduced overall network convergence time.

One BFD session is established per interface regardless of the actual number of routing protocols that are being used.

Implement and troubleshoot loop prevention mechanisms

Loops occur when routers act on the basis of inaccurate or old information. Link-state protocols like OSPF use reliable flooding mechanisms to ensure that all routers are acting on the basis of the same information. That is what link-state protocols avoid. All routers in a link-state database have the same view of the network.

Distance vector protocols are susceptible to routing loops. Split horizon is one of the features of distance vector routing protocols that prevents them. This feature prevents a router from advertising a route back onto the interface from which it was learned. Route poisoning is another method for preventing routing loops employed by distance vector routing protocols. When a router detects that one of its directly connected routes has failed, it sends the advertisement for that route with an infinite metric ("poisoning the route"). A router that receives the update knows that the route has failed and doesn't use it anymore. Holddown is also a loop-prevention mechanism employed by distance vector routing protocol. This feature prevents a router from learning new information about a failed route.

Route tagging, filtering

Users can define a route map to prevent OSPF routes from being added to the routing table. This filtering happens at the moment when OSPF is installing the route in the routing table. This feature has no effect on LSA flooding. In the route map, the user can match on any attribute of the OSPF route. That is, the route map could be based on the following match options:

match interface
match ip address
match ip next-hop
match ip route-source
match metric
match route-type
match tag

OSPF external LSAs have a tag. The value of the tag is examined before the prefix is installed in the routing table. All OSPF external prefixes that have the tag value of 999 are filtered (prevented from being installed in the routing table). The permit statement with sequence number 20 has no match conditions, and there are no other route-map statements after sequence number 20, so all other conditions are permitted.

route-map tag-filter deny 10
match tag 999
route-map tag-filter permit 20
router ospf 1
router-id 100.0.0.2
log-adjacency-changes
network 172.16.2.1 0.0.0.255 area 0
distribute-list route-map tag-filter in

Implement and troubleshoot routing protocol authentication

MD5

The integrity of routing information inside a network is of the utmost importance as it can influence how traffic reaches specific destinations. Configuring the use of routing protocol authentication is an easy option that ensures that the device on the other side of a connection is who they say they are.

There are two general ways that authentication is implemented by most routing protocols: using a routing protocol centric solution that configures the passwords or keys to use within the routing protocol configuration, or by using a general solution that utilizes separately configured keys that are able to be used by multiple routing protocols. Both OSPF and BGP use the former methods and configure the specific authentication type and passwords/keys within their specific respective configurations. RIP and EIGRP utilize the latter methods by utilizing a separate authentication key mechanism that is configured and then utilized for either RIP or EIGRP.

OSPF Authentication

The configuration of OSPF requires a couple of different commands; which commands are used is determined by the type of authentication and method of authentication exchange. OSPF supports two different types of authentication that can be configured: authentication limited to a specific interface, or authentication configured over an entire OSPF area. Regardless of which of these options is selected there are also two different methods of authentication exchange that can be configured for each, these include: cleartext simple exchange, or MD5 exchange. When using MD5 the password/key that is configured is not sent between the exchanging devices, instead a hash is calculated and sent; this hash is then verified by the remote device to ensure identity.

RIP and EIGRP

RIP and EIGRP utilize key chains for their authentication configuration. The key chain configuration provides the ability to setup multiple keys that can be used by the supporting features. This includes the ability to have keys that potentially overlap in the time that they are valid. Keys can also be configured with specific transmit (send) and receive (accept) lifetimes that provide the ability to have keys automatically change at a predetermined time.

Further Reading

http://goo.gl/KekdPi

Key-chain

Key chains consist of two mandatory and two optional components. The necessary components are key number and key string. Optionally it also include an accept-lifetime and a send-lifetime parameter.

Key chain configuration steps:
- First you need to configure key chain in global configuration mode.
- Under key chain you need to configure key number. Key number must be match on both side of router and should be active. If multiple key numbers are configured on a router, the router will select the lowest key ID number for outbound authentication however will accept any matching valid keys in the keychain upon receipt
- Once you configure key number you need to issue authentication string

EIGRP HMAC SHA2-256 bit

Packets exchanged between neighbors must be authenticated to ensure that a device accepts packets only from devices that have the same pre-shared authentication key. Enhanced Interior Gateway Routing Protocol (EIGRP) authentication is configurable on a per-interface basis; this means that packets exchanged between neighbors connected through an interface are authenticated.

EIGRP supports message digest algorithm 5 (MD5) authentication to prevent the introduction of unauthorized information from unapproved sources. MD5 authentication is defined in RFC 1321. EIGRP also supports the Hashed Message Authentication Code-Secure Hash

Algorithm-256 (HMAC-SHA-256) authentication method. When you use the HMAC-SHA-256 authentication method, a shared secret key is configured on all devices attached to a common network. For each packet, the key is used to generate and verify a message digest that gets added to the packet.

The message digest is a one-way function of the packet and the secret key. If HMAC-SHA-256 authentication is configured in an EIGRP network, EIGRP packets will be authenticated using HMAC-SHA-256 message authentication codes. The HMAC algorithm takes as input the data to be authenticated (that is, the EIGRP packet) and a shared secret key that is known to both the sender and the receiver; the algorithm gives a 256-bit hash output that is used for authentication. If the hash value provided by the sender matches the hash value calculated by the receiver, the packet is accepted by the receiver; otherwise, the packet is discarded.

Configuration Steps

1. router eigrp virtual-name
2. address-family ipv4 [multicast] [unicast] [vrf vrf-name] autonomous-system autonomous-system-number
3. address-family ipv6 [unicast] [vrf vrf-name] autonomous-system autonomous-system-number
4. network ip-address [wildcard-mask]
5. af-interface {default | interface-type interface-number}
6. authentication mode {hmac-sha-256 encryption-type password | md5}

Please note that step #4 is optional when you're configuring HMAC-SHA2.

Further Reading

http://goo.gl/m9ft5D

OSPFv2 SHA1-196bit

To prevent unauthorized or invalid routing updates in your network, Open Shortest Path First version 2 (OSPFv2) protocol packets must be authenticated. There are two methods of authentication that are defined for OSPFv2: plain text authentication and cryptographic authentication. This module describes how to configure cryptographic authentication using the Hashed Message Authentication Code - Secure Hash Algorithm (HMAC-SHA). OSPFv2 specification (RFC 2328) allows only the Message-Digest 5 (MD5) algorithm for cryptographic authentication. However, RFC 5709 (OSPFv2 HMAC-SHA Cryptographic Authentication) allows OSPFv2 to use HMAC-SHA algorithms for cryptographic authentication.

You can use show ip ospf command to see if authentication is turned on.

```
Router# show ip ospf interface serial0
Serial0 is up, line protocol is up
Internet Address 192.16.64.1/24, Area 0
Process ID 10, Router ID  172.16.10.36 , Network Type POINT_TO_POINT, Cost: 64
Transmit Delay is 1 sec, State POINT_TO_POINT,
Timer intervals configured, Hello 10, Dead 40, Wait 40, Retransmit 5
Hello due in 00:00:05
  Index 2/2, flood queue length 0
  Next 0x0(0)/0x0(0)
  Last flood scan length is 1, maximum is 1
  Last flood scan time is 0 msec, maximum is 4 msec
  Neighbor Count is 1, Adjacent neighbor count is 1
        Adjacent with neighbor 70.70.70.70
  Suppress hello for 0 neighbor(s)
  Message digest authentication enabled
        Youngest key id is 1
```

OSPFv3 IPsec authentication

In order to ensure that OSPFv3 packets are not altered and re-sent to the device, OSPFv3 packets must be authenticated.

OSPFv3 requires the use of IPsec to enable authentication. Crypto images are required to use authentication, because only crypto images include the IPsec code needed for use with OSPFv3. In OSPFv3, authentication fields have been removed from OSPFv3 packet headers. When OSPFv3 runs on IPv6, OSPFv3 requires the IPv6 authentication header (AH) or IPv6 ESP header to ensure integrity, authentication, and confidentiality of routing exchanges. IPv6 AH and ESP extension headers can be used to provide authentication and confidentiality to OSPFv3.

To use the IPsec AH and authentication, you must enable the ipv6 ospf authentication command. To use the IPsec ESP header and encryption, you must enable the ipv6 ospf encryption command. The ESP header may be applied alone or in combination with the AH, and when ESP is used, both encryption and authentication are provided.

Further Reading

http://goo.gl/IbMXmS

Exam Essentials

- Administrative distance is a measure of the trustworthiness of the source of the routing information. Administrative distance has only local significance, and is not advertised in routing updates. The smaller the administrative distance value, the more reliable the protocol
- In order to control the advertising and processing of routes in routing updates, use the distribute-list command
- When you are redistributing between two routing protocol eg. OSPF/EIGRP, if you don't configure filters or administrative distance modification then suboptimal routing may occur
- One BFD session is established per interface regardless of the actual number of routing protocols that are being used
- Holddown is also a loop-prevention mechanism employed by distance vector routing protocol
- Key chains consist of two necessary and two are optional components. The necessary components are key number and key string. Optionally it also include an accept-lifetime and a send-lifetime parameter
- Under key chain we need to configure key number. Key number must be match on both side of router and should be active. If multiple key numbers are configured on a router, the router will select the lowest key ID number for outbound authentication however will accept any matching valid keys in the keychain upon receipt
- OSPFv3 uses the IPsec secure to add authentication (using AH and/or ESP header) and encryption (using ESP header) to OSPFv3 packets.
- Asynchronous BFD mode uses half as many packets for failure detection compared to demand mode and periodic hello packets do not necessitate using echo function
- Bellman-ford algorithm is the basis of mechanism used by path vector protocols
- Passive-interface command allows admins to exclude an interface from becoming a peer during routing protocol bring up
- The BGP conditional advertisement feature uses the non-exist-map and the advertise-map keywords of the neighbor advertise-map command in order to track routes by the route prefix. If a route prefix is not present in output of the non-exist-map command, then the route specified by the advertise-map command is announced. This feature is useful for multihomed networks, in which some prefixes are advertised to

one of the providers only if information from the other provider is not present (this indicates a failure in the peering session or partial reachability).

Chapter 10: RIPv2 (IPv4/IPv6)

This chapter covers the following exam topics from Cisco's official 400-101 (v5) written exam curriculum.

- Implement and troubleshoot RIPv2
- RIPv6 (RIPng)

Chapter 10: RIPv2 (IPv4/IPv6)

Implement and troubleshoot RIPv2

The Cisco implementation of RIPv2 supports cleartext and Message Digest 5 (MD5) authentication, route summarization, classless inter-domain routing (CIDR), and variable-length subnet masks (VLSMs) over RIPv1.

RIP carries default, invalid, holddown and flush timers that are 60, 180 and 180 seconds respectively.

Further Reading
http://goo.gl/WJKLcY

Describe RIPv6 (RIPng)

RIPv6 Routing Information Protocol (RIP) functions the same and offers the same benefits as IPv4 RIP v2. RIP enhancements for IPv6, detailed in RFC 2080, include support for IPv6 addresses and prefixes and the use of the all-RIP-devices multicast group address, FF02::9, as the destination address for RIP update messages.

RIPng sends updates on UDP port 521 using the multicast group FF02::9.

Further Reading
http://goo.gl/GJc462

Exam Essentials
- RIP enhancements for IPv6, detailed in RFC 2080, include support for IPv6 addresses and prefixes and the use of the all-RIP-devices multicast group address, FF02::9, as the destination address for RIP update messages
- RIPng sends updates on UDP port 521 using the multicast group FF02::9

Chapter 11: EIGRP (IPv4/IPv6)

This chapter covers the following exam topics from Cisco's official 400-101 (v5) written exam curriculum.

- Packet types (hello, query, update)
- Route types (internal, external)
- Implement and troubleshoot neighbor relationship (multicast, unicast EIGRP peering, OTP p2p peering, OTP route-reflector peering, OTP multiple service providers scenario)
- Implement and troubleshoot loop free path selection (RD, FD, FC, successor, feasible successor, classic/wide metrics)
- Implement and troubleshoot operations (topology table, update, query, active/passive, stuck in active, graceful shutdown)
- Implement and troubleshoot EIGRP stub (stub, leak-map)
- Implement and troubleshoot load-balancing (equal-cost, unequal-cost, add-path)
- Implement, troubleshoot and optimize, EIGRP convergence and scalability (fast convergence requirements, control query boundaries, IP FRR, summary leak-map, summary metric)

Chapter 11: EIGRP (IPv4/IPv6)

EIGRP offers the following features:
- Fast convergence—The DUAL algorithm allows routing information to converge as quickly as any currently available routing protocol.
- Partial updates—EIGRP sends incremental updates when the state of a destination changes, instead of sending the entire contents of the routing table. This feature minimizes the bandwidth required for EIGRP packets.
- Less CPU usage than IGRP—This occurs because full update packets need not be processed each time they are received.
- Neighbor discovery mechanism—This is a simple hello mechanism used to learn about neighboring routers. It is protocol-independent. Security requirements do not allow dynamic learning of neighbors. BFD should be used to detect loss of a neighbor.
- Variable-length subnet masks (VLSMs).
- Arbitrary route summarization.
- Scaling—EIGRP scales to large networks.

EIGRP uses split horizon or advertises a route as unreachable when:
- two routers are in startup mode (exchanging topology tables for the first time)
- advertising a topology table change
- sending a query

Poison reverse is a loop avoidance mechanism that states that once you learn of a route through an interface, advertise it as unreachable back through that same interface.

Describe packet types

Packet types (hello, query, update, and such)

EIGRP uses five packet types:
- Hello/Acks
- Updates
- Queries
- Replies
- Requests

Hellos are multicast for neighbor discovery/recovery. They do not require acknowledgment. A hello with no data is also used as an acknowledgment (Ack). Acks are always sent using a unicast address and contain a non-zero acknowledgment number.

Updates are used to convey reachability of destinations. When a new neighbor is discovered, update packets are sent so the neighbor can build up its topology table. In this case, update packets are unicast. In other cases, such as a link cost change, updates are multicast. Updates are always transmitted reliably.

Queries and replies are sent when destinations go into Active state. Queries are always multicast unless they are sent in response to a received query. In this case, it is unicast back to the successor that originated the query. Replies are always sent in response to queries to indicate to the originator that it does not need to go into Active state because it has feasible successors. Replies are unicast to the originator of the query. Both queries and replies are transmitted reliably.

Request packets are used to get specific information from one or more neighbors. Request packets are used in route server applications. They can be multicast or unicast. Requests are transmitted unreliably.

The sequence TLV contains a list of the nodes that should not listen to multicast packets while the recovery takes place. While recovering, each reliable multicast packet transmitted has the CR (conditional receive) bit set to indicate that it should be processed only if the receiving node's was not present in the preceding sequence TLV packet.

Further Reading

http://goo.gl/LAhBON

Route types (internal, external)

EIGRP has the concept of internal and external routes. Internal routes are ones that have been originated within an EIGRP autonomous system (AS). Therefore, a directly attached network that is configured to run EIGRP is considered an internal route and is propagated with this information throughout the EIGRP AS. External routes are ones that have been learned by another routing protocol or reside in the routing table as static routes. These routes are tagged individually with the identity of their origination.

External routes are tagged with the following information:
- The router ID of the EIGRP router that redistributed the route.
- The AS number where the destination resides.
- A configurable administrator tag.
- Protocol ID of the external protocol.
- The metric from the external protocol.
- Bit flags for default routing.

Implement and troubleshoot neighbor relationship

Multicast, unicast EIGRP peering

To create an EIGRP routing process, use the following commands from within global configuration mode:

Router(config)# router eigrp autonomous-system
Router(config-router)# network network-number

EIGRP sends updates to the interfaces in the specified networks. If you do not specify the network of an interface, the interface will not be advertised in any EIGRP update.

IPv6 equivalent of 224.0.0.10 (group address that is used to send routing information to all EIGRP routers on a network segment) is FF02::A.

Further Reading

http://goo.gl/i6aPTK

OTP point-to-point peering

EIGRP Over-the-Top (OTP) is focused on simplifying the deployment of branch networks utilizing an end-to-end EIGRP solution over public and private networks. This simplicity is further enhanced with EIGRP use of OTP to support multiple service provider IP networks.

EIGRP Over the ToP allows the customer to establish EIGRP adjacencies across the MPLS/VPN provider cloud. An EIGRP targeted adjacency between CPEs is created. This EIGRP neighborship is done via unicast packets, using the CPE 'WAN' IP address. This "over the top" peering allows EIGRP to exchange customer prefixes directly between CPEs. Customer prefixes are NOT injected in the providers VRF routing table. In order to allow for proper forwarding of user traffic across the MPLS/VPN cloud, user packets are encapsulated on the CPE. The encapsulation header uses the WAN IP address of the CEs, which are known in the MPLS/VPN cloud.

OTP control plane consists in an EIGRP targeted adjacency between CPEs. Neighborship is established using the CPE WAN address, i.e. address of CPE on the PE/CPE link, so there is no need for any dynamic routing protocol between the PE/CPE. The PE just needs to redistribute the connected routes.

This adjacency is using unicast packets and the CPE needs to know the IP of the remote CPE. In the first phase of OTP, only static neighbors are allowed. With manual neighbor configuration, it wouldn't scale to establish full mesh peering between all CEs. Instead, the concept of Route Reflector, i.e. CPEs peer with RRs only is used and RRs reflect the routes they receive to other CPEs. Each CPE is configured with the RRs WAN address and each RR is configured in EIGRP promiscuous mode, i.e. to accept incoming 'connections' (similar to BGP listen feature).

OTP route-reflector peering

OTP offers Route Reflectors (RRs) to form a half-mesh topology and ensure connectivity among all sites in the network. A Route Reflector is an EIGRP peer that receives route updates from remote sites and "reflects" the routes to other sites. Route Reflectors are configured using the keyword "unicast-listen". This option enables the Route Reflectors to listen for unicast Hello messages from other sites, and upon receiving the first Hello message, automatically forms a peering relationship. OTP supports the use of dual or multiple Route Reflectors for redundancy.

OTP RRs should have split horizon disabled in addition to next-hop-self.

OTP multiple service providers scenario

The EIGRP OTP solution simplifies multi-provider IP WAN network designs. It simplifies the interface with the WAN providers and facilitates an end-to-end EIGRP network, which is easier to troubleshoot.

EIGRP OTP is configured in the Customer Edge (CE) routers. They include CE, CE1 and CE2. CE1 and CE2 establish an EIGRP neighbor association with CE, which maintains a database of all the Customer Edge routers and their associated prefixes. Essentially, the router CE is supporting a route reflector type functionality for EIGRP. This is accomplished with a single line of configuration on the each router. Once the EIGRP neighbor association is established the customer's traffic or data forwarding can start.

Further Reading

http://goo.gl/cbcOam

Implement and troubleshoot loop free path selection

RD, FD, FC, successor, feasible successor

Feasible distance is the best metric along a path to a destination network, including the metric to the neighbor advertising that path.

Reported distance is the total metric along a path to a destination network as advertised by an upstream neighbor. A feasible successor is a path whose reported distance is less than the feasible distance (current best path).

A feasible successor for a particular destination is a next hop router that is guaranteed not to be a part of a routing loop. This condition is verified by testing the feasibility condition. Thus, every successor is also a feasible successor. However, in most references about EIGRP the term feasible successor is used to denote only those routes which provide a loop-free path but which are not successors (i.e. they do not provide the least distance). From this point of view, for a reachable destination there is always at least one successor, however, there might not be any feasible successors.

The feasibility condition (FC) is a sufficient condition for routing loop prevention in EIGRP-routed network. It is used to select the successors and feasible successors that are guaranteed to be on a loop-free route to a destination. Its formulation is strikingly simple:

- If, for a destination, a neighbor router advertises a distance that is strictly lower than our feasible distance, then this neighbor lies on a loop-free route to this destination.
- or in other words,
- If, for a destination, a neighbor router tells us that it is closer to the destination than we have ever been, then this neighbor lies on a loop-free route to this destination.

Further Reading

http://goo.gl/zCHBBg

Classic metric

EIGRP historically has used five vector metrics: minimum throughput, latency, load, reliability, and Maximum Transmission Unit (MTU).

These values are accumulated from destination to source as follows:
- Throughput-minimum value
- Latency-accumulative

- Load-maximum
- Reliability-minimum
- MTU-minimum
- Hop count-accumulative

Wide metric

To this, there are two additional values being added: jitter and energy. These two new values are accumulated from destination to source:

- Jitter-accumulative
- Energy-accumulative

These extended attributes, as well as any future ones, will be controlled through K6. If K6 is non-zero, these will be an additive to the path's composite metric. Higher jitter or higher energy usage will result in paths which are worse than those paths that either do not monitor these attributes, or which have lower values. EIGRP will not send these attributes if the router does not provide them. If the attributes are received, then EIGRP will use them in the metric calculation (based on K6) and will forward them with that router's values, assumed to be "zero", and the accumulative values will be forwarded unchanged. Of these vector metric components, by default, only minimum throughput and latency are traditionally used to compute the best path. Unlike most metrics, minimum throughput is set to the minimum value of the entire path, and it does not reflect how many hops or low throughput links are in the path, nor does it reflect the availability of parallel links. Latency is calculated based on one-way delays, and is a cumulative value, which increases with each segment in the path.

Implement and troubleshoot operations

The following are the most common causes of problems with EIGRP neighbor relationships:

- Unidirectional link
- Uncommon subnet, primary, and secondary address mismatch
- Mismatched masks
- K value mismatches
- Mismatched AS numbers
- Stuck in active
- Layer 2 problem
- Access list denying multicast packets
- Manual change (summary router, metric change, route filter)

Topology table, update, query, active, passive

The show ip eigrp topology command displays the EIGRP router ID. The EIGRP router ID comes from the highest IP address assigned to a loopback interface. If no loopback interfaces are configured, the highest IP address assigned to any other active interface is chosen as the router ID. No two EIGRP routers can have the same EIGRP router ID. If they do, you will experience problems exchanging routes between the two routers with equal router IDs.

Route filtering enables routes to be filtered from an EIGRP routing advertisement as they come in from a neighbor or as they are sent out to a neighbor. These filters can cause routes to be missing from the routing table. The show ip protocols command shows whether any filter lists are applied to EIGRP.

Further Reading

http://goo.gl/4tGolG
http://goo.gl/iLXuwB

Stuck in active

Stuck in active means that an EIGRP router is involved in a diffusing computation (a process of asking the neighboring routers to assist in locating a replacement path to a network for which the usable path has been lost) for a new path to some network, and this computation seems to be stalled because some expected replies have not arrived in a reasonable time. Active timer expiration leads to stuck-in-active (SIA).

Graceful shutdown

With graceful shutdown, a goodbye message is broadcast when an EIGRP routing process is shutdown, to inform adjacent peers about the impending topology change. This feature allows supporting EIGRP peers to synchronize and recalculate neighbour relationships more efficiently than would occur if the peers discovered the topology change after the hold time expired.

EIGRP sends an interface goodbye message with all K values set to 255 towards neighbors connected to its different interfaces. If the IOS neighbor router supports this graceful shutdown then it says "interface goodbye received". If not, it says K values mismatch.

Implement and troubleshoot EIGRP stub

Stub

The Enhanced Interior Gateway Routing Protocol (EIGRP) Stub Routing feature improves network stability, reduces resource utilization, and simplifies stub router configuration. Stub routing is commonly used in a hub and spoke network topology.

In a hub and spoke network, one or more end (stub) networks are connected to a remote router (the spoke) that is connected to one or more distribution routers (the hub). The remote router is adjacent only to one or more distribution routers. The only route for IP traffic to follow into the remote router is through a distribution router. This type of configuration is commonly used in WAN topologies where the distribution router is directly connected to a WAN. The distribution router can be connected to many more remote routers. Often, the distribution router will be connected to 100 or more remote routers. In a hub and spoke topology, the remote router must forward all non local traffic to a distribution router, so it becomes unnecessary for the remote router to hold a complete routing table. Generally, the distribution router need not send anything more than a default route to the remote router.

When using the EIGRP Stub Routing feature, you need to configure the distribution and remote routers to use EIGRP, and to configure only the remote router as a stub. Only specified routes are propagated from the remote (stub) router, e.g. a stub router will not send dynamically learned prefixes to a hub router. The router responds to queries for summaries, connected routes, redistributed static routes, external routes, and internal routes with the message "inaccessible." A router that is configured as a stub will send a special peer information packet to all neighboring routers to report its status as a stub router.

Any neighbor that receives a packet informing it of the stub status will not query the stub router for any routes, and a router (such as a hub) that has a stub peer will not query that peer. The stub router will depend on the distribution router to send the proper updates to all peers.

Leak-map

To configure a summary aggregate address for a specified interface, use the ip summary-address eigrp command in interface configuration mode. To disable a configuration, use the no form of this command.

ip summary-address eigrp as-number ip-address mask [admin-distance] [leak-map name]

It allows propagation of a specific set of routes out of the summary in addition to the summary prefix itself. Manual summary route metric is derived from the best composite metric out of the routes that make up the summary.

Further Reading

http://goo.gl/we6Wy4

Implement and troubleshoot load-balancing

Equal-cost

Load balancing is the capability of a router to distribute traffic over all the router network ports that are the same distance from the destination address. Load balancing increases the utilization of network segments, and so increases effective network bandwidth. Equal cost path load balancing is applicable when different paths to a destination network report the same routing metric value. The maximum-paths command determines the maximum number of routes that the routing protocol can use.

Unequal-cost

Unequal cost path load balancing is applicable when different paths to a destination network are of different routing metric values. The variance command determines which of these routes is used by the router.

Add-path

The Add Path feature in EIGRP feature enables hubs in a single Dynamic Multipoint VPN (DMVPN) domain to advertise multiple best paths to connected spokes when the Enhanced Interior Gateway Routing Protocol (EIGRP) is the routing protocol between the hubs and the spokes.

add-paths number command enables EIGRP to advertise multiple paths as best paths to connected spokes in a single Dynamic Multipoint VPN (DMVPN) domain.

Implement EIGRP (multi-address) named mode

Types of families

To enter address-family configuration mode to configure an Enhanced Interior Gateway Routing Protocol (EIGRP) routing instance, use the address-family (EIGRP) command in router configuration mode. To remove the address-family from the EIGRP configuration, use the no form of this command. You will use named mode to configure VRF lite configuration.

EIGRP Autonomous-System Configuration

address-family ipv4 [unicast] vrf vrf-name [autonomous-system autonomous-system-number]

IPv4 address-family

EIGRP Named IPv4 Configuration

address-family ipv4 [multicast] [unicast] [vrf vrf-name] autonomous-system autonomous-system-number

IPv6 address-family

EIGRP Named IPv6 Configuration

address-family ipv6 [unicast] [vrf vrf-name] autonomous-system autonomous-system-number

Implement, troubleshoot and optimize EIGRP convergence and scalability

Describe fast convergence requirements

EIGRP has been designed and used to achieve sub-second convergence for years. Lab testing has shown that the key factor for EIGRP convergence is the presence or absence of a feasible successor. When there is no feasible successor, EIGRP uses queries to EIGRP peers and has to wait for responses. This slows convergence.

Proper network design is required for EIGRP to achieve fast convergence. Summarization helps limit the scope of EIGRP queries, indirectly speeding convergence. Summarization also shrinks the number of entries in the routing table, which speeds up various CPU operations. The effect of CPU operation on convergence is much less significant than the presence or absence of a feasible successor. A recommended way to ensure that a feasible successor is present is to use equal-cost routing.

EIGRP metrics can be tuned using the delay parameter. However, adjusting the delay on links consistently and tuning variance are next to impossible to do well at any scale. In general, it is unwise to have a large number of EIGRP peers. Under worst-case conditions, router CPU or other limiting factors might delay routing protocol convergence.

Further Reading

http://goo.gl/D6txcr

Control query boundaries

EIGRP is an advanced distance-vector protocol; it doesn't have LSA flooding like OSPF. EIGRP relies only on its neighbors for information on network reachability and availability. EIGRP keeps a list of backup routes called feasible successors. When the primary route is not available, EIGRP immediately uses the feasible successor as the backup route. This shortens convergence time. Now, if the primary route is gone and no feasible successor is available, the route is in active state. The only way for EIGRP to converge quickly is to query its neighbors about the unavailable route. If the neighbor doesn't know the status of the route, the neighbor asks its neighbors, and so on, until the edge of the network is reached.

The query stops if one of the following occurs:
- All queries are answered from all the neighbors.
- The end of network is reached.
- The lost route is unknown to the neighbors.

The problem is that, if there are no query boundaries, EIGRP potentially can ask every router in the network for a lost route. When EIGRP first queries its neighbor, a stuck in active timer starts. By default, the timer is 180 seconds. If, in three minutes, EIGRP doesn't receive the query response from all its neighbors, EIGRP declares that the route is stuck in active state and resets the neighbor that has not responded to the query.

IP FRR/fast reroute (single hop)

The EIGRP Loop-Free Alternate Fast Reroute feature allows the Enhanced Interior Gateway Routing Protocol (EIGRP) to reduce the routing transition time to less than 50 ms by pre-computing repair paths or backup routes and installing these paths or routes in the Routing Information Base (RIB). Fast Reroute (FRR) is the mechanism that enables traffic that traverses a failed link to be rerouted around the failure. In EIGRP networks, pre-computed backup routes or repair paths are known as feasible successors or loop-free alternates (LFAs).

Summary leak-map and metric

When EIGRP creates a summary route, it includes a metric with the route in order to advertise it. EIGRP searches for components of the summary to be suppressed and represented by the summary. EIGRP finds the component with the best metric and copies the metric from it into the summary. Components of the summary may come and go, which means that every time the best component changes, the summary needs to be re-advertised to all of its peers. Even if the best component is not the one that changed, EIGRP still has to search every topology entry to make sure the summary is not affected.

This can add significant processing overhead. Use the summary-metric command to mitigate this metric churn and processing overhead. Rather than searching for the best component metric, EIGRP uses the values configured with the summary-metric command.

Exam Essentials

- The sequence TLV contains a list of the nodes that should not listen to multicast packets while the recovery takes place. While recovering, each reliable multicast packet transmitted has the CR (conditional receive) bit set to indicate that it should be processed only if the receiving node's was not present in the preceding sequence TLV packet
- Request packets are used to get specific information from one or more neighbors. Request packets are used in route server applications. They can be multicast or unicast. Requests are transmitted unreliably
- IPv6 equivalent of 224.0.0.10 (group address that is used to send routing information to all EIGRP routers on a network segment) is FF02::A
- OTP RRs should have split horizon disabled in addition to next-hop-self
- Feasible distance is the best metric along a path to a destination network, including the metric to the neighbor advertising that path
- The feasibility condition (FC) is a sufficient condition for loop freedom in EIGRP-routed network
- The show ip eigrp topology command displays the EIGRP router ID. The EIGRP router ID comes from the highest IP address assigned to a loopback interface
- Any neighbor that receives a packet informing it of the stub status will not query the stub router for any routes, and a router (such as a hub) that has a stub peer will not query that peer
- The Add Path Support in EIGRP feature enables hubs in a single Dynamic Multipoint VPN (DMVPN) domain to advertise multiple best paths to connected spokes when the Enhanced Interior Gateway Routing Protocol (EIGRP) is the routing protocol between the hubs and the spokes
- To configure a summary aggregate address for a specified interface, use the ip summary-address eigrp command in interface configuration mode

- Use the summary-metric command to mitigate this metric churn and processing overhead
- Use the auto-summary command to summarize the external routes that are learned and overlap with the locally configured "network" statements
- Router ID, protocol ID and metric are three values that can be used to tag an external EIGRP route.
- EIGRP over the Top (EOT) uses LISP as its data plane.
- Feasible distance is the minimum metric to reach the final destination as per the EIGRP topology table
- EIGRP Retransmission Timeout (RTO) is six times as long as the Smooth Round Trip Time (SRTT)
- Configuring the **leak-map** keyword allows to advertise a component route that would otherwise be suppressed by the manual summary. Any component subset of the summary can be leaked. A route map and access list must be defined to source the leaked route.
- On a Cisco router, EIGRP external, internal and summary administrative distances are 90, 170 and 5 respectively
- The concept of EIGRP OTP SoO checking is follows:
    - During the import process the SoO value in BGP update is checked against the SoO value of the site-map attached to VRF interface. The update is propagated to CE only if there is no match (this check is done regardless of protocol used on PE/CE link).
    - At reception of EIGRP update, the SoO value in the EIGRP update is checked against the SoO value of site-map attached to the incoming interface. This update is accepted only if there is no match (this check can optionally be done on backdoor router).
- EIGRP delay metric is propagated to all neighbors on a given segment as opposed to bandwidth metric
- EIGRP delay metric is calculated as a sum of all paths from source to destination whereas only the minimum bandwidth is considered. Any changes to bandwidth metric also affect QoS
- EIGRP throttles to use 50 percent of the configured bandwidth. Lowering the bandwidth can cause problems like starving EIGRP neighbors from getting hello packets because of the throttling back.
- Reduced EIGRP timers can yield about 1-2 seconds convergence times at best whereas BFD can provide sub-second convergence times
- When RIP, IGRP, EIGRP are used as the routing protocol, enabling split horizon prevents the network of the secondary addresses from being advertised over the primary network. EIGRP can form neighbor relationship using only the primary address.
- EIGRP OTP allows EIGRP routes to go across a SP core without their involvement. It also allows for organization's EIGRP networks to be contiguous.

Chapter 12: OSPF (v2 and v3)

This chapter covers the following exam topics from Cisco's official 400-101 (v5) written exam curriculum.

- Packet types (LSA 1, 2, 3, 4, 5, 7, 9)
- Route types (N1, N2, E1, E2)
- Implement and troubleshoot neighbor relationship
- Implement and troubleshoot OSPFv3 address-family support
- Implement and troubleshoot network types, area types and router types (p2p, p2mp, broadcast, non-broadcast, LSA types, area type, backbone, normal, transit, stub, NSSA. totally stub, internal router, ABR, ASBR, virtual link)
- Implement and troubleshoot path preference
- Implement and troubleshoot operations (graceful shutdown, GTSM)
- Implement, troubleshoot and optimize OSPF convergence and scalability (metrics, LSA throttling, SPF tuning, fast hello, LSA propagation control, IP FRR, LFA/loop-free alternative, OSPFv3 prefix suppression)

Chapter 12: OSPF (v2 and v3)

Describe packet types

LSA types (1, 2, 3, 4, 5, 7, 9)

Table 12-1 summarizes various LSA types and their description

LSA Type	Description
1	Router Link advertisements. Generated by each router for each area it belongs to. They describe the states of the router's link to the area. These are only flooded within a particular area.
2	Network Link advertisements. Generated by Designated Routers. They describe the set of routers attached to a particular network. Flooded in the area that contains the network.
3 or 4	Summary Link advertisements. Generated by Area Border routers. They describe inter-area (between areas) routes. Type 3 describes routes to networks, also used for aggregating routes. Type 4 describes routes to ASBR.
5	AS external link advertisements. Originated by ASBR. They describe routes to destinations external to the AS. Flooded all over except stub areas.

A designated router (DR) is the router interface elected among all routers on a particular multi-access network segment, generally assumed to be broadcast multi-access. The basic neighbor discovery process (Hello), flooding (224.0.0.6), DR election (priority, RID). Special techniques, often vendor-dependent, may be needed to support the DR function on non-broadcast multi-access (NBMA) media. It is usually wise to configure the individual virtual circuits of a NBMA subnet as individual point-to-point lines.

DRs exist for the purpose of reducing network traffic by providing a source for routing updates. The DR maintains a complete topology table of the network and sends the updates to the other routers via multicast. All routers in a multi-access network segment will form a slave/master relationship with the DR. They will form adjacencies with the DR and BDR only. Every time a router sends an update, it sends it to the DR and BDR on the multicast address 224.0.0.6. The DR will then send the update out to all other routers in the area, to the multicast address 224.0.0.5. This way all the routers do not have to constantly update each other, and can rather get all their updates from a single source. The use of multicasting further reduces the network load. DRs and BDRs are always setup/elected on OSPF broadcast networks. DR's can also be elected on NBMA (Non-Broadcast Multi-Access) networks such as Frame Relay. DRs or BDRs are not elected on point-to-point links (such as a point-to-point WAN connection) because the two routers on either sides of the link must become fully adjacent and the bandwidth between them cannot be further optimized. DR and non-DR routers evolve from 2-way to full adjacency relationships by exchanging DD, Request, and Update.

Table 12-2, shows various OSPF network types and traffic that are allowed

Network Type	Traffic Type
non-broadcast p2mp broadcast	Unicast
broadcast p2p p2mp	Multicast
loopback	Stub

Route types (N1, N2, E1, E2)

There are several types of OSPF routes:
Intra-Area—In a multi-area OSPF network, routes, originated within an area, are known by the routers in the same area as Intra-Area routes. These routes are flagged as O in the show ip route command output.
- Inter-Area—When a route crosses an OSPF Area Border Router (ABR), the route is known as an OSPF Inter-Area route. These routes are flagged as O IA in the show ip route command output.
- Both Intra and Inter-Area routes are also called OSPF Internal routes, as they are generated by OSPF itself, when an interface is covered with the OSPF network command.
- External Type-2 or External Type-1—Routes which were redistributed into OSPF, such as Connected, Static, or other Routing Protocol, are known as External Type-2 or External Type-1. These routes are flagged as O E2 or O E1 in the show ip route command output.
- NSSA external type 2 or NSSA external type 1—When an area is configured as a Not-So-Stub Area (NSSA), and routes are redistributed into OSPF, the routes are known as NSSA external type 2 or NSSA external type 1. These routes are flagged as O N2 or O N1 in the show ip route command output.

Implement and troubleshoot neighbor relationship

You can use the show ip ospf neighbor command to determine the state of the OSPF neighbor or neighbors.

If the show ip ospf neighbor command reveals nothing at all—or reveals nothing about the particular neighbor you are analyzing—then this router has not seen any "valid" OSPF HELLOs from that neighbor. This means that OSPF either did not receive any HELLO packets from the neighbor or received HELLO packets that failed very basic sanity checks.

- state = down

A neighbor that is discovered dynamically through reception of HELLO packets can fall back to a down state if it is being deleted, for example when OSPF does not receive HELLO packets from the neighbor for period of time longer than the Dead timer interval. Therefore, the down state is transient for such neighbors; they will either advance to higher states or be completely deleted from the table of known neighbors. This is known as being "forgotten".

Usually, neighbors that are seen in the down state were manually configured with the neighbor command. Manually configured neighbors are always present in the OSPF neighbor table. If OSPF has never received HELLO packet from the manually configured neighbor, or if no HELLO packets were heard from the neighbor during the previous Dead timer interval, then the manually configured neighbor will be listed as down.

- state = init

The init state indicates that a router sees HELLO packets from the neighbor, but two-way communication has not been established. A Cisco router includes the Router IDs of all neighbors in the init (or higher) state in the Neighbor field of its HELLO packets. For two-way communication to be established with a neighbor, a router also must see its own Router ID in the Neighbor field of the neighbor's HELLO packets.

- state = exstart / exchange

OSPF neighbors that are in exstart or exchange state are trying to exchange DBD packets. The router and its neighbor form a master and slave relationship. The adjacency should continue past this state. If it does not, there is a problem with the DBD exchange, such as a maximum transmission unit (MTU) mismatch or the receipt of an unexpected DBD sequence number

- state = 2-way

The 2-way state indicates that the router has seen its own Router ID in the Neighbor field of the neighbor's HELLO packet. Receiving a Database Descriptor (DBD) packet from a neighbor in the init state will also a cause a transition to 2-way state. The OSPF neighbor 2-way state is not a cause for concern (e.g. for broadcast network type).

- state = loading

In the loading state, routers send link-state request packets. During the adjacency, if a router receives an outdated or missing link-state advertisement (LSA), it requests that LSA by sending a link-state request packet. Neighbors that do not transition beyond this state are most likely exchanging corrupted LSAs. This problem is usually accompanied by a %OSPF-4-BADLSA console message.

A common problem when using Open Shortest Path First (OSPF) is routes in the database don't appear in the routing table. In most cases OSPF finds a discrepancy in the database so it doesn't install the route in the routing table. Often, you can see the Adv Router is not-reachable message (which means that the router advertising the LSA is not reachable through OSPF) on top of the link-state advertisement (LSA) in the database when this problem occurs. Here is an example:

Router# show ip ospf database router 172.16.32.2

Adv Router is not-reachable
LS age: 418
Options: (No TOS-capability, DC)
LS Type: Router Links
Link State ID: 172.16.32.2
Advertising Router: 172.16.32.2
LS Seq Number: 80000002
Checksum: 0xFA63
Length: 60
 Number of Links: 3

There are several reasons for this problem, most of which deal with mis-configuration or a broken topology. When the configuration is corrected the OSPF database discrepancy goes away and the routes appear in the routing table.

When OSPF priority is set to zero for a given interface, it will never become a DR or BDR. When using "show ip ospf neighbor" command, the state will appear as 2WAY/DROTHER.

Further Reading

http://goo.gl/WmL2EB
http://goo.gl/A8N2zE

Implement and troubleshoot OSPFv3 address-family support

Configuration Steps

1. enable
2. configure terminal
3. router ospfv3 [process-id]
4. area area-ID [default-cost | nssa | stub]
5. auto-cost reference-bandwidth Mbps
6. bfd all-interfaces
7. default {area area-ID[range ipv6-prefix | virtual-link router-id]} [default-information originate [always | metric | metric-type | route-map] | distance | distribute-list prefix-list prefix-list-name {in | out} [interface] | maximum-paths paths | redistribute protocol | summary-prefix ipv6-prefix]
8. ignore lsa mospf
9. interface-id snmp-if-index
10. log-adjacency-changes [detail]
11. passive-interface [default | interface-type interface-number]
12. queue-depth {hello | update} {queue-size | unlimited}
13. router-id {router-id}

To filter outgoing link-state advertisements (LSAs) to an Open Shortest Path First (OSPF) interface, use the ip ospf database-filter all out command in interface or virtual network interface configuration modes. To restore the forwarding of LSAs to the interface, use the no form of this command.

Router(config-if)#ipv6 ospf neighbor 2002:234::2
OSPFv3:Neighbor address needs to be a link-local address

You need to add the additional static frame-relay DLCI mapping statement to neighbor's link local address before OSPF adjacency will form.

ip ospf database-filter all out [disable]

Verification Steps

- show ospfv3 [process-id] border-routers
- show ospfv3 [process-id [area-id]] database [database-summary | internal | external[ipv6-prefix] [link-state-id] | grace | inter-area prefix [ipv6-prefix | link-state-id] | inter-area router [destination-router-id | link-state-id] | link [interface interface-name |link-state-id] | network [link-state-id] | nssa-external [ipv6-prefix] [link-state-id] | prefix [ref-lsa {router | network} | link-state-id] | promiscuous | router [link-state-id] | unknown [{area | as | link} [link-state-id]] [adv-router router-id] [self-originate]
- show ospfv3 [process-id] events [generic | interface | lsa | neighbor | reverse | rib | spf]
- show ospfv3 [process-id] [area-id] flood-list interface-type interface-number
- show ospfv3 [process-id] graceful-restart
- show ospfv3 [process-id] [area-id] interface[type number] [brief]
- show ospfv3 [process-id] [area-id] neighbor[interface type interface-number] [neighbor-id] [detail]
- show ospfv3 [process-id] [area-id] request-list[neighbor] [interface] [interface neighbor]
- show ospfv3 [process-id] [area-id] retransmission-list [neighbor] [interface] [interface neighbor]
- show ospfv3 [process-id] statistic[detail]
- show ospfv3 [process-id] summary-prefix
- show ospfv3 [process-id] timers rate-limit
- show ospfv3 [process-id] traffic[interface-type interface-number]
- show ospfv3 [process-id] virtual-links

Further Reading

http://goo.gl/N8Z90m

IPv4/v6 address-family

The OSPFv3 address families feature enables both IPv4 and IPv6 unicast traffic to be supported. With this feature, users may have two router processes per interface, but only one process per AF. If the IPv4 AF is used, an IPv4 address must first be configured on the interface, but IPv6 must be enabled on the interface. A single IPv4 or IPv6 OSPFv3 process running multiple instances on the same interface is not supported.

Users with an IPv6 network that uses OSPFv3 as its IGP may want to use the same IGP to help carry and install IPv4 routes. All routers on this network have an IPv6 forwarding stack. Some (or all) of the links on this network may be allowed to do IPv4 forwarding and be configured with IPv4 addresses. Pockets of IPv4-only routers exist around the edges running an IPv4 static or dynamic routing protocol. In this scenario, users need the ability to forward IPv4 traffic between these pockets without tunneling overhead, which means that any IPv4 transit router has both IPv4 and IPv6 forwarding stacks (e.g., is dual stack). This feature allows a separate (possibly incongruent) topology to be constructed for the IPv4 AF. It installs IPv4 routes in IPv4 RIB, and then the forwarding occurs natively. The OSPFv3 process fully supports an IPv4 AF topology and can redistribute routes from and into any other IPv4 routing protocol.

An OSPFv3 process can be configured to be either IPv4 or IPv6. The address-family command is used to determine which AF will run in the OSPFv3 process, and only one address family can be configured per instance however multiple instances of OSPFv3 can be enabled on single interface. Once the AF is selected, users can enable multiple instances on a link and enable address-family-specific commands.

Different instance ID ranges are used for each AF (it is carried inside packet header as instance ID field and that's unique to IPv6). Each AF establishes different adjacencies, has a different link state database, and computes a different shortest path tree. The AF then installs the routes in AF-specific RIB. LSAs that carry IPv6 unicast prefixes are used without any modification in different instances to carry each AFs' prefixes.

The IPv4 subnets configured on OSPFv3-enabled interfaces are advertised through intra-area prefix LSAs, just as any IPv6 prefixes. External LSAs are used to advertise IPv4 routes redistributed from any IPv4 routing protocol, including connected and static. The IPv4 OSPFv3 process runs the SPF calculations and finds the shortest path to those IPv4 destinations. These computed routes are then inserted in the IPv4 RIB (computed routes are inserted into an IPv6 RIB for an IPv6 AF).

Because the IPv4 OSPFv3 process allocates a unique pdbindex in the IPv4 RIB, all other IPv4 routing protocols can redistribute routes from it. The parse chain for all protocols is same, so the ospfv3 keyword added to the list of IPv4 routing protocols causes OSPFv3 to appear in the redistribute command from any IPv4 routing protocol. With the ospfv3 keyword, IPv4 OSPFv3 routes can be redistributed into any other IPv4 routing protocol as defined in the redistribute ospfv3 command.

In case of using OSPF for IP VPNs as PE-CE protocol, the down bit helps prevent routing loops between MP-BGP and OSPF, but not when external routes are announced, such as when redistribution between multiple OSPF domains or when external routes are injected in an area that is dual-homed to the provider network. The PE router redistributes an OSPF route from a different OSPF domain into an OSPF domain as an external route. The down bit is not set because LSA Type 5 does not support the down bit. The redistributed route is propagated across the OSPF domain.

Implement and troubleshoot network types, area types and router types

Point-to-point, multipoint, broadcast, non-broadcast

The command used to set the network type of an OSPF interface is:

ip ospf network {broadcast | non-broadcast | point-to-multipoint}

Point-to-Point Sub-interfaces

A sub-interface is a logical way of defining an interface. The same physical interface can be split into multiple logical interfaces, with each sub-interface being defined as point-to-point. This was originally created in order to better handle issues caused by split horizon over NBMA and vector based routing protocols. A point-to-point sub-interface has the properties of any physical point-to-point interface. As far as OSPF is concerned, an adjacency is always formed over a point-to-point sub-interface with no DR or BDR election.

Point-to-Multipoint Interfaces

An OSPF point-to-multipoint interface is defined as a numbered point-to-point interface having one or more neighbors. This concept takes the previously discussed point-to-point concept one step further. Administrators do not have to worry about having multiple subnets for each point-to-point link. The cloud is configured as one subnet. This should work well for people who are migrating into the point-to-point concept with no change in IP addressing on the cloud. Also, they would not have to worry about DRs and neighbor statements. OSPF point-to-multipoint works by exchanging additional link-state updates that contain a number of information elements that describe connectivity to the neighboring routers.

Broadcast Interfaces

In case of broadcast, the interface will be logically set to broadcast (using ip ospf network broadcast command) and will behave as if the router were connected to a LAN. DR and BDR election will still be performed so special care should be taken to assure either a full mesh topology or a static selection of the DR based on the interface priority.

Table 12-3, shows the various OSPF network types and their associated default set of timers

OSPF network type	Default set of timers

point to point broadcast	Hello: 10 Dead: 40 Wait: 40
point to multipoint non-broadcast point to multipoint Non-broadcast	Hello: 30 Dead: 120 Wait: 120

LSA types, area type: backbone, normal, transit, stub, NSSA, totally stub

Table 12-4, shows the differences between the types of the OSPF areas.

Area Type	Description
Stub	No Type 5 AS-external LSA allowed
Totally Stub	No Type 3, 4 or 5 LSAs allowed except the default summary route
NSSA	No Type 5 AS-external LSAs allowed, but Type 7 LSAs that convert to Type 5 at the NSSA ABR can traverse
NSSA Totally Stub	No Type 3, 4 or 5 LSAs except the default summary route, but Type 7 LSAs that convert to Type 5 at the NSSA ABR are allowed

Internal router, ABR, ASBR

OSPF uses flooding to exchange link-state updates between routers. Any change in routing information is flooded to all routers in the network. Areas are introduced to put a boundary on the explosion of link-state updates. Flooding and calculation of the Dijkstra algorithm on a router is limited to changes within an area. All routers within an area have the exact link-state database. Routers that belong to multiple areas, and connect these areas to the backbone area are called area border routers (ABR). ABRs must therefore maintain information describing the backbone areas and other attached areas.

An area is interface specific. A router that has all of its interfaces within the same area is called an internal router (IR). A router that has interfaces in multiple areas is called an area border router (ABR). Routers that act as gateways (redistribution) between OSPF and other routing protocols (IGRP, EIGRP, IS-IS, RIP, BGP, Static) or other instances of the OSPF routing process are called autonomous system boundary router (ASBR). Any router can be an ABR or an ASBR. The P-bit is used in order to tell the NSSA ABR whether to translate type 7 into type 5.

Virtual link

Area 0 has to be at the center of all other areas. In some rare case where it is impossible to have an area physically connected to the backbone, a virtual link is used. The virtual link will provide the disconnected area a logical path to the backbone. The virtual link has to be established between two ABRs that have a common area, with one ABR connected to the backbone.

Packets sent on a virtual link with IPsec must use predetermined source and destination addresses. The first local area address found in the router's intra-area-prefix LSA for the area is used as the source address. This source address is saved in the area data structure and used when secure sockets are opened and packets sent over the virtual link. The virtual link will not transition to the point-to-point state until a source address is selected. Also, when the source or destination address changes, the previous secure sockets must be closed and new secure sockets opened.

Implement and troubleshoot path preference

The order of preference for OSPF routes is:
- intra-area routes, O
- inter-area routes, O IA
- external routes type 1, O E1
- external routes type 2, O E2

This rule of preference cannot be changed. However, it applies only within a single OSPF process. If a router is running more than one OSPF process, route comparison occurs. With route comparison, the metrics and administrative distances (if they have been changed) of the OSPF processes are compared. Route types are disregarded when routes supplied by two different OSPF processes are compared.

Further Reading

http://goo.gl/We0UP3

Implement and troubleshoot operations

General operations
The most common reasons for OSPF neighborship to not form are:
- MTU mismatch
- Area type mismatch
- Network type mismatch

Further Reading
http://goo.gl/yJmqbg
http://goo.gl/zkztmu

Graceful shutdown
The Graceful Shutdown for OSPFv3 feature provides the ability to temporarily shut down the OSPFv3 protocol in the least disruptive manner and to notify its neighbors that it is going away. All traffic that has another path through the network will be directed to that alternate path. A graceful shutdown of the OSPFv3 protocol can be initiated using the shutdown command in router configuration mode or in address family configuration mode.

This feature also provides the ability to shut down OSPFv3 on a specific interface. In this case, OSPFv3 will not advertise the interface or form adjacencies over it; however, all of the OSPFv3 interface configuration will be retained. To initiate a graceful shutdown of an interface, use the ipv6 ospf shutdown or the ospfv3 shutdown command in interface configuration mode.

Generic TTL Security Mechanism (GTSM)
OSPF is a link state protocol that requires networking devices to detect topological changes in the network, flood Link State Advertisement (LSA) updates to neighbors, and quickly converge on a new view of the topology. However, during the act of receiving LSAs from neighbors, network attacks can occur, because there are no checks that unicast or multicast packets are originating from a neighbor that is one hop away or multiple hops away over virtual links.

For virtual links, OSPF packets travel multiple hops across the network; hence, the TTL value can be decremented several times. For these type of links, a minimum TTL value must be allowed and accepted for multiple-hop packets.

To filter network attacks originating from invalid sources traveling over multiple hops, the Generalized TTL Security Mechanism (GTSM), RFC 3682, is used to prevent the attacks. GTSM filters link-local addresses and allows for only one-hop neighbor adjacencies through the configuration of TTL value 255. The TTL value in the IP header is set to 255 when OSPF packets are originated, and checked on the received OSPF packets against the default GTSM TTL value 255 or the user configured GTSM TTL value, blocking unauthorized OSPF packets originated from TTL hops away.

Further Reading

http://goo.gl/czri2f

Implement, troubleshoot and optimize OSPF convergence and scalability

Metrics

OSPF convergence is extremely fast when compared to other protocols. To keep this desirable behavior fully functional in your network, you need to consider the three components that determine how long it takes for OSPF to converge:
- The length of time it takes OSPF to detect a link or interface failure
- The length of time it takes the routers to exchange routing information via LSAs, rerun the Shortest Path First algorithm, and build a new routing table
- A built-in SPF delay time of five seconds (default value)

Thus, the average time for OSPF to propagate LSAs and rerun the SPF algorithm is approximately 1 second. Then the SPF delay timer of five seconds must elapse. Therefor OSPF convergence can be a anything from 6 to 46 seconds, depending upon the type of failure, SPF timer settings, size of the network, and size of the LSA database. The worst case scenario is when a link fails but the destination is still reachable via an alternate route, because the 40 second default dead timer will need to expire before the SPF is rerun.

If OSPF interface costs are auto-calculated based on interface bandwidth then the OSPF reference bandwidth on a router should be at least twice the highest interface bandwidth configured on any of the router's interfaces. OSPF link cost is an integer value calculated by dividing the reference bandwidth by the interface's bandwidth value. If interface bandwidth values are large and the reference bandwidth is too small, this calculation will result in interfaces with different bandwidths being assigned a metric of 1. To avoid such issues, you can use auto-cost reference-bandwidth command.

LSA throttling, SPF tuning, fast hello

The OSPF Link-State Advertisement (LSA) Throttling feature provides a dynamic mechanism to slow down link-state advertisement (LSA) updates in OSPF during times of network instability. It also allows faster Open Shortest Path First (OSPF) convergence by providing LSA rate limiting in milliseconds.

The use of SPF throttle timer tuning can aid in improving the convergence of the campus network to within the sub-second threshold, but is not sufficient to ensure optimal convergence times. Two factors impact the ability of OSPF to converge: the time waiting for an SPF calculation, and the time waiting for an LSA to be received indicating a network topology change. Before the 12.2S release, Cisco IOS implemented two internal timers affecting the generation of LSAs. The first was an internal delay timer that throttled the generation of router (type-1) and network (type-2) LSAs for 500 msec after a network interface change. A second timer throttled the generation of any specific updated LSA for at least five seconds after having sent the same LSA. These two timers could impact the speed at which the network was able to converge. On the detection of any interface change, OSPF would not generate an LSA indicating the link status change for 500 msec, thus preventing the SPF process from responding to the link failure for at least 500 additional msec. After this occurred, any additional change such as link restoration was throttled for a further five seconds, also potentially impacting recovery. The presence of these delay timers, like the SPF timers, was based on a need to ensure the stability of the network and mitigate against OSPF thrashing in the event of a flapping link or other network problem.

The same design and physical factors that allow for SPF tuning in the campus environment also make it amenable to tuning of the LSA timers. The use of routed point-to-point interfaces in the campus removes the need to consider the loss of multiple logical links in the event of a single interface failure (as is the case in a multi-point WAN environment). The use of direct fiber connections between devices also reduces the probability for link loss and ensures a higher degree of accurate link status detection (no LMI or other soft WAN-like failures need to be considered). Interface-specific features such as debounce timers and IP event dampening also lessen the probability of false or flapping interface conditions. The combination of these factors serves to mitigate the factors with which the LSA timers were initially designed to address.

Tuning LSA throttle timers uses an approach similar to that described above for SPF. Three configuration values are used: an initial delay timer, a hold timer, and a maximum hold timer. Using a similar approach to that discussed above results in the use of the same timer values for the LSA configuration as for the SPF configuration.

The recommended values are as follows:

lsa-start: 10 msec
lsa-hold: 100 to 500 msec
lsa-max-wait: 5 seconds

router ospf 100
router-id 10.120.250.101
log-adjacency-changes
auto-cost reference-bandwidth 10000
area 120 stub no-summary
timers throttle spf 10 100 5000
timers throttle lsa all 10 100 5000
network 10.120.0.0 0.0.255.255 area 120

Using this configuration for both LSA and SPF throttle timers produces a further reduction in network convergence from 0.72 to 0.24 seconds. The combination of tuning LSA and SPF timers from their defaults values down to the values shown above provides an overall improvement in convergence time from 5.68 seconds to 0.24 seconds.

In tuning the throttle timer controlling the generation of LSAs, it is necessary to make a similar configuration to the throttle timer controlling the receipt of LSAs. The "lsa arrival" timer controls the rate at which a switch accepts a second LSA with the same LSA ID. If distribution switch A is configured to generate LSAs with a hold time of 100 msec, it is necessary for the adjacent switches, such as distribution switch B for example, to be configured to accept LSAs at a rate at least equal to that with which they are generated. It is considered best practice to tune the arrival rate at some value less than the generated rate to accommodate for any buffering or internal process timer scheduling delays. Using a hold time of 100 msec, an LSA arrival value of 80 msec is considered sufficient.

router ospf 100
router-id 10.120.250.1
log-adjacency-changes
auto-cost reference-bandwidth 10000
area 120 stub no-summary
timers throttle spf 10 100 5000
timers throttle lsa all 10 100 5000
timers lsa arrival 80
network 10.120.0.0 0.0.255.255 area 120

The timers throttle lsa all command controls the generation (sending) of LSAs. The first LSA is always generated immediately upon an OSPF topology change, and the next LSA generated is controlled by the minimum start interval. The subsequent LSAs generated for the same LSA are rate-limited until the maximum interval is reached. The "same LSA" is defined as an LSA instance that contains the same LSA ID number, LSA type, and advertising router ID.

The timers lsa arrival command controls the minimum interval for accepting the same LSA. If an instance of the same LSA arrives sooner than the interval that is set, the LSA is dropped. It is recommended that the arrival interval be less than or equal to the hold-time interval of the timers throttle lsa all command.

LSA propagation control (area types, ISPF)

By default, OSPF LSA propagation is controlled by three parameters:

- OSPF_LSA_DELAY_INTERVAL: Controls the length of time that the router should wait before generating a type 1 router LSA or type 2 network LSA. By default, this parameter is set at 500 ms.
- MinLSInterval: Defines the minimum time between distinct originations of any particular LSA. The value of MinLSInterval is set to 5 seconds.
- MinLSArrival: The minimum time that must elapse between reception of new LSA instances during flooding for any particular LSA. LSA instances received at higher frequencies are discarded. The value of MinLSArrival is set to 1 second.

IP FRR/fast reroute (single and multi hop)

The OSPFv2 Loop-Free Alternate Fast Reroute feature uses a pre-computed alternate next hop to reduce failure reaction time when the primary next hop fails. It lets you configure a per-prefix loop-free alternate (LFA) path that redirects traffic to a next hop other than the primary neighbor. The forwarding decision is made and service is restored without other routers' knowledge of the failure.

Further Reading
http://goo.gl/IfU3LV

OSPFv3 prefix suppression

Open Shortest Path First version 3 (OSPFv3) can hide the IPv4 and IPv6 prefixes of connected networks from link-state advertisements (LSAs). When OSPFv3 is deployed in large networks, limiting the number of IPv4 and IPv6 prefixes that are carried in the OSPFv3 LSAs can speed up OSPFv3 convergence. The OSPFv3 prefix suppression feature allows you to hide IPv4 and IPv6 prefixes that are configured on interfaces running OSPFv3.

In OSPFv3, addressing semantics have been removed from the OSPF protocol packets and the main LSA types, leaving a network-protocol-independent core. This means that

Router-LSAs and network-LSAs no longer contain network addresses, but simply express topology information. The process of hiding prefixes is simpler in OSPFv3 and suppressed prefixes are simply removed from the intra-area-prefix-LSA. Prefixes are also propagated in OSPFv3 via link LSAs.

The OSPFv3 Prefix Suppression feature provides a number of benefits. The exclusion of certain prefixes from advertisements means that there is more memory available for LSA storage, bandwidth and buffers for LSA flooding, and CPU cycles for origination and flooding of LSAs and for SPF computation. Prefixes are also filtered from link LSAs. A device only filters locally configured prefixes, not prefixes learnt via link LSAs. In addition, security has been improved by reducing the possibility of remote attack with the hiding of transit-only networks.

Further Reading

http://goo.gl/5stkhh

Exam Essentials

- You can use the show ip ospf neighbor command to determine the state of the OSPF neighbor or neighbors
- The OSPF neighbor 2-way state is not a cause for concern (e.g. for broadcast network type)
- If interface bandwidth values are large and the reference bandwidth is too small, this calculation will result in interfaces with different bandwidths being assigned a metric of 1. To avoid such issues, you can use auto-cost reference-bandwidth command
- The OSPFv2 Loop-Free Alternate Fast Reroute feature uses a precomputed alternate next hop to reduce failure reaction time when the primary next hop fails
- When a router receives two type 5 LSAs to the same destination with the forwarding addresses set on both LSAs, the router makes a comparison based on the metric to the forwarding addresses. The LSA with a forwarding address that offers the smaller metric is placed into the routing table. If the metric of the redistributed routes are different, the routers prefer the route with the lowest metric and not the lowest metric to the forwarding address.
- When the type 5 LSAs generated by two routers contain zero forwarding addresses, then the LSA to be installed in the receiving routers is determined by comparing the metrics to the ASBRs generating the LSAs.
- "ipv6 ospf authentication" command is a must have when you configure IPSec AH algorithm and it allows an administrator to configure a SPI value
- OSPF Loop-Free Alternate (LFA) feature is supported within the VRF based OSPF instances

- default-information originate always command configures a router to always advertise a default route regardless of the fact if that exists in the routing table o not
- When OSPF authentication is configured, an interface can be in "Going up" or "Down" states as witnessed within the "debug ip ospf adj" command output
- If an OSPF router receives an identical LSA when configured with SPF throttling and before an interval is set, it will simply ignore the LSA
- When an OSPF adjacency is established on a link but LDP-OSPF Synchronization is not yet achieved or is lost, the IGP advertises the max-metric on that link.

Chapter 13: BGP

This chapter covers the following exam topics from Cisco's official 400-101 (v5) written exam curriculum.

- Implement and troubleshoot peer relationships (peer-group, template, active/passive, states, timers, dynamic neighbors)
- Implement and troubleshoot operations IBGP and EBGP (4-byte AS number, private AS)
- Implement, troubleshoot and optimize routing policies (attribute manipulation, conditional advertisement, outbound route filtering, communities, extended communities, multi-homing)
- Implement and troubleshoot scalability (route-reflector. cluster, confederations, aggregation, AS set)
- Implement and troubleshoot multiprotocol BGP (IPv4, IPv6, address-family)
- Implement and troubleshoot AS path manipulations (local AS, allow AS in, remove private AS, prepend, regex)
- Implement and troubleshoot other features (multipath, synchronization, soft reconfiguration, route refresh)
- Fast convergence features (prefix independent convergence, add-path, next-hop address tracking)

Chapter 13: BGP

Describe, implement and troubleshoot peer relationships

Peer-group, template

In older versions of Cisco IOS software, BGP update messages were grouped based on peer group configurations. This method of grouping neighbors for BGP update message generation reduced the amount of system processing resources needed to scan the routing table. This method, however, had the following limitations:
- All neighbors that shared the same peer group configuration also had to share the same outbound routing policies.
- All neighbors had to belong to the same peer group and address family. Neighbors configured in different address-families could not belong to different peer groups.

These limitations existed to balance optimal update generation and replication against peer group configuration. These limitations also caused the network operator to configure smaller peer groups, which reduced the efficiency of update message generation and limited the scalability of neighbor configuration.

A peer template is a configuration pattern that can be applied to neighbors that share common policies. Peer templates are reusable and support inheritance, which allows the network operator to group and apply distinct neighbor configurations for BGP neighbors that share common policies. Peer templates also allow the network operator to define very complex configuration patterns through the capability of a peer template to inherit a configuration from another peer template.

There are two types of peer templates:
- Peer session templates are used to group and apply the configuration of general session commands that are common to all address family and Network Layer Reachability Information (NLRI) configuration modes.
- Peer policy templates are used to group and apply the configuration of commands that are applied within specific address-families and NLRI configuration modes.

Peer templates improve the flexibility and enhance the capability of neighbor configuration. Peer templates also provide an alternative to peer group configuration and overcome some limitations of peer groups. With the configuration of the BGP Configuration Using Peer Templates feature and the support of the BGP Dynamic Update Peer-Groups feature, the network operator no longer needs to configure peer groups in BGP and can benefit from improved configuration flexibility and faster convergence.

This command can be used to check whether the routes are being advertised:

Router#show ip bgp 172.16.10.0/24
BGP routing table entry for 172.16.10.0/24, version 24480684
    Bestpath Modifiers: deterministic-med
    Paths: (4 available, best #3)
    Not advertised to any peer ←

Typical reasons for this include:

- absence of network statement with the exact prefix and mask
- exact route is not in the IP routing table

Further Reading

http://goo.gl/yxdoju

Active, passive

When a BGP speaker first initializes, it uses a local ephemeral TCP port, or random port number greater than 1024, and attempts to contact each configured BGP speaker on TCP port 179 (the well known BGP port). The speaker initiating the session performs an active open, while the peer performs a passive open. It's possible for two speakers to attempt to connect to one another at the same time; this is known as a connection collision. When two speakers collide, each speaker compares the local router ID to the router ID of the colliding neighbor. The BGP speaker with the higher router ID value drops the session on which it is passive, and the BGP speaker with the lower router ID value drops the session on which it is active (i.e., only the session initiated by the BGP speaker with the larger router ID value is preserved).

States, timers

- Idle State:
    - Refuse all incoming BGP connections
    - Start the initialization of event triggers.
    - Initiates a TCP connection with its configured BGP peer.
    - Listens for a TCP connection from its peer.
    - Changes its state to Connect.

If an error occurs at any state of the FSM process, the BGP session is terminated immediately and returned to the Idle state. Some of the reasons why a router does not progress from the Idle state are:

TCP port 179 is not open
A random TCP port over 1023 is not open
- Peer address configured incorrectly on either router
- AS number configured incorrectly on either router

- Connect State:
    - Waits for successful TCP negotiation with peer.
    - BGP does not spend much time in this state if the TCP session has been successfully established.
    - Sends Open message to peer and changes state to OpenSent.
    - If an error occurs, BGP moves to the Active state. Some reasons for the error are:
    - TCP port 179 is not open.
    - A random TCP port over 1023 is not open.
    - Peer address configured incorrectly on either router.
    - AS number configured incorrectly on either router.

- Active State:
    - If the router was unable to establish a successful TCP session, then it ends up in the Active state.
    - BGP FSM tries to restart another TCP session with the peer and, if successful, then it sends an Open message to the peer.
    - If it is unsuccessful again, the FSM is reset to the Idle state.
    - Repeated failures may result in a router cycling between the Idle and Active states. Some of the reasons for this include:
    - TCP port 179 is not open.
    - A random TCP port over 1023 is not open.
    - BGP configuration error.
    - Network congestion.
    - Flapping network interface.

- OpenSent State:
    - BGP FSM listens for an Open message from its peer.
    - Once the message has been received, the router checks the validity of the Open message.
    - If there is an error it is because one of the fields in the Open message does not match between the peers, e.g., BGP version mismatch, MD5 password mismatch, the peering router expects a different My AS, etc. The router then sends a Notification message to the peer indicating why the error occurred.

If there is no error, a Keepalive message is sent, various timers are set and the state is changed to OpenConfirm.

- OpenConfirm State:
    - The peer is listening for a Keepalive message from its peer.
    - If a Keepalive message is received and no timer has expired before reception of the Keepalive, BGP transitions to the Established state.
    - If a timer expires before a Keepalive message is received, or if an error condition occurs, the router transitions back to the Idle state.

- Established State:
    - In this state, the peers send Update messages to exchange information about each route being advertised to the BGP peer.
    - If there is any error in the Update message then a Notification message is sent to the peer, and BGP transitions back to the Idle state.
    - If a timer expires before a Keepalive message is received, or if an error condition occurs, the router transitions back to the Idle state.

BGP keepalive timer is 60 seconds and the hold-timer is 180 seconds. When a BGP connection negotiate the hold-timer between two BGP peers started, the smaller of the two hold-timers will be chosen. Internet is not a stable network, setting the hold-timer too low will be bad to router CPU as the route will keep on withdrawing and adding. We usually keep the BGP hold-timer as it is. However, if you use BGP in a stable WAN environment, you may choose to reduce the hold-timer for fast convergence.

Dynamic neighbors

BGP dynamic neighbor support allows BGP peering to a group of remote neighbors that are defined by a range of IP addresses. Each range can be configured as a subnet IP address. BGP dynamic neighbors are configured using a range of IP addresses and BGP peer groups. After a subnet range is configured for a BGP peer group and a TCP session is initiated by another router for an IP address in the subnet range, a new BGP neighbor is dynamically created as a member of that group. After the initial configuration of subnet ranges and activation of the peer group (referred to as a listen range group), dynamic BGP neighbor creation does not require any further CLI configuration on the initial router. Other routers can establish a BGP session with the initial router, but the initial router need not establish a BGP session to other routers if the IP address of the remote peer used for the BGP session is not within the configured range.

Implement and troubleshoot IBGP and EBGP

EBGP, IBGP

BGP is an exterior gateway protocol (EGP), used to perform inter-domain routing in TCP/IP networks. A BGP router needs to establish a connection (on TCP port 179) to each of its BGP peers before BGP updates can be exchanged. The BGP session between two BGP peers is said to be an external BGP (eBGP) session if the BGP peers are in different autonomous systems (AS) . A BGP session between two BGP peers is said to be an internal BGP (iBGP) session if the BGP peers are in the same autonomous systems.

By default, the peer relationship is established using the IP address of the interface closest to the peer router. However, using the neighbor update-source command, any operational interface, including the loopback interface, can be specified to be used for establishing TCP connections. This method of peering using a loopback interface is useful since it will not bring down the BGP session when there are multiple paths between the BGP peers, which would otherwise result in tearing down the BGP session if the physical interface used for establishing the session goes down. In addition to that, it also allows the routers running BGP with multiple links between them to load balance over the available paths.

To allow the redistribution of i-BGP routes into an interior gateway protocol such as IS-IS or OSPF or EIGRP, use the bgp redistribute-internal command in router configuration mode.

4-bytes AS number

During the early time of BGP development and standardization, it was assumed that availability of a 16 bit binary number to identify the Autonomous System (AS) within BGP would have been more than sufficient. The 16 bit AS number, also known as the 2-byte AS number, provides a pool of 65,536 unique Autonomous System numbers. The IANA manages the available BGP Autonomous System Numbers (ASN) pool, with the assignments being carried out by the Regional Registries. 2 byte ASN is now regarded as historical.

A solution to this depletion is the expansion of the existing 2-byte AS number to a 4-byte AS number, which provides a theoretical 4,294,967,296 unique AS numbers.

The Cisco IOS BGP "4-byte ASN" feature allows BGP to carry a Autonomous System Number (ASN) encoded as a 4-byte entity.

Private AS

Private autonomous system (AS) numbers which range from 64,512 to 65,535 are used to conserve globally unique AS numbers. Globally unique AS numbers (1 - 64,511) are assigned by InterNIC. These private AS number cannot be leaked to a global Border Gateway Protocol (BGP) table because they are not unique (BGP best path calculation expects unique AS numbers). It allows the stripping of private AS numbers out of the AS_PATH list before the routes are propagated to a BGP peer.

Generally customer networks and their routing policies are an extension of the respective Internet Service Providers (ISPs). When a customer network is large, the service provider may assign an AS number using a couple of different methods in order to manage the network and routing policies.
- One way is by permanently assigning an AS number in the range of 1 to 64511. This is done when a customer network connects to two different ISPs, such as multi-homing. This situation mandates that customer network should have a unique AS number so that it can uniquely propagate its BGP routes to a global BGP mesh via two ISPs.
- A second way is by assigning a Private AS number in the range of 64,512 to 65,535. This is done when a customer network connects to a single ISP (either single-homed or dual-homed to the same ISP) and the intention is to conserve the AS numbers. It is not recommended that you use a private AS number if you are planning to connect to multiple ISPs in the future.

When a private AS number is allocated to the customer network, the BGP updates from the customer network to ISP will have the private AS number in its AS_PATH list. When the ISP propagates its network information to the global BGP table (Internet), it should not propagate the AS_PATH with the private AS number of the customer to the Internet. To help the ISP remove the private AS number from its AS_PATH list, use the Cisco IOS remove-private-as command.

To remove the private AS number, use the neighbor x.x.x.x remove-private-as router configuration command. The neighbor x.x.x.x remove-private-as per-neighbor configuration command forces BGP to drop the private AS numbers. You can configure this command for external BGP neighbors. When the outbound update contains a sequence of private AS numbers, this sequence is dropped.

Explain attributes and best-path selection

BGP assigns the first valid path as the current best path. BGP then compares the best path with the next path in the list, until BGP reaches the end of the list of valid paths. This list provides the rules that are used to determine the best path:

1. Prefer the path with the highest WEIGHT.
2. Prefer the path with the highest LOCAL_PREF.
3. Prefer the path that was locally originated via a network or aggregate BGP subcommand or through redistribution from an IGP.
4. Prefer the path with the shortest AS_PATH
5. Prefer the path with the lowest origin type.
6. Prefer the path with the lowest multi-exit discriminator (MED).
7. Prefer eBGP over iBGP paths.
8. Prefer the path with the lowest IGP metric to the BGP next hop.
9. When both paths are external, prefer the path that was received first (the oldest one).
10. Prefer the route that comes from the BGP router with the lowest router ID.
11. If the originator or router ID is the same for multiple paths, prefer the path with the minimum cluster list length.
12. Prefer the path that comes from the lowest neighbor address.

Further Reading

http://goo.gl/jTwpaQ

Implement, optimize and troubleshoot routing policies

Attribute manipulation

BGP is a protocol that uses route attributes to select the best path to a destination.

BGP Path Attributes

BGP uses several attributes for the path-selection process. BGP uses path attributes to communicate routing policies. BGP path attributes include next hop, local preference, AS path, origin, multi-exit discriminator (MED), atomic aggregate, and aggregator. Of these, the AS path is one of the most important attributes: It lists the number of AS paths to reach a destination network.

BGP attributes can be categorized as well-known or optional. Well-known attributes are recognized by all BGP implementations. Optional attributes do not have to be supported by the BGP process; they are used on a test or experimental basis. Well-known attributes can be further subcategorized as mandatory or discretionary. Mandatory attributes are always included in BGP update messages. Discretionary attributes might or might not be included in the BGP update message.

Next-Hop Attribute

The next-hop attribute is the IP address of the next IP hop that will be used to reach the destination. The next-hop attribute is a well-known mandatory attribute. With eBGP, the eBGP peer sets the next hop when it announces the route. Multi-access networks use the next-hop attribute where there is more than one BGP router.

Local Preference Attribute

The local preference attribute indicates which path to use to exit the AS. It is a well-known discretionary attribute used between iBGP peers and is not passed on to external BGP peers. In Cisco IOS Software, the default local preference is 100. The higher local preference is preferred.

Origin Attribute

Origin is a well-known mandatory attribute that defines the source of the path information. Do not confuse the origin with comparing whether the route is external (eBGP) or internal (iBGP). The origin attribute is received from the source BGP router.

There are three types of origin attributes:
- IGP—Indicated by an i in the BGP table. Present when the route is learned by way of the network statement.
- EGP—Indicated by an e in the BGP table. Learned from EGP.
- Incomplete—Indicated by a ? in the BGP table. Learned from redistribution of the route.

In terms of choosing a route based on origin, BGP prefers routes that have been verified by an IGP over routes that have been learned from EGP peers, and BGP prefers routes learned from eBGP peers over incomplete paths.

AS_Path Attribute

The AS path is a well-known mandatory attribute that contains a list of AS numbers in the path to the destination. Each AS prepends its own AS number to the AS path. The AS path describes all the autonomous systems a packet would have to travel to reach the destination IP network. It is used to ensure that the path is loop-free. When the AS path attribute is used to select a path, the route with the fewest AS hops is preferred.

MED Attribute

The MED attribute, also known as a metric, tells external BGP peers the preferred path into the AS when multiple paths into the AS exist. In other words, MED influences which one of many paths a neighboring AS uses to reach destinations within the AS. It is an optional non-transitive attribute carried in eBGP updates. The MED attribute is not used with iBGP peers. The lowest MED value is preferred, and the default value is 0. Paths received with no MED are assigned a MED of 0. The MED is carried into an AS but does not leave the AS.

Community Attribute

Although it is not an attribute used in the routing-decision process, the community attribute groups routes and applies policies or decisions (accept, prefer) to those routes. It is a group of destinations that share some common property. The community attribute is an optional transitive attribute of variable length.

Atomic Aggregate and Aggregator Attributes

The atomic aggregate attribute informs BGP peers that the local router used a less specific (aggregated) route to a destination without using a more specific route.
If a BGP router selects a less specific route when a more specific route is available, it must attach the atomic aggregate attribute when propagating the route. The atomic aggregate attribute lets the BGP peers know that the BGP router used an aggregated route. A more specific route must be in the advertising router's BGP table before it propagates an aggregate route.

Table 13-1, shows BGP attributes and the category they belong to

BGP Attribute	Category
AS_PATH Origin Next-Hop	BGP well known mandatory
Originator ID Cluster List MED Multiprotocol Reachable/UnReachable NLRI	BGP optional nontransitive
Aggregator Community	BGP optional transitive

Local_Pref Atomic_Aggregate	BGP well known discretionary

Conditional advertisement

Normally, routes are propagated regardless of the existence of a different path. The BGP conditional advertisement feature uses the non-exist-map and the advertise-map keywords of the neighbor advertise-map command in order to track routes by the route prefix. If a route prefix is not present in output of the non-exist-map command, then the route specified by the advertise-map command is announced.

This feature is useful for multi-homed networks, in which some prefixes are advertised to one of the providers only if information from the other provider is not present (this indicates a failure in the peering session or partial reachability). The conditional BGP announcements are sent in addition to the normal announcements that a BGP router sends to its peers.

Outbound route filtering

The BGP Prefix-Based Outbound Route Filtering feature uses Border Gateway Protocol (BGP) outbound route filter (ORF) send and receive capabilities to minimize the number of BGP updates that are sent between BGP peers. Configuring this feature can help reduce the amount of system resources required for generating and processing routing updates by filtering out unwanted routing updates at the source. For example, this feature can be used to reduce the amount of processing required on a router that is not accepting full routes from a service provider network.

Communities, extended communities

A community is a BGP attribute that may be added to each prefix. Communities are transitive optional attributes, meaning BGP implementations do not have to recognize the attribute and at the network operator's discretion carry it through an AS or pass it on to another AS. The community attribute can be thought of as simply a flat, 32-bit value that can be applied to any set of prefixes. It can be read as a 32-bit value or split into two portions, the first 2 bytes representing an ASN and the last 2 bytes as a value with a predetermined meaning.

The values 0x00000000 through 0x0000FFFF and 0xFFFF0000 through 0xFFFFFFFF are reserved. Most modern router software displays communities as ASN:VALUE. In this format the communities 1:0 through 65534:65535 are available for use. The convention is to use the ASN of your own network as the leading 16 bits for your internal communities and communities that you accept from and send to your customers.

When OSPF is used as PE-CE routing protocol, BGP uses extended communities to convey various OSPF attributes however there are a few exceptions (e.g. network type) to what attributes are conveyed.

Multi-homing

Border Gateway Protocol (BGP) is one of the key protocols to use to achieve Internet connection redundancy. When you connect your network to two different Internet service providers (ISPs), it is called multi-homing. Multi-homing provides redundancy and network optimization. It selects the ISP which offers the best path to a resource. When you are running BGP with more than one service provider, you run the risk that your autonomous system (AS) will become a transit AS. This causes Internet traffic to pass through your AS and potentially consume all of the bandwidth and resources on the CPU of your router.

Implement and troubleshoot scalability

Route-reflector, cluster

BGP requires that all iBGP speakers be fully meshed. However, this requirement does not scale well when there are many iBGP speakers. Instead of configuring a confederation, another way to reduce the iBGP mesh is to configure a route reflector.

When the route reflector receives an advertised route, depending on the neighbor, it takes the following actions:
- A route from an external BGP speaker is advertised to all clients and non-client peers.
- A route from a non-client peer is advertised to all clients.
- A route from a client is advertised to all clients and non-client peers. Hence, the clients need not be fully meshed.

To configure a route reflector and its clients, use the following command in router configuration mode:

Router(config-router)# neighbor ip-address | peer-group-name route-reflector-client

Whenever an IBGP route is reflected (propagated to another IBGP peer), the route reflector appends two optional, non-transitive attributes to the BGP route:

- If the route does not have the Originator ID attribute (it has not been reflected before), the router ID of the IBGP peer from which the route has been received is copied into the Originator ID attribute.

- If the route does not have the Cluster list attribute, it's added to the route.
- The value configured with the bgp cluster-id router configuration command (or the router ID of the route reflector if the cluster-id is not configured) is prepended to the Cluster list attribute.

Route reflector does not change or remove any other attributes of the reflected routes (even non-transitive attributes), ensuring that the iBGP routes are not changed within the autonomous system.

Confederations

The implementation of BGP confederation reduces the iBGP mesh inside an AS. The key is to divide an AS into multiple ASs and assign the whole group to a single confederation. Each AS alone has iBGP fully meshed and has connections to other ASs inside the confederation. Even though these ASs have eBGP peers to ASs within the confederation, the ASs exchange routing as if they used iBGP. In this way, the confederation preserves next hop, metric, and local preference information. To the outside world, the confederation appears to be a single AS.

In order to configure a BGP confederation, issue this command:

bgp confederation identifier autonomous-system

The confederation identifier is the AS number of the confederation group. The issue of this command performs peering between multiple ASs within the confederation:

bgp confederation peers autonomous-system [autonomous-system]

Further Reading

http://goo.gl/oQ2Etm

Aggregation, AS set

Border Gateway Protocol (BGP) allows the aggregation of specific routes into one route with use of the aggregate-address address mask [as-set] [summary-only] [suppress-map map-name] [advertise-map map-name] [attribute-map map-name] command. When you issue the aggregate-address command without any arguments, there is no inheritance of the individual route attributes (such as AS_PATH or community), which causes a loss of granularity.

Use of the as-set argument creates an aggregate address with a mathematical set of autonomous systems (ASs). This as-setargument summarizes the AS_PATH attributes of all the individual routes. These sample configurations enable you to examine this feature and how this argument helps BGP detect and avoid loops.

In some cases, you can require a change in the attributes of the aggregate route. Examples of such attributes include metric, community, and origin.

Implement and troubleshoot multiprotocol BGP

IPv4, IPv6, VPN address-family

Border Gateway Protocol (BGP) is one of the key protocols to use to achieve Internet connection redundancy. When you connect your network to two different Internet service providers (ISPs), it is called multi-homing. Multi-homing provides redundancy and network optimization. It selects the ISP which offers the best path to a resource. When you run BGP with more than one service provider, you run the risk that your autonomous system (AS) will become a transit AS. This causes Internet traffic to pass through your AS and potentially consume all of the bandwidth and resources on the CPU of your router.

The router using Multiprotocol BGP (MP-BGP) distributes the VPN routing information using the MP-BGP extended communities.

```
Router> show ip bgp
BGP table version is 5, local router ID is 200.200.200.1
Status codes: s suppressed, d damped, h history, * valid, > best, i - internal, r RIB-failure
Origin codes: i - IGP, e - EGP, ? - incomplete

   Network      Next Hop      Metric LocPrf Weight Path
r> 6.6.6.0/24   10.10.13.3         0    130      0 30 i
*> 7.7.7.0/24   10.10.13.3         0    125      0 30 i
```

When BGP tries to install the best path prefix into Routing Information Base (RIB) (for example, the IP Routing table), RIB might reject the BGP route due to any of these reasons:
- Route with better administrative distance already present in IGP. For example, if a static route already exists in IP Routing table.
- Memory failure.
- The number of routes in VPN routing/forwarding (VRF) exceeds the route-limit configured under the VRF instance.

In such cases, the prefixes that are rejected for these reasons are identified by "r RIB-failure" in the show ip bgp command output and are not advertised to the peers.

With Route Target Constraint (RTC), the RR sends only wanted VPN4/6 prefixes to the PE. The support is through a new address family rtfilter for both VPNv4 and VPNv6.

The Route Target (RT) filtering information is obtained from the VPN RT import list from all the VRFs on the PE router. The PE router sends this filtering information as a BGP update in the address family rtfilter to the RR. This filtering information or RT membership is encoded in the Network Layer Reachability Information (NLRI) of the MP_REACH_NLRI and MP_UNREACH_NLRI attributes. The receiving BGP peer translates this NLRI into a filter and installs this filter outbound to the sending peer. The receiving BGP peer uses this filter to decide which VPNv4/6 prefixes to send or not send, dependent upon the presence of attached RTs.

Further Reading

http://goo.gl/BzTJGh

Implement and troubleshoot AS path manipulations

Local AS, allow AS in, remove private AS

The local-AS feature allows a router to appear to be a member of a second autonomous system (AS), in addition to its real AS. This feature can only be used for true eBGP peers. You cannot use this feature for two peers that are members of different confederation sub-ASs. neighbor allowas-in command is issued in order to allow BGP at the other side to inject updates.

To remove the private AS number, use the neighbor x.x.x.x remove-private-as router configuration command.

The debug ip bgp updates command displays the received prefixes with its attributes from the neighbor.

Prepend

AS-path prepending is configured in Cisco IOS with route-map based per-neighbor outbound filter. The actual prepending is specified within the route-map with the set as-path prepend command.

Regexp

You can use regular expressions in the ip as-path access-list command with Border Gateway Protocol (BGP).

Table 13-2, shows various regular expressions and their description

RegEx	Description
?	repeats the previous character one or zero times
*	repeats the previous character zero or many times
+	repeats the previous character one or more times
^	matches the beginning of a string
$	matches the end of a string
[]	is a range
_	matches the space between AS numbers or the end of the AS PATH list
\	is an escape character

"^[0-9]+$" regular expression string means routes originated in any directly connected single AS, or in other words, the routes directly originated by the peers of your AS.

Further Reading

http://goo.gl/zwXNPX

Implement and troubleshoot other features

Multipath

The BGP Multipath Load Sharing for eBGP and iBGP feature allows you to configure multipath load balancing with both external BGP (eBGP) and internal BGP (iBGP) paths in Border Gateway Protocol (BGP) networks that are configured to use Multiprotocol Label Switching (MPLS) Virtual Private Networks (VPNs). This feature provides improved load balancing deployment and service offering capabilities and is useful for multi-homed autonomous systems and Provider Edge (PE) routers that import both eBGP and iBGP paths from multi-homed and stub networks.

BGP synchronization

If your AS passes traffic from another AS to a third AS, BGP should not advertise a route before all routers in your AS learn about the route via IGP. BGP waits until IGP propagates the route within the AS and then advertises it to external peers. A BGP router with synchronization enabled does not install iBGP learned routes into its routing table if it is not able to validate those routes in its IGP. Issue the no synchronization command under router bgp in order to disable synchronization. This prevents BGP from validating iBGP routes in IGP.

Soft reconfiguration, route refresh

When the routing policy of a BGP neighbor changes, the session must be reset (cleared) for the changes to take effect. Because resetting a BGP session can be disruptive to networks, a soft reset method is recommended for reconfiguring the routing table.

Previously, in order to reconfigure the inbound routing table, both the local BGP router and the BGP peer first needed to be configured to store incoming routing policy updates using the neighbor soft-reconfiguration command. Additional resources, particularly memory, were required to store the inbound routing table updates. The clear ip bgp command could then initiate the soft reset, which generated a new set of inbound routing table updates using the stored information.

This feature provides an additional method for soft reset that allows the dynamic exchange of route refresh requests and routing information between BGP routers, and the subsequent re-advertisement of the respective outbound routing table. Soft reset using the route refresh capability does not require pre-configuration and consumes no additional memory resources.

Describe BGP fast convergence features

Prefix independent convergence

The BGP Prefix Independent Convergence (PIC) improves convergence after a network failure. This convergence is applicable to both core and edge failures on IP and MPLS networks. You can use this feature to create and store an alternate path in the routing information base (RIB), forwarding information base (FIB) and the Cisco Express Forwarding (CEF). When a failure is detected, the alternate path immediately takes over, enabling fast failover.

These are the benefits of the feature:
- An alternate path for failover allows faster restoration of connectivity.

- Reduced traffic loss.
- Constant convergence time so that the switching time is the same for all prefixes.

CEF recursion is disabled with BGP PIC configuration when either next-hop is directly connected or learned with a /32 mask.

Add-path

The BGP Additional Paths feature allows the advertisement of multiple paths through the same peering session for the same prefix without the new paths implicitly replacing any previous paths. This behavior promotes path diversity and reduces multi-exit discriminator (MED) oscillations.

BGP routers and route reflectors (RRs) propagate only their best path over their sessions. The advertisement of a prefix replaces the previous announcement of that prefix (this behavior is known as an implicit withdraw). The implicit withdraw can achieve better scaling, but at the cost of path diversity.

Path hiding can prevent efficient use of BGP multipath, prevent hitless planned maintenance, and can lead to MED oscillations and suboptimal hot-potato routing. Upon nexthop failures, path hiding also inhibits fast and local recovery because the network has to wait for BGP control plane convergence to restore traffic. The BGP Additional Paths feature provides a generic way of offering path diversity; the Best External or Best Internal features offer path diversity only in limited scenarios.

The BGP Additional Paths feature provides a way for multiple paths for the same prefix to be advertised without the new paths implicitly replacing the previous paths. Thus, path diversity is achieved instead of path hiding.

Next-hop address tracking

The BGP Support for Next-Hop Address Tracking feature is enabled by default when a supporting Cisco IOS software image is installed. Border Gateway Protocol (BGP) next-hop address tracking is event driven. BGP prefixes are automatically tracked as peering sessions are established. Next-hop changes are rapidly reported to the BGP routing process as they are updated in the Routing Information Base (RIB). This optimization improves overall BGP convergence by reducing the response time to next-hop changes for routes installed in the RIB. When a best-path calculation is run in between BGP scanner cycles, only next-hop changes are tracked and processed.

You can use bgp nexthop command to configure next-hop address tracking.

Exam Essentials

- To allow the redistribution of i-BGP routes into an interior gateway protocol such as IS-IS or OSPF or EIGRP, use the bgp redistribute-internal command in router configuration mode
- The Cisco IOS BGP "4-byte ASN" feature allows BGP to carry a Autonomous System Number (ASN) encoded as a 4-byte entity
- To remove the private AS number, use the neighbor x.x.x.x remove-private-as router configuration command
- When OSPF is used as PE-CE routing protocol, BGP uses extended communities to convey various OSPF attributes however there are a few exceptions (e.g. network type) to what attributes are conveyed
- When BGP tries to install the best path prefix into Routing Information Base (RIB) (for example, the IP Routing table), RIB might reject the BGP route due to any of these reasons:
    - Route with better administrative distance already present in IGP. For example, if a static route already exists in IP Routing table.
    - Memory failure.
    - The number of routes in VPN routing/forwarding (VRF) exceeds the route-limit configured under the VRF instance
- When the routing policy of a BGP neighbor changes, the session must be reset (cleared) for the changes to take effect. Because resetting a BGP session can be disruptive to networks, a soft reset method is recommended for reconfiguring the routing table
- The BGP Prefix Independent Convergence (PIC) improves convergence after a network failure. This convergence is applicable to both core and edge failures on IP and MPLS networks
- In such cases, the prefixes that are rejected for these reasons are identified by "r RIB-failure" in the show ip bgp command output and are not advertised to the peers.
- The BGP Additional Paths feature provides a way for multiple paths for the same prefix to be advertised without the new paths implicitly replacing the previous paths. Thus, path diversity is achieved instead of path hiding
- show ip bgp summary command can be used to discern, among other things, if a router is running out of memory due to BGP table
- Soft reconfiguration feature allows BGP routes to be refreshed without bringing down the established BGP sessions
- When configuring route reflectors, you can use CLUSTER_ID attribute to identify the routes that belong to same group
- RD and v4 address are essential components of an MP-BGP VPNv4 address
- BGP PIC feature allows you to install a backup path in the FIB
- BGP ASN can be either 2 or 4 bytes long
- iBGP peers and confederation peers share BGP cost community

Chapter 14: ISIS (IPv4/IPv6)

This chapter covers the following exam topics from Cisco's official 400-101 (v5) written exam curriculum.

- Basic ISIS network (single area, single topology)
- Neighbor relationship
- Network types, levels, and router types (NSAP addressing, p2p, broadcast)
- Operations
- Optimization features (metrics, wide metric)

Chapter 14: ISIS (IPv4/IPv6)

Describe basic ISIS network

IS-IS requires configuration on both the router and the interface. An IS-IS process is created when you enable IS-IS on a router and define a specific tag to identify that routing process. Interfaces configured with a specific tag will be part of the corresponding router process. More than one IS-IS process can run on a router for Connectionless Network Service (CLNS), but only one IS-IS process can run for IP.

Small IS-IS networks are built as a single area that includes all the routers in the network. As the network grows larger, it is usually reorganized into a backbone area made up of the connected set of all Level 2 routers from all areas. The areas are connected to local areas. Within a local area, routers know how to reach all system IDs. Between areas, routers know how to reach the backbone, and the backbone routers know how to reach other areas. Routers establish Level 1 adjacencies to perform routing within a local area (intra-area routing). Routers establish Level 2 adjacencies to perform routing between Level 1 areas (inter-area routing).

If the network administrator does not specify Level 1 or Level 2 routing for the routing process being configured, the default routing behavior for the routing process will be Level 1-2.
If Level 2 routing is configured on any process, additional processes are automatically configured as Level 1, with the exception of previously configured Level 2 process, which will remain Level 2. You can have only one Level-2 process. You can configure the Level-2 process to perform Level-1 routing at the same time. If Level-2 routing is not desired for a router instance, use the is-type command in router configuration mode to remove the Level-2 capability. You can also use the is-type command to configure a different router instance as a Level-2 router. Some networks use legacy equipment that supports only Level 1 routing. These devices are typically organized into many small areas that cannot be aggregated due to performance limitations. Cisco routers are used to interconnect each area to the Level 2 backbone.

The idea behind the Designated Intermediate System (DIS) is similar to that behind the designated router in OSPF. The DIS creates a pseudo node (a virtual node), and all the routers on a LAN, including the DIS, form an adjacency with the pseudo node instead of forming n*(n-1) order adjacencies with each other in a full mesh.

On a LAN, one of the routers will elect itself the DIS based on interface priority (the default is 64). If all interface priorities are the same, the router with the highest subnetwork point of attachment (SNPA) is selected. MAC addresses are the SNPA on LANs. On Frame Relay networks, the local data-link connection identifier (DLCI) is the SNPA. If the SNPA is a DLCI and is the same at both sides of a link, the router with the higher system ID (in the NSAP address) will become the DIS.

A pseudo node LSP represents a LAN, including all ISs attached to that LAN, just as a non-pseudo node LSP represents a router, including all ISs and LANs connected with the router.

The DIS election is pre-emptive (unlike with OSPF). If a new router boots on the LAN with a higher interface priority, it becomes the DIS, purges the old pseudo node LSP, and a new set of LSPs will be flooded. The DIS sends CSNPs describing all the LSPs in the database every 3 seconds. If a router needs an LSP because it is older than the LSP advertised by the DIS in its CSNP or it is missing an LSP that is listed in the CSNP, it will send a PSNP to the DIS and receive the LSP in return. This mechanism can work both ways: If a router sees that it has a newer version of an LSP, or it has an LSP that the DIS does not advertise in its CSNP, the router will send the newer or missing LSP to the DIS.

The Cisco IS-IS implementation offers an authentication mechanism to prevent unauthorized routers from forming adjacencies or injecting TLVs. Currently, only plain-text authentication is available where the configured password is transmitted inside the IS-IS PDUs unencrypted in plain text. As such, the password can be determined by sniffing the packets. Future Cisco IOS Software releases will also contain Hashed Message Authentication Codes with MD5 (HMAC-MD5) with encrypted passwords as specified in the corresponding IETF draft.
IS-IS authentication is configured independently for adjacency establishment (hello) and for LSP authentication.

Single area, Single topology

Small IS-IS networks are built as a single area that includes all the routers in the network. As the network grows larger, it is usually reorganized into a backbone area made up of the connected set of all Level 2 routers from all areas, which is in turn connected to local areas. Within a local area, routers know how to reach all system IDs. Between areas, routers know how to reach the backbone, and the backbone routers know how to reach other areas.

Routers establish Level 1 adjacencies to perform routing within a local area (intra-area routing). Routers establish Level 2 adjacencies to perform routing between Level 1 areas (inter-area routing). Some networks use legacy equipment that supports only Level 1 routing. These devices are typically organized into many small areas that cannot be aggregated due to performance limitations. Cisco routers are used to interconnect each area to the Level 2 backbone.

Describe neighbor relationship

Table 14-1, describes the configuration steps to enable ISIS

Step 1	Define areas, prepare an addressing plan for the routers (including defining the NETs), and determine interfaces that will run Integrated IS-IS.
Step 2	Enable IS-IS as an IP routing protocol on the routers, and assign a tag to the process (if required).
Step 3	Configure the NETs on the routers. This identifies the routers for IS-IS.
Step 4	Enable Integrated IS-IS on the proper interfaces on the routers. Do not forget interfaces to stub IP networks, such as loopback interfaces (although there will not be any CLNS neighbors on these interfaces).

ISO has developed standards for two types of routing protocols:

- ES-IS discovery protocol—ES-IS performs "routing" between End Systems and Intermediate Systems referred as Level 0 "routing." ES-IS is analogous to the Address Resolution Protocol (ARP) in IP. Although it is not explicitly a routing protocol, ES-IS is included here because it is commonly used with routing protocols to provide end-to-end data movement through an internetwork.
- IS-IS routing protocols—IS-IS performs hierarchical (Level 1, Level 2, and Level 3) routing between intermediate systems. Level 3 routing is done between separate domains. However, note that the IS-IS routing protocol is not itself capable of Level 3 routing.

There is no Address Resolution Protocol (ARP), Internet Control Message Protocol (ICMP) or Inter-domain Routing Protocol (IDRP) for CLNS, but End System-to-Intermediate System (ES-IS) Protocol provides the same kind of reporting functions for ISs and ESs.

Further Reading

http://goo.gl/OqIRQP

Describe network types, levels and router types

NSAP addressing

NSAP is the network-layer address for CLNS packets. An NSAP describes an attachment to a particular service at the network layer of a node, similar to the combination of IP destination address and IP protocol number in an IP packet. NSAP encoding and format are specified by ISO 8348/Ad2.

ISO 8348/Ad2 uses the concept of hierarchical addressing domains. The global domain is the highest level. This global domain is subdivided into sub-domains, and each sub-domain is associated with an addressing authority that has a unique plan for constructing NSAP addresses.

An NSAP address has two major parts: the initial domain part (IDP) and the domain specific part (DSP). The IDP consists of a 1-byte authority and format identifier (AFI) and a variable-length initial domain identifier (IDI), and the DSP is a string of digits identifying a particular transport implementation of a specified AFI authority. Everything to the left of the system ID can be thought of as the area address of a network node.

The LSP identifier is derived from the system ID (along with the pseudonode ID and LSP number). Each IS is usually configured with one NET and in one area; each system ID within an area must be unique.

Further Reading
http://goo.gl/s31fz4

Point-to-point, broadcast

When a network consists of only two networking devices connected to broadcast media and uses the integrated IS-IS protocol, it is better for the system to handle the link as a point-to-point link instead of as a broadcast link. This feature introduces a new command to make IS-IS behave as a point-to-point link between the networking devices.

Router(config-if)# isis network point-to-point | broadcast

Describe operations

From a high level, IS-IS operates as follows:

- Routers running IS-IS will send hello packets out all IS-IS-enabled interfaces to discover neighbors and establish adjacencies.
- Routers sharing a common data link will become IS-IS neighbors if their hello packets contain information that meets the criteria for forming an adjacency. The criteria differ slightly depending on the type of media being used (p2p or broadcast). The main criteria are matching authentication, IS-type and MTU size.
- Routers may build a link-state packet (LSP) based upon their local interfaces that are configured for IS-IS and prefixes learned from other adjacent routers.
- Generally, routers flood LSPs to all adjacent neighbors except the neighbor from which they received the same LSP. However, there are different forms of flooding and also a number of scenarios in which the flooding operation may differ.
- All routers will construct their link-state database from these LSPs.
- A shortest-path tree (SPT) is calculated by each IS, and from this SPT the routing table is built.

Describe optimization features

To minimize the number of adjacencies, LSDBs, and related SPF and PRC computations that are performed, it is recommended that you have configured all Level 1 routers as Level 1 by using the is-type command. We recommend that you use the metric-style wide command because some features, such as setting prefix tags and MPLS traffic engineering, require that routers that are running IS-IS generate the new-style TLVs that have wider metric fields. If you use the default narrow metric style for IS-IS, the router generates and accepts old-style type, length, and value objects (TLVs).

Metrics, wide metric

Cisco IOS Software allows for wide metrics with the support of a 24-bit metric field. Using the new metric style, link metrics now have a maximum value of 16777215 (2^{24}-1) with a total path metric of 4261412864 (254 x 2^{24}). Deploying IS-IS in the IP network with wide metrics is recommended to enable finer granularity and to support future applications such as Traffic Engineering.

Running different metric styles within one network poses a serious problem: Link-state protocols calculate loop-free routes because all routers (within one area) calculate their routing table based on the same link-state database. This principle is violated if some routers look at old-style (narrow), and some at new-style (wider) TLVs. However, if the same interface cost is used for both the old- and new-style metrics, then the SPF will compute a loop-free topology.

Exam Essentials

- NSAP is the network-layer address for CLNS packets. An NSAP describes an attachment to a particular service at the network layer of a node, similar to the combination of IP destination address and IP protocol number in an IP packet
- The LSP identifier is derived from the system ID (along with the pseudonode ID and LSP number). Each IS is usually configured with one NET and in one area; each system ID within an area must be unique
- ISIS pads hello packets to MTU size to avoid MTU issues
- Overload bit is special bit in the IS-IS LSP used to inform the network that the advertising router is not yet ready to forward transit traffic.
- ISIS uses 0XFEFE as EtherType and its packets are directly encapsulated using L2 as opposed to IP
- ISIS system ID is 6 bytes long
- ISIS hello and dead intervals are set to 10 and 30 seconds by default
- "isis hello-multiplier"interface command can be used to modify ISIS hello interval
- The ISIS Attach Bit (or ATT bit) is set by L1L2 routers to notify L1 routers that they can reach the rest of the network i.e. default routing.

Part 4 VPN Technologies

Chapter 15: Tunneling
Chapter 16: Encryption

Chapter 15: Tunneling

This chapter covers the following exam topics from Cisco's official 400-101 (v5) written exam curriculum.

- Tunneling (Label stack, LSR, LSP, LDP, MPLS ping/traceroute)
- Implement and troubleshoot basic MPLS L3VPN (CE/PE/P, extranet/route leaking)
- Implement and troubleshoot encapsulation (GRE, dynamic GRE, LISP encapsulation principles supporting EIGRP OTP)
- Implement and troubleshoot DMVPN (single hub, NHRP, pre-shared key, QoS profile, pre-classify)
- IPv6 tunneling techniques (6in4, 6to4, ISATAP, 6RD, 6PE/6VPE)
- Basic L2 VPN (L2TPv3, ATOM)
- asic L2 VPN (MPLS/VPLS, OTV)

Chapter 15: Tunneling

Implement and troubleshoot MPLS operations

Label stack, LSR, LSP

As packets are forwarded in a label-switching framework, MPLS routers encapsulate the packets with special headers called labels. A label basically tells the router which Label Switched Path (LSP) it belongs to. The router can then use the ingress port and the LSP information to determine where the next hop in the LSP is. You can actually add labels to packets that already have labels (known as label stacking).

A MPLS router that performs routing based only on the label is called a label switch router (LSR) or transit router.

An LSP is a path through an MPLS network, set up by a signaling protocol such as LDP, RSVP-TE, BGP or CR-LDP. The path is set up based on criteria in the Forwarding Equivalence Class (FEC).

In order to scale an MPLS network, where there are different types of platforms and services in parts of the network, it makes sense to split the network into different areas. A typical design introduces a hierarchy that has a core in the center with aggregation on the side. In order to scale, there can be different Interior Gateway Protocols (IGPs) in the the core versus the aggregation. In order to scale, you cannot distribute the IGP prefixes from one IGP into the other. If you do not distribute the IGP prefixes from one IGP into the other IGP, the end-to-end Label-Switched Paths (LSPs) are not possible. In order to deliver the MPLS services end-to-end, you need the LSP to be end-to-end. The goal is to keep the MPLS services (MPLS VPN, MPLS L2VPN) as they are, but introduce greater scalability. In order to do this, move some of the IGP prefixes into Border Gateway Protocol (BGP) (the loopback prefixes of the Provider Edge (PE) routers), which then distributes the prefixes end-to-end. This is called unified or seamless MPLS.

RRs advertise the BGP prefixes with the next hop set to themselves, they assign a local MPLS label to the BGP prefixes. This means that in the data plane, the packets forwarded on these end-to-end LSPs have an extra MPLS label in the label stack. The RRs are in the forwarding path. In order to set the next hop to self for reflected iBGP routes, you must configure the neighbor x.x.x.x next-hop-self all command.

Further Reading
http://goo.gl/2KtrRv

LDP

MPLS LDP provides the means for LSRs to request, distribute, and release label prefix binding information to peer routers in a network. LDP enables LSRs to discover potential peers and to establish LDP sessions with those peers for the purpose of exchanging label binding information.

MPLS LDP enables one LSR to inform another LSR of the label bindings it has made. Once a pair of routers communicate the LDP parameters, they establish a label-switched path (LSP). MPLS LDP enables LSRs to distribute labels along normally routed paths to support MPLS forwarding. This method of label distribution is also called hop-by-hop forwarding. With IP forwarding, when a packet arrives at a router the router looks at the destination address in the IP header, performs a route lookup, and forwards the packet to the next hop. With MPLS forwarding, when a packet arrives at a router the router looks at the incoming label, looks up the label in a table, and then forwards the packet to the next hop. MPLS LDP is useful for applications that require hop-by-hop forwarding, such as MPLS VPNs.

When you enable MPLS LDP, the LSRs send out messages to try to find other LSRs with which they can create LDP sessions. An LSR engages in discovery by periodically transmitting LDP Hello messages to signal its desire to advertise label bindings. The LSR sends the LDP Hello messages as UDP packets to the well known LDP port (646).

LDP defines two types of discovery:
- Basic discovery—Used to discover directly connected LDP LSRs. For basic discovery, an LSR sends Hellos messages to the "all routers on this subnet" multicast address on interfaces for which LDP has been configured.
- Extended discovery—Used between nondirectly connected LDP LSRs. For extended discovery, an LSR sends targeted Hello messages to a specific IP address.

The Hello messages carry the LDP ID of the label space that the sending LSR wants to advertise, as well as other information. When an LSR receives an LDP Hello message from another LSR, it considers that LSR and the specified label space to be "discovered." After two LSRs discover each other in this manner, they attempt to establish an LDP session

Further Reading

http://goo.gl/jDYfzO

MPLS ping, MPLS traceroute

MPLS LSP ping uses MPLS echo request and reply packets to validate an LSP. You can use MPLS LSP ping to validate IPv4 LDP, AToM, and IPv4 RSVP FECs by using appropriate keywords and arguments with the ping mpls command. The MPLS echo request packet is sent to a target router through the use of the appropriate label stack associated with the LSP to be validated. Use of the label stack causes the packet to be forwarded over the LSP itself.

The destination IP address of the MPLS echo request packet is different from the address used to select the label stack. The destination IP address is defined as a 127.x.y.z/8 address. The 127.x.y.z/8 address prevents the IP packet from being IP switched to its destination if the LSP is broken.

An MPLS echo reply is sent in response to an MPLS echo request. The reply is sent as an IP packet and it is forwarded using IP, MPLS, or a combination of both types of switching. The source address of the MPLS echo reply packet is an address obtained from the router generating the echo reply. The destination address is the source address of the router that originated the MPLS echo request packet. The MPLS echo reply destination port is set to the echo request source port.

MPLS LSP traceroute uses MPLS echo request and reply packets to validate an LSP. You can use MPLS LSP traceroute to validate IPv4 LDP and IPv4 RSVP FECs by using appropriate keywords and arguments with the trace mpls command.

The MPLS LSP Traceroute feature uses TTL settings to force expiration of the TTL along an LSP. MPLS LSP Traceroute incrementally increases the TTL value in its MPLS echo requests (TTL = 1, 2, 3, 4) to discover the downstream mapping of each successive hop. The success of the LSP traceroute depends on the transit router processing the MPLS echo request when it receives a labeled packet with a TTL = 1. On Cisco routers, when the TTL expires, the packet is sent to the Route Processor (RP) for processing. The transit router returns an MPLS echo reply containing information about the transit hop in response to the TTL-expired MPLS packet. The MPLS echo reply destination port is set to the echo request source port.

Further Reading

http://goo.gl/V1Z2kN

Implement and troubleshoot basic MPLS L3VPN

L3VPN, CE, PE, P

Multiprotocol Label Switching (MPLS) was originally derived from Tag Switching, and various other vendor methods of IP-switching support enhancements in the scalability and performance of IP-routed networks by combining the intelligence of routing with the high performance of switching.

MPLS is now used for VPNs, which is an appropriate combination because MPLS decouples information used for forwarding of the IP packet (the label) from the information carried in the IP header.

MPLS VPNs can combine any of the following:
- Globally unique and routable addresses
- Globally unique, non-routable addresses
- Private addresses (RFC1918)
- Addresses that are neither globally unique nor private.

Label Switched Paths are bound to VPN-IP routes and are confined to the VPN Service Provider.

P Router or Provider Router is a Label Switch Router (LSR) that functions as a transit router of the core network. A Provider Edge router (PE router) is a router between one network service provider's area and areas administered by other network providers.

The customer edge (CE) is the router at the customer premises that is connected to the provider edge of a service provider IP/MPLS network. CE peers with the Provider Edge (PE) and exchanges routes with the corresponding VRF inside the PE. The routing protocol used could be static or dynamic (an Interior Gateway Protocol like OSPF or an Exterior Gateway Protocol like BGP).

Extranet (route leaking)

There are two primary uses of route leaking in MPLS VPN context.

- Route leaking from a global routing table into a VPN routing/forwarding instance (VRF) and route leaking from a VRF into a global routing table
- Route leaking between different VRFs

Further Reading

http://goo.gl/FXrVOO

Implement and troubleshoot encapsulation

GRE

Tunneling provides a mechanism to transport packets of one protocol within another protocol, the indirection. The protocol that is carried is known as the passenger protocol, and the protocol that is used for carrying the passenger protocol is known as the transport protocol. Generic Routing Encapsulation (GRE) is one of the available tunneling mechanisms which uses IP as the transport protocol and can be used for carrying many different passenger protocols. The tunnels behave as virtual point-to-point links that have two endpoints identified by the tunnel source and tunnel destination addresses at each endpoint.

Configuring a GRE tunnel involves creating a tunnel interface, which is a logical interface. Then you must configure the tunnel endpoints for the tunnel interface.

To configure the tunnel source and destination, issue the
tunnel source {ip-address | interface-type} and tunnel destination {host-name | ip-address} commands under the interface configuration mode for the tunnel.

Dynamic GRE

NHRP is used similarly to the Address Resolution Protocol (ARP) on Ethernet, it provides the ability to map a tunnel IP address with a logical Non-Broadcast Multi-Access (NBMA) IP address; this allows multipoint (mGRE) to have dynamically set up tunnels without having to explicitly configure a mapping entry between each potential next-hop destination. Dynamic GRE is configured using the NHRP based address resolution for mGRE. Multipoint GRE can be used both at hub and at spokes. Dynamic GRE or Dynamic Multipoint VPNs (DMVPNs) can be configured with or without IPSec.

The "%TUN-5-RECURDOWN: Tunnel0 temporarily disabled" is caused due to recursive routing. The error message means that the GRE tunnel router has discovered a recursive routing problem. Tunnel interface status depends on the IP reachability to the tunnel destination. When the router detects a recursive routing failure for the tunnel destination, it shuts the tunnel interface down for a few minutes so that the situation causing the problem can resolve itself as routing protocols converge. If the problem is caused by misconfiguration, the link can oscillate indefinitely. Another symptom of this problem is continuously flapping Enhanced Interior Gateway Routing Protocol (EIGRP), Open Shortest Path First (OSPF), or Border Gateway Protocol (BGP) neighbors, when the neighbors are over a GRE tunnel.

This condition is usually due to one of these causes:
- A misconfiguration that causes the router to try to route to the tunnel destination address using the tunnel interface itself (recursive routing)
- A temporary instability caused by route flapping elsewhere in the network

LISP encapsulation principles supporting EIGRP OTP

EIGRP Over the Top (OTP) allows the customer to establish EIGRP adjacencies across the MPLS/VPN provider cloud. An EIGRP targeted adjacency between CEs is created. This EIGRP neighborship is done via unicast packets, using the CE 'WAN' IP address. This "over the top" peering allows EIGRP to exchange customer prefixes directly between CEs. Customer prefixes are NOT injected in the providers VRF routing table. In order to allow for proper forwarding of user traffic across the MPLS/VPN cloud, user packets are encapsulated on the CE. The encapsulation header uses the WAN IP address of the CEs, which are known in the MPLS/VPN cloud.

Control Plane
OTP control plane consists in an EIGRP targeted adjacency between CEs. Neighborship is established using the CE WAN address, i.e. address of CE on the PE/CE link, so there is no need for any dynamic routing protocol between the PE/CE. The PE just needs to redistribute the connected routes.

Data Plane
Since the customer prefixes are not known in the VRF of provider, customer traffic can't be natively forwarded through the provider cloud, but needs to be encapsulated by CEs before being sent through the provider cloud.

OTP leverages existing LISP encapsulation which:
- Allows dynamic multi-point tunneling

- Provides instance ID field to optionally support virtualization across WAN

OTP does not use LISP control plane (map server/resolver, etc.) instead it uses EIGRP to exchange routes and provide the next-hop, which LISP encapsulation uses to reach remote prefixes.

Further Reading

http://goo.gl/GnFijf

Implement and troubleshoot DMVPN (single hub)

NHRP

NHRP is an ARP-like protocol that alleviates these NBMA network problems. With NHRP, systems attached to an NBMA network dynamically learn the NBMA address of the other systems that are part of that network, allowing these systems to directly communicate without requiring traffic to use an intermediate hop.

NHRP allows Next Hop Clients (NHCs) to dynamically register with Next Hop Servers (NHSs). This allows the NHCs to join the NBMA network without configuration changes on the NHSs, especially in cases where the NHC has a dynamic physical IP address or is behind a Network Address Translation (NAT) router that dynamically changes the physical IP address. In these cases it would be impossible to preconfigure the logical virtual private network (VPN IP) to physical (NBMA IP) mapping for the NHC on the NHS. This function is called NHRP registration.

NHRP also allows one NHC client (spoke) to dynamically discover the logical VPN IP to physical NBMA IP mapping for another NHC client (spoke) within the same NBMA network. Without this discovery, IP packets traversing from hosts behind one spoke to hosts behind another spoke would have to traverse by way of the NHS (hub) router. This would increase the utilization of the hub's physical bandwidth and CPU to process these packets that come into the hub on the multipoint interface and go right back out the multipoint interface. This is often called hairpinning. With NHRP, systems attached to an NBMA network dynamically learn the NBMA address of the other systems that are part of that network, allowing these systems to directly communicate without requiring traffic to use an intermediate hop. This alleviates the load on the intermediate hop (NHS) and can increase the overall bandwidth of the NBMA network to be greater than the bandwidth of the hub router.

NHRP is used to facilitate building a VPN. In this context, a VPN consists of a virtual Layer 3 network that is built on top of an actual Layer 3 network. The topology you use over the VPN is largely independent of the underlying network, and the protocols you run over it are completely independent of it. The Dynamic Multipoint VPN network (DMVPN) is based on GRE IP logical tunnels that can be protected by adding in IPsec to encrypt the GRE IP tunnels.

You can use debug nhrp to troubleshoot NHRP related problems (e.g. authentication errors).

Further Reading

http://goo.gl/hCBkGD

DMVPN with IPsec using pre-shared key

The feature works according to the following rules.
- Each spoke has a permanent IPSec tunnel to the hub, not to the other spokes within the network. Each spoke registers as clients of the NHRP server.
- When a spoke needs to send a packet to a destination (private) subnet on another spoke, it queries the NHRP server for the real (outside) address of the destination (target) spoke.
- After the originating spoke learns the peer address of the target spoke, it can initiate a dynamic IPSec tunnel to the target spoke.
- The spoke-to-spoke tunnel is built over the multipoint GRE (mGRE) interface.
- The spoke-to-spoke links are established on demand whenever there is traffic between the spokes. Thereafter, packets are able to bypass the hub and use the spoke-to-spoke tunnel.
- If an IP multicast stream originates from a spoke location, a rendezvous point (RP) must be deployed at the hub site in order for other spoke site clients to receive the stream
- mGRE Tunnel Interface allows a single GRE interface to support multiple IPSec tunnels and simplifies the size and complexity of the configuration.

Hub Router
crypto isakmp policy 100 hash md5 authentication pre-share !--- Add dynamic pre-shared keys for all the remote VPN !--- routers. crypto isakmp key cciein8weeks address 0.0.0.0 0.0.0.0 !--- Create the Phase 2 policy for actual data encryption. crypto ipsec transform-set strong esp-3des esp-md5-hmac

!
!--- Create an IPSec profile to be applied dynamically to the
!--- GRE over IPSec tunnels.

crypto ipsec profile cciein8weeks
set security-association lifetime seconds 120
set transform-set strong

!--- Create a GRE tunnel template which will be applied to
!--- all the dynamically created GRE tunnels.

interface Tunnel0
ip address 192.168.1.1 255.255.255.0
no ip redirects
ip mtu 1440
ip nhrp authentication cciein8weeks
ip nhrp map multicast dynamic
ip nhrp network-id 1
no ip split-horizon eigrp 90
no ip next-hop-self eigrp 90
tunnel source FastEthernet0/0
tunnel mode gre multipoint
tunnel key 0
tunnel protection ipsec profile cciein8weeks

!--- This is the outbound interface.

interface FastEthernet0/0
ip address 209.168.202.225 255.255.255.0
duplex auto
speed auto

!--- This is the inbound interface.

interface FastEthernet0/1
ip address 1.1.1.1 255.255.255.0
duplex auto
speed auto
!
!--- Enable a routing protocol to send and receive
!--- dynamic updates about the private networks.

router eigrp 10
network 1.1.1.0 0.0.0.255
network 192.168.1.0
no auto-summary

Spoke 1 (DMVPN Phase II)

```
crypto isakmp policy 10
hash md5
authentication pre-share

!--- Add dynamic pre-shared keys for all the remote VPN
!--- routers and the hub router.

crypto isakmp key cciein8weeks address 0.0.0.0 0.0.0.0
!
!--- Create the Phase 2 policy for actual data encryption.
crypto ipsec transform-set strong esp-3des esp-md5-hmac

!--- Create an IPSec profile to be applied dynamically to
!--- the GRE over IPSec tunnels.

crypto ipsec profile cciein8weeks
set security-association lifetime seconds 120
set transform-set strong

!--- Create a GRE tunnel template to be applied to
!--- all the dynamically created GRE tunnels.

interface Tunnel0
ip address 192.168.1.2 255.255.255.0
no ip redirects
ip mtu 1440
ip nhrp authentication cciein8weeks
ip nhrp map multicast dynamic
ip nhrp map 192.168.1.1 209.168.202.225
ip nhrp map multicast 209.168.202.225
ip nhrp network-id 1
ip nhrp nhs 192.168.1.1
tunnel source FastEthernet0/0
tunnel mode gre multipoint <- facilitates spoke to spoke communication
tunnel key 0
tunnel protection ipsec profile cciein8weeks
!
!--- This is the outbound interface.
interface FastEthernet0/0
ip address 209.168.202.131 255.255.255.0
duplex auto
```

```
speed auto
!
!--- This is the inbound interface.
interface FastEthernet0/1
ip address 2.2.2.2 255.255.255.0
duplex auto
speed auto

!--- Enable a routing protocol to send and receive
!--- dynamic updates about the private networks.

router eigrp 10
network 2.2.2.0 0.0.0.255
network 192.168.1.0
no auto-summary
```

Spoke 2

```
crypto isakmp policy 10
hash md5
authentication pre-share

!--- Add dynamic pre-shared keys for all the remote VPN
!--- routers and the hub router.

crypto isakmp key cciein8weeks address 0.0.0.0 0.0.0.0
!--- Create the Phase 2 policy for actual data encryption.
crypto ipsec transform-set strong esp-3des esp-md5-hmac

!--- Create an IPSec profile to be applied dynamically to
!--- the GRE over IPSec tunnels.

crypto ipsec profile cciein8weeks
set security-association lifetime seconds 120
set transform-set strong
!--- Create a GRE tunnel template to be applied to
!--- all the dynamically created GRE tunnels.

interface Tunnel0
ip address 192.168.1.3 255.255.255.0
no ip redirects
ip mtu 1440
ip nhrp authentication cciein8weeks
ip nhrp map multicast dynamic
ip nhrp map 192.168.1.1 209.168.202.225
ip nhrp map multicast 209.168.202.225
```

```
ip nhrp network-id 1
ip nhrp nhs 192.168.1.1
tunnel source FastEthernet0/0
tunnel mode gre multipoint
tunnel key 0
tunnel protection ipsec profile cciein8weeks
!

!--- This is the outbound interface.

interface FastEthernet0/0
ip address 209.168.202.130 255.255.255.0
duplex auto
speed auto
!
!--- This is the inbound interface.

interface FastEthernet0/1
ip address 3.3.3.3 255.255.255.0
duplex auto
speed auto
!
!--- Enable a routing protocol to send and receive
!--- dynamic updates about the private networks.

router eigrp 10
network 3.3.3.0 0.0.0.255
network 192.168.1.0
no auto-summary
```

QoS profile

The Per-Tunnel QoS for DMVPN feature introduces per-tunnel quality of service (QoS) support for Dynamic Multipoint VPN (DMVPN) and increases per-tunnel QoS performance for Internet Protocol Security (IPsec) tunnel interfaces. This feature allows you to apply a QoS policy on a DMVPN hub on a tunnel instance (per-endpoint or per-spoke basis) in the egress direction for DMVPN hub-to-spoke tunnels. The QoS policy on a DMVPN hub on a tunnel instance allows you to shape the tunnel traffic to individual spokes (parent policy) and to differentiate individual data flows going through the tunnel for policing (child policy).

The QoS policy that is used by the hub for a particular endpoint or spoke is selected by the Next Hop Resolution Protocol (NHRP) group in which the spoke is configured. Even though many spokes may be configured in the same NHRP group, the tunnel traffic of each spoke is measured individually for shaping and policing.

The following example shows how to map NHRP groups to a QoS policy on the hub. The example shows a hierarchical QoS policy (parent: group1_parent/group2_parent; child: group1/group2) that will be used for configuring per-tunnel QoS for DMVPN feature. The example also shows how to map the NHRP group spoke_group1 to the QoS policy group1_parent and map the NHRP group spoke_group2 to the QoS policy group2_parent on the hub:

DMVPN Hub and QoS Configuration

class-map match-all group1_Routing
 match ip precedence 6
class-map match-all group2_Routing
 match ip precedence 6
class-map match-all group2_voice
 match access-group 100
class-map match-all group1_voice
 match access-group 100
 	
policy-map group1
 class group1_voice
    priority 1000
 class group1_Routing
    bandwidth percent 20
policy-map group1_parent
 class class-default
    shape average 3000000
  service-policy group1
policy-map group2
 class group2_voice
    priority percent 20
 class group2_Routing
    bandwidth percent 10
policy-map group2_parent
 class class-default
    shape average 2000000
  service-policy group2
 	
interface tunnel 1
ip address 209.165.200.225 255.255.255.224
no ip redirects
ip mtu 1400
ip nhrp authentication testing

```
ip nhrp map multicast dynamic
ip nhrp map group spoke_group1 service-policy output group1_parent
ip nhrp map group spoke_group2 service-policy output group2_parent
ip nhrp network-id 172176366
ip nhrp holdtime 300
ip nhrp registration no-unique
tunnel source fastethernet 2/1/1
tunnel mode gre multipoint
tunnel protection ipsec profile DMVPN

interface fastethernet 2/1/1
ip address 209.165.200.226 255.255.255.224
```

Pre-classify

Configure qos pre-classify in VPN designs where both QoS and IPsec occur on the same system and QoS needs to match on parameters in the cleartext packet other than the DSCP/ToS byte.

Further Reading

http://goo.gl/cb0HLi

Describe IPv6 tunneling techniques

6in4, 6to4

6in4 is an Internet transition mechanism for migrating from Internet Protocol version 4 (IPv4) to IPv6. 6in4 uses tunneling to encapsulate IPv6 traffic over explicitly-configured IPv4 links as defined in RFC 4213. The 6in4 traffic is sent over the IPv4 Internet inside IPv4 packets whose IP headers have the IP protocol number set to 41. This protocol number is specifically designated for IPv6 encapsulation. In 6in4, the IPv4 packet header is immediately followed by the IPv6 packet being carried. This means that the encapsulation overhead is simply the size of the IPv4 header of 20 bytes. With an Ethernet Maximum Transmission Unit (MTU) of 1500 bytes, one can thus send IPv6 packets of 1480 bytes without fragmentation. 6in4 tunneling is also referred to as proto-41 static because the endpoints are configured statically.

6to4 Tunneling is one of the IPv6 translation mechanism which encapsulates the IPv6 packets into IPv4 which allows remote IPv6 networks to communicate across the IPv4 infrastructure(core network or Internet). The main difference between the manual tunnels and automatic 6to4 tunnels is that the tunnel is not point-to-point but it is point-to-multipoint. In automatic 6to4 tunnels, the IPv4 infrastructure is treated as a virtual non-broadcast multi-access (NBMA) link routers are not configured as point-to-point. The IPv4 address embedded in the IPv6 address is used to find the other end of the automatic tunnel.

Point-to-multipoint 6to4 tunnels that can be used to connect isolated IPv6 sites can use addresses from the 2002::/16 prefix.

Further Reading

http://goo.gl/xEL1XF

ISATAP

ISATAP is an automatic overlay tunneling mechanism that uses the underlying IPv4 network as a NBMA link layer for IPv6.

Overlay tunneling encapsulates IPv6 packets in IPv4 packets for delivery across an IPv4 infrastructure (a core network). By using overlay tunnels, you can communicate with isolated IPv6 networks without upgrading the IPv4 infrastructure between them. Overlay tunnels can be configured between border devices or between a border device and a host; however, both tunnel endpoints must support both the IPv4 and IPv6 protocol stacks.

IPv6 supports the following types of overlay tunneling mechanisms:
- Manual
- Generic routing encapsulation (GRE)
- IPv4-compatible
- 6to4
- Intra-site Automatic Tunnel Addressing Protocol (ISATAP)

6RD

IPv6 Rapid Deployment (6rd) is a stateless tunneling mechanism which allows a Service Provider to rapidly deploy IPv6 in a lightweight and secure manner without requiring upgrades to existing IPv4 access network infrastructure. While there are a number of methods for carrying IPv6 over IPv4, 6rd has been particularly successful due to its stateless mode of operation which is lightweight and naturally scalable, resilient, and simple to provision.

Further Reading

http://goo.gl/JXYWEc

6VPE

The 6PE feature is particularly applicable to Service Providers who already run an MPLS network or plan to do it. One of the Cisco 6PE advantages is that there is no need to upgrade the hardware, software or configuration of the core network. Thus it eliminates the impact on the operations and the revenues generated by the existing IPv4 traffic. MPLS has been chosen by many Service Providers as a vehicle to deliver services to customers. MPLS as a multi-service infrastructure technology is able to provide layer 3 VPN, QoS, traffic engineering, fast re-routing and integration of ATM and IP switching. It is in a very natural manner that MPLS is put to contribution to ease IPv6 introduction in existing production networks.

MPLS de-coupling of the control plane and data plane provide an interesting alternative to the integration and co-existence of IPv4, IPv6 and ATM over a single infrastructure, thus fulfilling environments such as 3G networks where UMTS Release 5 needs in terms of transport: Cisco 6PE for IPv6 traffic, ATM over MPLS and regular IPv4 switching with its VPN, traffic engineering and QoS extensions. From an operational standpoint, new CEs introduction is straightforward and painless as it leverages the Layer 3 VPN scalability. Using tunnels on the CE routers is the simplest way to deploy IPv6 over MPLS networks. It has no impact on the operation or infrastructure of MPLS, and requires no changes to either the P routers (they don't have to be IPv6 aware) in the core or the PE routers connected to the customers.

6VPE is a technology that allows IPv6 VPN customers to communicate with each other over an IPv4 MPLS Provider without any tunnel setup, by having the customer VPNv6 prefixes using a v4-mapped IPv6 address as next-hop inside the provider's network and using IPv4 LSPs between the 6VPEs. In 6VPE, labels must be exchanged between the 6VPEs for their VPNv6 prefixes, which means that the VPNv6 address-family must be activated on the IPv4 iBGP session between the 6VPEs.

By default, the mpls ip propagate-ttl command is enabled and the IP TTL value is copied to the MPLS TTL field during label imposition. To disable TTL propagation for all packets, use the no mpls ip propagate-ttl command. To disable TTL propagation for only forwarded packets, use the no mpls ip propagate forwarded command. Disabling TTL propagation of forwarded packets allows the structure of the MPLS network to be hidden from customers, but not the provider.

Further Reading

http://goo.gl/vuPAxm
http://goo.gl/Hu78Cr

Describe basic layer 2 VPN —wireline

L2TPv3 general principles

The Layer 2 Tunneling Protocol version 3 (L2TPv3) feature employs L2TPv3 and pseudowire (PW) technology to provide tunneling service to Ethernet traffic. A L2TPv3 tunnel is a control connection between two PE routers. One L2TPv3 tunnel can have multiple data connections, and each data connection is termed as an L2TPv3 session. The control connection is used to establish, maintain, and release sessions. Each session is identified by a session ID which is unique across the entire router. L2TPv3 carries frames inside IP packets.

Further Reading

http://goo.gl/V9egil

ATOM general principles

Any Transport over MPLS (AToM) transports Layer 2 packets over a Multiprotocol Label Switching (MPLS) backbone. AToM uses a directed Label Distribution Protocol (LDP) session between edge routers for setting up and maintaining connections. Forwarding occurs through the use of two levels of labels, switching between the edge routers. The external label (tunnel label) routes the packet over the MPLS backbone to the egress Provider Edge (PE) at the ingress PE. The VC label is a de-multiplexing label that determines the connection at the tunnel endpoint (the particular egress interface on the egress PE as well as the virtual path identifier [VPI]/virtual channel identifier [VCI] value for an ATM Adaptation Layer 5 [AAL5] protocol data unit [PDU], the data-link connection identifier [DLCI] value for a Frame Relay PDU, or the virtual LAN [VLAN] identifier for an Ethernet frame). EoMPLS carries frames inside MPLS packets.

Because the control word is included by default, so it may be necessary to explicitly disable this command in static pseudowire configurations. You can use mpls control-word command is used in static pseudowire configurations, the command must be configured the same way on both ends of the connection to work correctly. Otherwise, the provider edge routers cannot exchange control messages to negotiate inclusion or exclusion of the control word.

To specify the path that traffic uses a Multiprotocol Label Switching (MPLS) Traffic engineering (TE) tunnel or destination IP address and Domain Name Server (DNS) name), use the preferred-path command in pseudowire configuration mode. To disable tunnel selection, use the no form of this command.

preferred-path {interface tunnel tunnel-number | peer {ip-address | host-name}} [disable-fallback]
no preferred-path {interface tunnel tunnel-number | peer {ip-address | host-name}} [disable-fallback]

Further Reading

http://goo.gl/6RsX89

Describe basic L2VPN — LAN services

MPLS-VPLS general principles

VPLS is a technology that allows Multiprotocol Label Switching (MPLS) networks to offer Layer 2 Ethernet services. It provides multipoint Ethernet service as compared to Ethernet over MPLS (EoMPLS) that is point to point. VPLS emulates a virtual IEEE Ethernet bridge network. It uses flooding to communicate MAC address reachability information. VPLS can carry single VLAN within each instance. It supports MAC address aging and replicates broadcast and multicast traffic. A point to point Ethernet Virtual Circuit (EVC) connecting a pair of physical UNIs is also known as Ethernet Wire Service (EWS) or Ethernet Private Line (EPL). EPL provides VLAN transparency and control protocol tunneling are supplied by the implementation of 802.1Q-in-Q tag-stacking technology. Ethernet Virtual Private Line (EVPL) and EPL are also considered E-Line services.

Unlike Layer 3 VPN, there is no routing interaction between customer and service provider networks.
- Multipoint-to-multipoint configuration
- Forwarding of frames based on learned MAC addresses
- Uses virtual forwarding instance (VFI, like VLAN) for customer separation

VPLS Components:
- User-facing PE (U-PE): The U-PE is the device to which the functions needed to take forwarding or switching decisions at the ingress of the provider network.
- Network PE (N-PE): The N-PE is the device to which the signaling and control functions are allocated when a VPLS-PE is distributed across more than one box.
- Virtual switching instance (VSI): Virtual switching instance that serves one single VPLS A VSI performs standard LAN (that is, Ethernet) bridging functions, including forwarding done by a VSI based on MAC addresses and VLAN tags.
- Pseudowire (PW): PWE3 is a mechanism that emulates the essential attributes of a telecommunications service (such as a T1 leased line or Frame Relay) over a PSN.

- Attachment circuit (AC): The physical or virtual circuit attaching (AC) a CE to a PE. An attachment circuit may be, for example, a Frame Relay DLCI, an ATM VPI/VCI, an Ethernet port, a VLAN, or an MPLS LSP. One or multiple ACs can belong to same VFI.
- VC (virtual circuit): Martini-based data encapsulation, tunnel label is used to reach remote PE, VC label is used to identify VFI. One or multiple VCs can belong to same VFI

Virtual Forwarding Instance (VFI):
- VFI creates L2 multipoint bridging among all ACs and VCs. It's an L2 broadcast domain such as VLAN.
- Multiple VFIs can exist on the same PE box to separate user traffic such as VLANs.
- Signaling

Signaling uses LDP to establish and tear down PWs. Using LDP as the signaling VPLS control plane does not have inherent support of auto-discovery. Therefore, LDP-VPLS relies on manual configuration to identify all PE routers. MPLS in the core, normal LDP sessions per hop to exchange tunnel label or IGP label. Targeted or directed LDP session between PEs to exchange VC label. Tunnel label is used to forward packet from PE to PE VC label and is used to identify L2VPN circuit.

Further Reading

http://goo.gl/KwPVFS

OTV general principles

OTV is a "MAC address in or over IP" technique for supporting Layer 2 VPNs to extend LANs over any transport. The transport can be Layer 2 based, Layer 3 based, IP switched, label switched, or anything else as long as it can carry IP packets. By using the principles of MAC routing, OTV provides an overlay that enables Layer 2 connectivity between separate Layer 2 domains while keeping these domains independent and preserving the fault-isolation, resiliency, and load-balancing benefits of an IP-based interconnection.

The core principles on which OTV operates are the use of a control protocol to advertise MAC address reachability information (instead of using data plane learning) and packet switching of IP encapsulated Layer 2 traffic (instead of using circuit switching) for data forwarding. These features are a significant departure from the core mechanics of traditional Layer 2 VPNs. In traditional Layer 2 VPNs, a static mesh of circuits is maintained among all devices in the VPN to enable flooding of traffic and source-based learning of MAC addresses. This full mesh of circuits is an unrestricted flood domain on which all traffic is forwarded. Maintaining this full mesh of circuits severely limits the scalability of existing Layer 2 VPN approaches. At the same time, the lack of a control plane limits the extensibility of current Layer 2 VPN solutions to properly address the requirements for extending LANs across data centers.

OTV uses a control protocol to map MAC address destinations to IP next hops that are reachable through the network core. OTV can be thought of as MAC routing in which the destination is a MAC address, the next hop is an IP address, and traffic is encapsulated in IP so it can simply be carried to its MAC routing next hop over the core IP network. Thus a flow between source and destination host MAC addresses is translated in the overlay into an IP flow between the source and destination IP addresses of the relevant edge devices. This process is called encapsulation rather than tunneling as the encapsulation is imposed dynamically and tunnels are not maintained. Since traffic is IP forwarded, OTV is as efficient as the core IP network and will deliver optimal traffic load balancing, multicast traffic replication, and fast failover just like the core would. OTV also supports detection of multi-homing.

Table 15-1 shows the OTV entities/roles and their description

OTV Entity	Description
edge device	This is a device which performs all OTV functions. The OTV Edge device is connected to Layer 2 segments and IP transport network.
join interfaces	These are Layer 3 interfaces on the OTV Edge device which connects to the IP transport network
internal interface	These are Layer 2 interfaces on the OTV Edge device. These can be "trunk" or "access" ports.
overlay interface	This is a multicast-enabled multi-access network over which all OTV encapsulated Layer 2 frames are carried.
site VLAN	OTV Edge devices need to elect an Authoritative Edge Device (AED) per VLAN so that only one device forwards traffic for that VLAN. For this election, the OTV Edge devices use Site VLAN for communication on the local site.

authoritative edge device	The authoritative edge device is responsible for all MAC address reachability updates for a VLAN.

Further Reading

http://goo.gl/XioB96

Exam Essentials

- In order to set the next hop to self for reflected iBGP routes, you must configure the neighbor x.x.x.x next-hop-self all command
- The "%TUN-5-RECURDOWN: Tunnel0 temporarily disabled" is caused due to recursive routing. The error message means that the GRE tunnel router has discovered a recursive routing problem
- OTP does NOT use LISP control plane (map server/resolver, etc.) instead it uses EIGRP to exchange routes and provide the next-hop, which LISP encapsulation uses to reach remote prefixes
- You can use debug nhrp to troubleshoot NHRP related problems (e.g. authentication errors)
- Configure qos pre-classify in VPN designs where both QoS and IPsec occur on the same system and QoS needs to match on parameters in the cleartext packet other than the DSCP/ToS byte
- ISATAP is an automatic overlay tunneling mechanism that uses the underlying IPv4 network as a NBMA link layer for IPv6
- L2TPv3 carries frames inside IP packets
- OTV is a "MAC address in IP" technique for supporting Layer 2 VPNs to extend LANs over any transport. The transport can be Layer 2 based, Layer 3 based, IP switched, label switched, or anything else as long as it can carry IP packets
- Since traffic is IP forwarded, OTV is as efficient as the core IP network and will deliver optimal traffic load balancing, multicast traffic replication, and fast failover just like the core would. OTV also supports detection of multi-homing
- Unified MPLSABRs (edge routers) are iBGP route reflectors set with next-hop self
- Address family rtfilter is used with Route Target Constraints or RTC
- RLOCs are used by routers in the public IP network to route traffic between two networks
- The NHRP network ID is used to define the NHRP domain for an NHRP interface and differentiate between multiple NHRP domains
- 2002/16 prefix is used for 6to4 tunnel addresses

- Depending on the Don't Fragment (DF) bit, L2TP routers will either fragment or drop a packet that exceeds the path MTU
- Tunnel auto mode feature eases the configuration by automatically selecting the tunneling and transport protocols
- MPLS EXP and Traffic class bits describe the MPLS QoS behaviors
- Tunnel mode is recommended as best practice when using DMVPN
- If you configure manual tunneling, it would nail up a permanent link between IPv6 domains (over IPv4)
- PW FEC contains PW ID, Type and Control Word (CW)
- v6in4 can operate in either transport or tunnel mode

Chapter 16: Encryption

This chapter covers the following exam topics from Cisco's official 400-101 (v5) written exam curriculum.

- Implement and troubleshoot IPSec with pre-shared key (IPv4 site to site, IPv6 in IPv4 tunnels, VTI)
- GETVPN

Chapter 16: Encryption

Implement and troubleshoot IPsec with pre-shared key

IPv4 site to IPv4 site

IPSec between two sites such as branch and a headquarter is known as site to site or LAN to LAN tunnel. It can be configured with or without GRE. IKE has two modes of operation, aggressive or main mode. Main mode hides IKE/IPSec peer identities.

Router B
crypto isakmp policy 2 authentication pre-share crypto isakmp key cciein8weeks address 172.16.1.1 ! ! !--- Configuration for IPsec policies. !--- Enables the crypto transform configuration mode, !--- where you can specify the transform sets that are used !--- during an IPsec negotiation. crypto ipsec transform-set Router-IPSEC esp-des esp-sha-hmac ! !--- Indicates that IKE is used to establish !--- the IPsec Security Association for protecting the !--- traffic specified by this crypto map entry. crypto map cciein8weeks 1 ipsec-isakmp description Tunnel to172.16.1.1 !--- Sets the IP address of the remote end.   set peer 172.16.1.1 !--- Configures IPsec to use the transform-set !--- "Router-IPSEC" defined earlier in this configuration.   set transform-set Router-IPSEC !--- Specifies the interesting traffic to be encrypted.

```
   match address 100
!
!--- Configures the interface to use the
!--- crypto map " cciein8weeks" for IPsec.

interface FastEthernet0
 ip address 172.17.1.1 255.255.255.0
 duplex auto
 speed auto
 crypto map cciein8weeks
```

IPSec(validate_transform_proposal): proxy identities not supported
ISAKMP: IPSec policy invalidated proposal
ISAKMP (0:2): SA not acceptable!

Above messages are indicative of the fact that access lists (as referenced in match address command inside a crypto map) for IPsec interesting traffic do not match between peers.

Further Reading

http://goo.gl/PmO6l4

IPv6 in IPv4 tunnels

Generic routing encapsulation (GRE) tunnels sometimes are combined with IPSec, because IPSec does not support IPv6 multicast packets. This function prevents dynamic routing protocols from running successfully over an IPSec VPN network. Because GRE tunnels do support IPv6 multicast , a dynamic routing protocol can be run over a GRE tunnel. Once a dynamic routing protocol is configured over a GRE tunnel, you can encrypt the GRE IPv6 multicast packets using IPSec.

IPSec can encrypt GRE packets using a crypto map or tunnel protection. Both methods specify that IPSec encryption is performed after GRE encapsulation is configured. When a crypto map is used, encryption is applied to the outbound physical interfaces for the GRE tunnel packets. When tunnel protection is used, encryption is configured on the GRE tunnel interface.

"%CRPTO-4-IKMP_BAD_MESSAGE: IKE" message from 150.150.150.1 failed its sanity check or is malformed appears if the pre-shared keys on the peers do not match. In order to fix this issue, check the pre-shared keys on both sides.

Further Reading
http://goo.gl/pqy0E8
http://goo.gl/RhXJDZ

Virtual tunneling Interface (VTI)

The use of IPsec VTIs both greatly simplifies the configuration process when you need to provide protection for remote access and provides a simpler alternative to using generic routing encapsulation (GRE) or Layer 2 Tunneling Protocol (L2TP) tunnels for encapsulation and crypto maps with IPsec. A major benefit associated with IPsec VTIs is that the configuration does not require a static mapping of IPsec sessions to a physical interface. The IPsec tunnel endpoint is associated with an actual (virtual) interface. Because there is a routable interface at the tunnel endpoint, many common interface capabilities can be applied to the IPsec tunnel.

The IPsec VTI allows for the flexibility of sending and receiving both IP unicast and multicast encrypted traffic on any physical interface, such as in the case of multiple paths. Traffic is encrypted or decrypted when it is forwarded from or to the tunnel interface and is managed by the IP routing table. Using IP routing to forward the traffic to the tunnel interface simplifies the IPsec VPN configuration compared to the more complex process of using access control lists (ACLs) with the crypto map in native IPsec configurations. DVTIs function like any other real interface so that you can apply quality of service (QoS), firewall, and other security services as soon as the tunnel is active.

IPsec VTIs allow you to configure a virtual interface to which you can apply features. Features for clear-text packets are configured on the VTI. Features for encrypted packets are applied on the physical outside interface. When IPsec VTIs are used, you can separate the application of features such as NAT, ACLs, and QoS and apply them to clear-text or encrypted text, or both. When crypto maps are used, there is no simple way to apply encryption features to the IPsec tunnel.

There are two types of VTI interfaces:
- Static VTIs (SVTIs)
- Dynamic VTIs (DVTIs)

SVTI configurations can be used for site-to-site connectivity in which a tunnel provides always-on access between two sites. The advantage of using SVTIs as opposed to crypto map configurations is that users can enable dynamic routing protocols on the tunnel interface without the extra 4 bytes required for GRE headers, thus reducing the bandwidth for sending encrypted data. Additionally, multiple Cisco IOS software features can be configured directly on the tunnel interface and on the physical egress interface of the tunnel interface. This direct configuration allows users to have solid control on the application of the features in the pre- or post-encryption path.

DVTIs can provide highly secure and scalable connectivity for remote-access VPNs. The DVTI technology replaces dynamic crypto maps and the dynamic hub-and-spoke method for establishing tunnels. Dynamic VTIs can be used for both the server and remote configuration. The tunnels provide an on-demand separate virtual access interface for each VPN session. The configuration of the virtual access interfaces is cloned from a virtual template configuration, which includes the IPsec configuration and any Cisco IOS software feature configured on the virtual template interface, such as QoS, NetFlow, or ACLs.

Dynamic VTIs function like any other real interface so that you can apply QoS, firewall, other security services as soon as the tunnel is active. QoS features can be used to improve the performance of various applications across the network. Any combination of QoS features offered in Cisco IOS software can be used to support voice, video, or data applications.

Further Reading
http://goo.gl/0yHAkK

Describe GET VPN

The IOS GETVPN is a tunnel-less (i.e. no overlay) VPN technology that provides end-to-end security for network traffic in a native mode and maintaining the fully meshed topology. It uses the core network's ability to route and replicate the packets between various sites within the enterprise. Cisco IOS GETVPN preserves the original source and destination IP addresses information in the header of the encrypted packet for optimal routing. Hence, it is largely suited for an enterprise running over a private Multiprotocol Label Switching (MPLS)/IP-based core network. It is also better suited to encrypt multicast traffic. Cisco IOS GET VPN uses Group Domain of Interpretation (GDOI) as the keying protocol and IPSec for encryption.

A GETVPN deployment has primarily three components, Key Server (KS), Group Member (GM), and Group Domain of Interpretation (GDOI) protocol. GMs do encrypt/decrypt the traffic and KS distribute the encryption key to all the group members. The KS decides on one single data encryption key for a given life time. Since all GMs use the same key, any GM can decrypt the traffic encrypted by any other GM. GDOI protocol is used between the GM and KS for group key and group SA management. Minimum one KS is required for a GETVPN deployment.
Unlike traditional IPSec encryption solutions, GET VPN uses the concept of group SA. All members in the GETVPN group can communicate with each other using a common

encryption policy and a shared SA and therefore no need to negotiate IPSec between GMs on a peer to peer basis; thereby reducing the resource load on the GM routers.

Group Member

The group member registers with the key server to get the IPSec SA that is necessary to encrypt data traffic within the group. The group member provides the group ID to the key server to get the respective policy and keys for this group. These keys are refreshed periodically by KS, and before the current IPSec SAs expire, so that there is no loss of traffic.

Key Server

Key server is responsible for maintaining security policies, authenticating the GMs and providing the session key for encrypting traffic. KS authenticates the individual GMs at the time of registration. Only after successful registration the GMs can participate in group SA. A group member can register at any time and receive the most current policy and keys. When a GM registers with the key server, the key server verifies the group id number of the GM. If this id number is a valid and the GM has provided valid Internet Key Exchange (IKE) credentials, the key server sends the SA policy and the Keys to the group member.

There are two types of keys that the GM will receive from the KS:

- Key Encryption Key (KEK), for securing control plane
- Traffic Encryption Key (TEK), for securing data plane

The TEK becomes part of the IPSec SA with which the group members within the same group encrypt the data. KEK is used to secure rekey messages (i.e. control plane) between the key server and the group members.

The Key Server sends out rekey messages either because of an impending IPSec SA expiration or because the security policy has changed on the key server. Keys can be distributed during rekey using either multicast or unicast transport. Multicast method is more scalable as keys need not be transmitted to each group member individually. Unlike in unicast, KS will not receive acknowledgement from GM about the success of the rekey reception in multicast rekey method. In unicast rekey method, KS will delete a GM from its database if three consecutive rekeys are not acknowledged by that particular GM.

Further Reading

http://goo.gl/mxG401

Exam Essentials

- "%CRPTO-4-IKMP_BAD_MESSAGE: IKE" message from 150.150.150.1 failed its sanity check or is malformed appears if the pre-shared keys on the peers do not match. In order to fix this issue, check the pre-shared keys on both sides
- A GETVPN deployment has primarily three components, Key Server (KS), Group Member (GM), and Group Domain of Interpretation (GDOI) protocol
- There are two types of keys that the GM will receive from the KS:
    - Key Encryption Key (KEK), securing control plane
    - Traffic Encryption Key (TEK), securing data plane
- If a GETVPN GM is unable to register to a KS, it will send all traffic encrypted
- GET VPN uses the Synchronous Anti-Replay (SAR) mechanism to provide anti-replay
- Cisco IOS GET VPN uses the IETF's standard RFC3547 Group Domain of Interpretation (GDOI) as the key management protocol
- In Cisco IOS, the most secure way to protect preshared key is to use secure type 6 format. For security reasons, neither the removal of the master key, nor the removal of the password encryption aes command unencrypts the passwords in the router configuration. Once passwords are encrypted, they are not unencrypted. Existing encrypted keys in the configuration are still able to be unencrypted provided the master key is not removed.

Part 5 Infrastructure Security

Chapter 17: Device Security
Chapter 18: Network Security

Chapter 17: Device Security

This chapter covers the following exam topics from Cisco's official 400-101 (v5) written exam curriculum.

- Implement and troubleshoot IOS AAA using local database
- Implement and troubleshoot device access control (VTY/AUX/Console, SNMP, management plane protection, password encryption)
- Implement and troubleshoot control plane policing
- Device security using IOS AAA with TACACS+ and RADIUS (AAA, local privilege authorization fallback)

Chapter 17: Device Security

Implement and troubleshoot IOS AAA using local database

The Local AAA Server feature allows you to configure your router so that user authentication and authorization attributes currently available on AAA servers are available locally on the router. The attributes can be added to existing framework, such as the local user database or subscriber profile. The local AAA server provides access to the complete dictionary of Cisco IOS supported attributes.

You can configure your router so that AAA authentication and authorization attributes currently available on AAA servers are made available on existing Cisco IOS devices. The attributes can be added to existing framework, such as the local user database or subscriber profile. For example, an attribute list can now be added to an existing username, providing the ability for the local user database to act as a local AAA server. For situations in which the local username list is relatively small, this flexibility allows you to provide complete user authentication or authorization locally within the Cisco IOS software without having a AAA server. This ability can allow you to maintain your user database locally or provide a failover local mechanism without having to sacrifice policy options when defining local users.

A subscriber profile allows domain-based clients to have policy applied at the end-user service level. This flexibility allows common policy to be set for all users under a domain in one place and applied there whether or not user authorization is done locally.

Further Reading

http://goo.gl/aaTqf5

Implement and troubleshoot device access control

Lines (VTY, AUX, Console)

The use of password protection to control or restrict access to the command line interface (CLI) of your router is one of the fundamental elements of an overall security plan. Protecting the router from unauthorized remote access, typically Telnet, is the most common security that needs configuring, but protecting the router from unauthorized local access cannot be overlooked.

The VTY lines are the Virtual Terminal lines of the router, used solely to control inbound Telnet connections. They are virtual, in the sense that they are a function of software - there is no hardware associated with them. They appear in the configuration as line vty 0 4.

Each of these types of lines can be configured with password protection. Lines can be configured to use one password for all users, or for user-specific passwords. User-specific passwords can be configured locally on the router, or you can use an authentication server to provide authentication.

To specify a password on a line, use the password command in line configuration mode. To enable password checking at login, use the login command in line configuration mode.

While transport preferred none provides the same output, it also disables auto telnet for the defined host that are configured with the ip host command. This is unlike the no logging preferred command, which stops it for undefined hosts and lets it work for the defined ones.

In this example, passwords are configured for users attempting to connect to the router on the VTY lines using Telnet.

From the privileged EXEC (or "enable") prompt, enter configuration mode and enter username/password combinations, one for each user for whom you want to allow access to the router:

1. router#configure termina

Enter configuration commands, one per line. End with CNTL/Z.
2. router(config)#username russ password montecito
3. router(config)#username cindy password belgium
4. router(config)#username mike password rottweiler

Switch to line configuration mode, using the following commands. Notice that the prompt changes to reflect the current mode.
5. router(config)#line vty 0 4
6. router(config-line)#

Configure password checking at login.
7. router(config-line)#login local

8. Exit configuration mode.

You will see "% Error in authentication" error message as you attempt to enter "enable" or privileged mode if you are using local database for authentication without setting an enable password.

Further Reading

http://goo.gl/4lCTlk
http://goo.gl/0mfGTv

SNMP

SNMP is an application-layer protocol that provides a message format for communication between SNMP managers and agents. SNMP provides a standardized framework and a common language used for the monitoring and management of devices in a network.

The SNMP framework has three components:

- An SNMP manager
- An SNMP agent
- A MIB

The SNMP manager is the system used to control and monitor the activities of network hosts using SNMP. The most common managing system is called a Network Management System (NMS). The term NMS can be applied to either a dedicated device used for network management, or the applications used on such a device. A variety of network management applications are available for use with SNMP. These features range from simple command-line applications to feature-rich graphical user interfaces (such as the CiscoWorks2000 line of products).

The SNMP agent is the software component within the managed device that maintains the data for the device and reports these data, as needed, to managing systems. The agent and MIB reside on the routing device (router, access server, or switch). To enable the SNMP agent on a Cisco routing device, you must define the relationship between the manager and the agent.
The Management Information Base (MIB) is a virtual information storage area for network management information, which consists of collections of managed objects. Within the MIB there are collections of related objects, defined in MIB modules.

The SNMP agent contains MIB variables whose values the SNMP manager can request or change through Get or Set operations. A manager can get a value from an agent or store a value into that agent. The agent gathers data from the MIB, the repository for information about device parameters and network data. The agent can also respond to manager requests to Get or Set data.

Further Reading

http://goo.gl/WjvDT3

Management plane protection

The Management Plane Protection (MPP) feature in Cisco IOS provides the capability to restrict the interfaces on which network management packets are allowed to enter a device. The MPP feature allows a network operator to designate one or more router interfaces as management interfaces.

Device management traffic is permitted to enter a device only through these management interfaces. After MPP is enabled, no interfaces except designated management interfaces will accept network management traffic destined to the device. Restricting management packets to designated interfaces provides greater control over management of a device, providing more security for that device. Other benefits include improved performance for data packets on non management interfaces, support for network scalability, need for fewer access control lists (ACLs) to restrict access to a device, and management packet floods on switching and routing interfaces are prevented from reaching the CPU.

Further Reading

http://goo.gl/w1vvxh

Password encryption

The enable password command is not recommended since password is stored in cleartext. Use the enable secret command instead for better security. Enable secrets are hashed using the MD5 algorithm. As far as anyone at Cisco knows, it is impossible to recover an enable secret based on the contents of a configuration file (other than by obvious dictionary attacks).

Almost all passwords and other authentication strings in Cisco IOS configuration files are encrypted using the weak, reversible scheme used for user passwords.
To determine which scheme has been used to encrypt a specific password, check the digit preceding the encrypted string in the configuration file. If that digit is a 7, the password has been encrypted using the weak algorithm. If the digit is a 5, the password has been hashed using the stronger MD5 algorithm.

For example, in the configuration command:

enable secret 5 1iUjJ$cDZ03KKGh7mHfX2RSbDqP.

The enable secret has been hashed with MD5, whereas in the command:

username abc password 7 07362E590E1B1C041B1E124C0A2F2E206832752E1A01134D

The password has been encrypted using the weak reversible algorithm.

Because protocol analyzers can examine packets (and read passwords), you can increase access security by configuring the Cisco IOS software to encrypt passwords. Encryption prevents the password from being readable in the configuration file.

To configure the Cisco IOS software to encrypt passwords, use the following command in global
configuration mode:

Router(config)# service password-encryption

The actual encryption process occurs when the current configuration is written or when a password is configured. Password encryption is applied to all passwords, including authentication key passwords, the privileged command password, console and virtual terminal line access passwords, and BGP neighbor passwords. The service password-encryption command is primarily useful for keeping unauthorized individuals from viewing your password in your configuration file.

Further Reading

http://goo.gl/qlilER

Implement and troubleshoot control plane policing

Control Plane Policing (CoPP) is a Cisco IOS-wide feature designed to allow users to manage the flow of traffic handled by the route processor of their network devices. CoPP is designed to prevent unnecessary traffic from overwhelming the route processor that, if left unabated, could affect system performance. Route processor resource exhaustion, in this case, refers to all resources associated with the punt path and route processor(s) such as Cisco IOS process memory and buffers, and ingress packet queues.

More than just control plane packets can punt and affect the route processor and system resources. Management plane traffic, as well as certain data plane exceptions IP packets and some services plane packets, may also require the use of route processor resources. Even so, it is common practice to identify the resources associated with the punt path and route processor(s) as the Control Plane. The feature in Cisco IOS is CoPP.

CoPP protects the route processor on network devices by treating route processor resources as a separate entity with its own ingress interface (and in some implementations, egress also). Because of this behavior, a CoPP policy can be developed and applied only to those packets within the control plane. Unlike interface ACLs, for example, no effort is wasted investigating data plane (transit) packets that will never reach the control plane. This action has a significant simplifying implication on the construction of policies for CoPP.

CoPP is implemented using the Cisco IOS Modular QoS CLI (MQC), a highly flexible framework that allows users to create and attach traffic polices to interfaces The Cisco Modular QoS CLI (MQC) mechanisms are used by CoPP to define the classification and policing descriptions for its policies. In this way, in addition to the limited permit and deny actions associated with simple ACLs, specific packets may be permitted but rate-limited when using the MQC structure. For example, you may wish to permit certain ICMP packet types, but rate limit them so that the route processor is not adversely impacted. This action adds tremendously to the capabilities and flexibility of developing and deploying a useable CoPP policy.

CoPP doesn't encompass SMTP and RPC protocols.

Further Reading
http://goo.gl/swi8DE

Describe device security using IOS AAA with TACACS+ and RADIUS

AAA with TACACS+ and RADIUS
RADIUS is an access server that uses AAA protocol and combines authentication and authorization. It is a system of distributed security that secures remote access to networks and network services against unauthorized access. TACACS+ provides session encryption and can provide CLI authorization by user groups.

RADIUS comprises of three components:
- A protocol with a frame format that utilizes User Datagram Protocol (UDP)/IP
- A server
- A client

RADIUS uses UDP while TACACS+ uses TCP. TCP offers several advantages over UDP. TCP offers a connection-oriented transport, while UDP offers best-effort delivery. RADIUS requires additional programmable variables such as retransmit attempts and time-outs to compensate for best-effort transport, but it lacks the level of built-in support that a TCP transport offers:

- TCP usage provides a separate acknowledgment that a request has been received, within (approximately) a network round-trip time (RTT), regardless of how loaded and slow the backend authentication mechanism (a TCP acknowledgment) might be.
- TCP provides immediate indication of a crashed, or not running, server by a reset (RST). You can determine when a server crashes and returns to service if you use long-lived TCP connections. UDP cannot tell the difference between a server that is down, a slow server, and a non-existent server.
- Using TCP keepalives, server crashes can be detected out-of-band with actual requests. Connections to multiple servers can be maintained simultaneously, and you only need to send messages to the ones that are known to be up and running.
- TCP is more scalable and adapts to growing, as well as congested, networks.

Local privilege authorization fallback

The local database can act as a fallback method for several functions. This behavior is designed to help prevent accidental lockout. For users who need fallback support, it is recommended that their usernames and passwords in the local database match their usernames and passwords in the AAA servers. This provides transparent fallback support. Because the user cannot determine whether a AAA server or the local database is providing the service, using usernames and passwords on AAA servers that are different than the usernames and passwords in the local database means that the user cannot be certain which username and password should be given.

The local database supports the following fallback functions:
- Console and enable password authentication—When you use the aaa authentication console command, you can add the LOCAL keyword after the AAA server group tag. If the servers in the group all are unavailable, the security appliance uses the local database to authenticate administrative access. This can include enable password authentication, too.
- Command authorization—When you use the aaa authorization command command, you can add the LOCAL keyword after the AAA server group tag. If the TACACS+ servers in the group all are unavailable, the local database is used to authorize commands based on privilege levels.
- VPN authentication and authorization—VPN authentication and authorization are supported to enable remote access to the security appliance if AAA servers that normally support these VPN services are unavailable. The authentication-server-group

command, available in tunnel-group general attributes mode, lets you specify the LOCAL keyword when you are configuring attributes of a tunnel group. When VPN client of an administrator specifies a tunnel group configured to fallback to the local database, the VPN tunnel can be established even if the AAA server group is unavailable, provided that the local database is configured with the necessary attributes.

Exam Essentials

- The Local AAA Server feature allows you to configure your router so that user authentication and authorization attributes currently available on AAA servers are available locally on the router
- While transport preferred none provides the same output, it also disables auto telnet for the defined host that are configured with the ip host command. This is unlike the no logging preferred command, which stops it for undefined hosts and lets it work for the defined ones
- You will see "% Error in authentication" error message as you attempt to enter "enable" or privileged mode if you are using local database for authentication without setting an enable password.
- The enable password command is not recommended since password is stored in cleartext. Use the enable secret command instead for better security
- RADIUS is an access server that uses AAA protocol and combines authentication and authorization. It is a system of distributed security that secures remote access to networks and network services against unauthorized access. TACACS+ provides session encryption and can provide CLI authorization by user groups
- The local database can act as a fallback method for several functions. This behavior is designed to help prevent accidental lockout. For users who need fallback support, it is recommended that their usernames and passwords in the local database match their usernames and passwords in the AAA servers
- A router can be configured to authenticate for its enable password against a AAA server
- AAA local database allows for command authorization and network access authentication

Chapter 18: Network Security

This chapter covers the following exam topics from Cisco's official 400-101 (v5) written exam curriculum.

- Implement and troubleshoot switch security features (VACL, PACL, stormcontrol, DHCP snooping, IP source-guard, dynamic ARP inspection, port-security, private VLAN)
- Implement and troubleshoot router security features (IPv4 access control lists, standard/extended, time-based, IPv6 traffic filter, uRPF)
- Implement and troubleshoot IPv6 first hop security (RA guard, DHCP guard, binding table, device tracking, ND inspection/snooping, source guard, PACL)
- 802.1x (802.1x, EAP, RADIUS, MAC authentication bypass)

Chapter 18: Network Security

Implement and troubleshoot switch security features

VACL, PACL

VLAN ACLs (VACLs) can provide access control for all packets that are bridged within a VLAN or that are routed into or out of a VLAN or a WAN interface for VACL capture. Unlike Cisco IOS ACLs that are applied on routed packets only, VACLs apply to all packets and can be applied to any VLAN or WAN interface. VACLs are processed in the ACL TCAM hardware. VACLs ignore any Cisco IOS ACL fields that are not supported in hardware.

You can configure VACLs for IP and MAC-layer traffic. VACLs applied to WAN interfaces support only IP traffic for VACL capture. If a VACL is configured for a packet type, and a packet of that type does not match the VACL, the default action is to deny the packet.

The port ACL (PACL) feature provides the ability to perform access control on specific Layer 2 ports. A Layer 2 port is a physical LAN or trunk port that belongs to a VLAN. Port ACLs are applied only on the ingress traffic. The port ACL feature is supported only in hardware (port ACLs are not applied to any packets routed in software). They apply to both voice and data VLANs.

When you create a port ACL, an entry is created in the ACL TCAM. You can use the show tcam counts command to see how much TCAM space is available. The PACL feature does not affect Layer 2 control packets received on the port.

You can use the access-group mode command to change the way that PACLs interact with other ACLs.

PACLs use the following modes:

Prefer port mode—If a PACL is configured on a Layer 2 interface, the PACL takes effect and overwrites the effect of other ACLs (Cisco IOS ACL and VACL). If no PACL feature is configured on the Layer 2 interface, other features applicable to the interface are merged and are applied on the interface.
Merge mode—In this mode, the PACL, VACL, and Cisco IOS ACLs are merged in the ingress direction following the logical serial. This is the default access group mode.

You configure the access-group mode command on each interface. The default is merge mode.

Further Reading

http://goo.gl/I1YMZD

Stormcontrol

A traffic storm occurs when packets flood the LAN, creating excessive traffic and degrading network performance. The traffic storm control feature prevents LAN ports from being disrupted by a broadcast, multicast, or unicast traffic storm on physical interfaces. Traffic storm control (also called traffic suppression) monitors incoming traffic levels over a 1-second traffic storm control interval, and during the interval it compares the traffic level with the traffic storm control level that you configure. The traffic storm control level is a percentage of the total available bandwidth of the port. Each port has a single traffic storm control level that is used for all types of traffic (broadcast, multicast, and unicast).

Traffic storm control monitors the level of each traffic type for which you enable traffic storm control in 1-second traffic storm control intervals.

DHCP snooping

DHCP snooping is a security feature that acts like a firewall between untrusted hosts and trusted DHCP servers. The DHCP snooping feature performs the following activities:

- Validates DHCP messages received from untrusted sources and filters out invalid messages.
- Rate-limits DHCP traffic from trusted and untrusted sources.
- Builds and maintains the DHCP snooping binding database, which contains information about untrusted hosts with leased IP addresses.
- Utilizes the DHCP snooping binding database to validate subsequent requests from untrusted hosts.
- Other security features, such as dynamic ARP inspection (DAI), also use information stored in the DHCP snooping binding database.

DHCP snooping is enabled on a per-VLAN basis. By default, the feature is inactive on all VLANs. You can enable the feature on a single VLAN or a range of VLANs. The DHCP snooping feature is implemented in software on the route processor (RP). Therefore, all DHCP messages for enabled VLANs are intercepted in the Policy Feature Card (PFC) and directed to the RP for processing.

IP source-guard

IP source guard provides source IP address filtering on a Layer 2 port to prevent a malicious host from impersonating a legitimate host by assuming the legitimate host's IP address. The feature uses dynamic DHCP snooping and static IP source binding to match IP addresses to hosts on untrusted Layer 2 access ports.

Initially, all IP traffic on the protected port is blocked except for DHCP packets. After a client receives an IP address from the DHCP server, or after static IP source binding is configured by the administrator, all traffic with that IP source address is permitted from that client. Traffic from other hosts is denied. This filtering limits a host's ability to attack the network by claiming a neighbor host's IP address. IP source guard is a port-based feature that automatically creates an implicit port access control list (PACL).

Further Reading

http://goo.gl/QJPgaJ

Dynamic ARP inspection

ARP spoofing attacks and ARP cache poisoning can occur because ARP allows a gratuitous reply from a host even if an ARP request was not received. After the attack, all traffic from the device under attack flows through the attacker's computer and then to the router, switch, or host.

An ARP spoofing attack can target hosts, switches, and routers connected to your Layer 2 network by poisoning the ARP caches of systems connected to the subnet and by intercepting traffic intended for other hosts on the subnet

Hosts A, B, and C are connected to the switch on interfaces A, B and C, all of which are on the same subnet. Their IP and MAC addresses are shown in parentheses; for example, Host A uses IP address IA and MAC address MA. When Host A needs to communicate to Host B at the IP layer, it broadcasts an ARP request for the MAC address associated with IP address IB. When the switch and Host B receive the ARP request, they populate their ARP caches with an ARP binding for a host with the IP address IA and a MAC address MA; for example, IP address IA is bound to MAC address MA. When Host B responds, the switch and Host A populate their ARP caches with a binding for a host with the IP address IB and the MAC address MB.

Host C can poison the ARP caches of the switch for Host A, and Host B by broadcasting forged ARP responses with bindings for a host with an IP address of IA (or IB) and a MAC address of MC. Hosts with poisoned ARP caches use the MAC address MC as the destination MAC address for traffic intended for IA or IB. This means that Host C intercepts that traffic. Because Host C knows the true MAC addresses associated with IA and IB, it can forward the intercepted traffic to those hosts by using the correct MAC address as the destination. Host C has inserted itself into the traffic stream from Host A to Host B, which is the topology of the classic man-in-the middle attack.

Port-security

You can use port security with dynamically learned and static MAC addresses to restrict a port's ingress traffic by limiting the MAC addresses that are allowed to send traffic into the port. When you assign secure MAC addresses to a secure port, the port does not forward ingress traffic that has source addresses outside the group of defined addresses. If you limit the number of secure MAC addresses to one and assign a single secure MAC address, the device attached to that port has the full bandwidth of the port.

A security violation occurs in either of these situations:
- When the maximum number of secure MAC addresses is reached on a secure port and the source MAC address of the ingress traffic is different from any of the identified secure MAC addresses, port security applies the configured violation mode.
- If traffic with a secure MAC address that is configured or learned on one secure port attempts to access another secure port in the same VLAN, applies the configured violation mode.

Private VLAN

A private VLAN partitions the Layer 2 broadcast domain of a VLAN into sub-domains, allowing you to isolate the ports on the switch from each other. A sub-domain consists of a primary VLAN and one or more secondary VLANs.

All VLANs in a private VLAN domain share the same primary VLAN. The secondary VLAN ID differentiates one sub-domain from another. The secondary VLANs may either be isolated VLANs or community VLANs. A host on an isolated VLAN can only communicate with the associated promiscuous port in its primary VLAN. Hosts on community VLANs can communicate among themselves and with their associated promiscuous port but not with ports in other community VLANs.

Implement and troubleshoot router security features

IPv4 access control lists (standard, extended, time-based)

Cisco provides basic traffic filtering capabilities with access control lists (also referred to as access lists). Access lists can be configured for all routed network protocols (IP, AppleTalk, and so on) to filter the packets of those protocols as the packets pass through a router.

Access lists filter network traffic by controlling whether routed packets are forwarded or blocked at the router's interfaces. Your router examines each packet to determine whether to forward or drop the packet, on the basis of the criteria you specified within the access lists. Access list criteria could be the source address of the traffic, the destination address of the traffic, the upper-layer protocol, or other information. Note that sophisticated users can sometimes successfully evade or fool basic access lists because no authentication is required.

Standard ACLs are the oldest type of ACL. Standard ACLs control traffic by the comparison of the source address of the IP packets to the addresses configured in the ACL.

This is the command syntax format of a standard ACL.
access-list access-list-number {permit|deny} {host|source source-wildcard|any}

A source/source-wildcard setting of 0.0.0.0/255.255.255.255 can be specified as any. The wildcard can be omitted if it is all zeros. Therefore, host 10.1.1.2 0.0.0.0 is the same as host 10.1.1.2. After the ACL is defined, it must be applied to the interface (inbound or outbound). In early software releases, out was the default when a keyword out or in was not specified. The direction must be specified in later software releases.

interface <interface>
ip access-group number {in|out}

This is an example of the use of a standard ACL in order to block all traffic except that from source 10.1.1.x.

interface Ethernet0/0
ip address 10.1.1.1 255.255.255.0
ip access-group 1 in
access-list 1 permit 10.1.1.0 0.0.0.255

Zone-Based Policy Firewall (also known as Zone-Policy Firewall, or ZFW) changes the firewall configuration from the older interface-based model to a more flexible, more easily understood zone-based model. Interfaces are assigned to zones, and inspection policy is applied to traffic moving between the zones. Inter-zone policies offer considerable flexibility and granularity, so different inspection policies can be applied to multiple host groups connected to the same router interface.

When ZBF is enabled on an IOS router, any traffic to the self zone (that is, traffic destined to the router's management plane) is allowed by default in the IOS 15.x train of code. If you have created a policy for any zone (such as 'inside' or 'outside') to the self zone (out-to-self policy) or the reverse (self-to-out policy), you must explicitly define permissible traffic in the policies attached to these zones. Use the inspect or pass action in order to define the permissible traffic.

Zone-Based Firewall as DHCP Client with Pass Action for UDP Traffic Configuration

This example configuration utilizes the pass action set instead of the inspect action in the policy-map for all UDP traffic to or from the router.

```
zone security outside
zone security inside

interface Ethernet0/1
zone-member security outside
interface Ethernet0/2
zone-member security inside

class-map type inspect match-all dhcp
match protocol udp

policy-map type inspect out-to-self
class type inspect dhcp
 pass
class class-default
 drop
policy-map type inspect self-to-out
class type inspect dhcp
 pass
class class-default
 drop

zone-pair security out-to-self source outside destination self
zone-pair security self-to-out source self destination outside
```

Zone-Based Firewall with Pass Action for DHCP Traffic Configuration

This example configuration shows how to prevent all UDP traffic from a zone into your router's self zone except for DHCP packets. Use an access-list with specific ports in order to allow just DHCP traffic; in this example, UDP port 67 and UDP port 68 are specified to be matched. A class-map that references the access-list has the pass action applied.

```
access-list extended 111
10 permit udp any any eq 67

access-list extended 112
10 permit udp any any eq 68

class-map type inspect match-any self-to-out
match access-group 111
class-map type inspect match-any out-to-self
match access-group 112

zone security outside
zone security inside

interface Ethernet0/1
zone-member security outside
interface Ethernet0/2
zone-member security inside

policy-map type inspect out-to-self
class type inspect out-to-self
 pass
class class-default
 drop
policy-map type inspect self-to-out
class type inspect self-to-out
 pass
class class-default
 drop

zone-pair security out-to-self source outside destination self
zone-pair security self-to-out source self destination outside
```

Further Reading

http://goo.gl/TwuLVY

IPv6 traffic filter

To filter incoming or outgoing IPv6 traffic on an interface, use the ipv6 traffic-filter command in interface configuration mode. To disable the filtering of IPv6 traffic on an interface, use the no form of this command.

ipv6 traffic-filter access-list-name {in | out}
no ipv6 traffic-filter access-list-name

Further Reading

http://goo.gl/v7dzXe

Unicast reverse path forwarding

Network administrators can use Unicast Reverse Path Forwarding (Unicast RPF) to help limit the malicious traffic on an enterprise network. This security feature works by enabling a router to verify the reachability of the source address in packets being forwarded. This capability can limit the appearance of spoofed addresses on a network. If the source IP address is not valid, the packet is discarded. Unicast RPF works in one of three different modes: strict mode, loose mode, or VRF mode. Unicast RPF requires CEF to be enabled.

When administrators use Unicast RPF in strict mode, the packet must be received on the interface that the router would use to forward the return packet. Unicast RPF configured in strict mode may drop legitimate traffic that is received on an interface that was not the router's choice for sending return traffic. Dropping this legitimate traffic could occur when asymmetric routing paths are present in the network.

When administrators use Unicast RPF in loose mode, the source address must appear in the routing table. Administrators can change this behavior using the allow-default option, which allows the use of the default route in the source verification process. Additionally, a packet that contains a source address for which the return route points to the Null 0 interface will be dropped. An access list may also be specified that permits or denies certain source addresses in Unicast RPF loose mode.

Care must be taken to ensure that the appropriate Unicast RPF mode (loose or strict) is configured during the deployment of this feature because it can drop legitimate traffic. Although asymmetric traffic flows may be of concern when deploying this feature, Unicast RPF loose mode is a scalable option for networks that contain asymmetric routing paths.

Implement and troubleshoot IPv6 first hop security

RA guard

The IPv6 RA Guard feature provides support for allowing the network administrator to block or reject unwanted or rogue router advertisement (RA) guard messages that arrive at the network device platform. RAs are used by devices to announce themselves on the link. The IPv6 RA Guard feature analyzes these RAs and filters out RAs that are sent by unauthorized devices. In host mode, all RA and router redirect messages are disallowed on the port. The RA guard feature compares configuration information on the Layer 2 (L2) device with the information found in the received RA frame. Once the L2 device has validated the content of the RA frame and router redirect frame against the configuration, it forwards the RA to its unicast or multicast destination. If the RA frame content is not validated, the RA is dropped. You can use show ipv6 snooping command to get details of both RA guard and ND inspection features.

Further Reading
http://goo.gl/776y5S

DHCP guard

The DHCPv6 Guard feature blocks reply and advertisement messages that come from unauthorized DHCP servers and relay agents. Packets are classified into one of the three DHCP type messages. All client messages are always switched regardless of device role. DHCP server messages are only processed further if the device role is set to server. Further processing of server messages includes DHCP server advertisements (for source validation and server preference) and DHCP server replies (for permitted prefixes).

If the device is configured as a DHCP server, all the messages need to be switched, regardless of the device role configuration.

Further Reading
http://goo.gl/uyCyAx

Binding table

A database table of IPv6 neighbors connected to the device is created from information sources such as NDP snooping. This database, or binding table, is used by various IPv6 guard features to validate the link-layer address (LLA), the IPv4 or IPv6 address, and the prefix binding of the neighbors to prevent spoofing and redirect attacks.

The IPv6 first-hop security binding table recovery mechanism enables the binding table to recover in the event of a device reboot. The recovery mechanism will block any data traffic sourced from an unknown source, that is a source not already specified in the binding table and previously learnt via NDP or Dynamic Host Configuration Protocol (DHCP) gleaning. The IPv6 First-Hop Security Binding Table Recovery Mechanism feature recovers the missing binding table entries when the resolution for a destination address fails in the destination guard. Upon a failure, a binding table entry is recovered by querying the DHCP server or the destination host depending on the configuration.

Further Reading
http://goo.gl/CkmbLH

Device tracking

The IPv6 Device Tracking feature provides IPv6 host liveness tracking so that a neighbor table can be immediately updated when an IPv6 host disappears. The feature tracks the liveness of the neighbors connected through the Layer 2 device on a regular basis in order to revoke network access privileges as they become inactive.

Further Reading
http://goo.gl/Fg1jWP

ND inspection/snooping

IPv6 Neighbor Discovery (ND) inspection learns and secures bindings for stateless auto-configuration addresses in Layer 2 neighbor tables. IPv6 ND inspection analyzes neighbor discovery messages in order to build a trusted binding table database, and IPv6 neighbor discovery messages that do not have valid bindings are dropped. A neighbor discovery message is considered trustworthy if its IPv6-to-MAC mapping is verifiable.

This feature mitigates some of the inherent vulnerabilities for the neighbor discovery mechanism, such as attacks on duplicate address detection (DAD), address resolution, device discovery, and the neighbor cache.

Further Reading
http://goo.gl/IQyw9k

Source guard

IPv6 source guard is an interface feature between the populated binding table and data traffic filtering. This feature enables the device to deny traffic when it is originated from an address that is not stored in the binding table. IPv6 source guard does not inspect ND or DHCP packets; rather, it works in conjunction with IPv6 neighbor discovery (ND) inspection or IPv6 address glean, both of which detect existing addresses on the link and store them into the binding table.

IPv6 source guard is an interface between the populated binding table and data traffic filtering, and the binding table must be populated with IPv6 prefixes for IPv6 source guard to work.

IPv6 source guard can deny traffic from unknown sources or unallocated addresses, such as traffic from sources not assigned by a DHCP server. When traffic is denied, the IPv6 address glean feature is notified so that it can try to recover the traffic by querying the DHCP server or by using IPv6 ND. The data-glean function prevents the device and end user from getting deadlocked, whereupon a valid address fails to be stored into the binding table, there is no recovery path, and the end user is unable to connect.

Further Reading
http://goo.gl/6YGjus

PACL

The IPv6 PACL feature provides the ability to provide access control (permit or deny) on Layer 2 switch ports for IPv6 traffic. IPv6 PACLs are similar to IPv4 PACLs, which provide access control on Layer 2 switch ports for IPv4 traffic. They are supported only in the ingress direction and in hardware. A PACL can filter ingress traffic on Layer 2 interfaces based on Layer 3 and Layer 4 header information or non-IP Layer 2 information.

Further Reading
http://goo.gl/H3Y1GD

Describe 802.1x

The IEEE 802.1X standard defines a client-server-based access control and authentication protocol that restricts unauthorized devices from connecting to a LAN through publicly accessible ports. The authentication server authenticates each client connected to a switch port before making available any services offered by the switch or the LAN. Until the client is authenticated, 802.1X access control allows only Extensible Authentication Protocol over LAN

(EAPOL) traffic through the port to which the client is connected. After authentication is successful, normal traffic can pass through the port.

Further Reading
http://goo.gl/LE4d55

802.1x, EAP, RADIUS

With 802.1X port-based authentication, the devices in the network have specific roles.

Client—the device (workstation) that requests access to the LAN and switch services and responds to the requests from the switch. The workstation must be running 802.1X-compliant client software such as that offered in the Microsoft Windows XP operating system. (The client is the supplicant in the IEEE 802.1X specification.)

Authentication server—performs the actual authentication of the client. The authentication server validates the identity of the client and notifies the switch whether or not the client is authorized to access the LAN and switch services. Because the switch acts as the proxy, the authentication service is transparent to the client. In this release, the Remote Authentication Dial-In User Service (RADIUS) security system with Extensible Authentication Protocol (EAP) extensions is the only supported authentication server; it is available in Cisco Secure Access Control Server version 3.0. RADIUS operates in a client/server model in which secure authentication information is exchanged between the RADIUS server and one or more RADIUS clients.

Switch (edge switch or wireless access point)—controls the physical access to the network based on the authentication status of the client. The switch acts as an intermediary or proxy between the client and the authentication server, requesting identity information from the client, verifying that information with the authentication server, and relaying a response to the client. The switch includes the RADIUS client, which is responsible for encapsulating and decapsulating the Extensible Authentication Protocol (EAP) frames and interacting with the authentication server.

When the switch receives EAPOL frames and relays them to the authentication server, the Ethernet header is stripped and the remaining EAP frame is re-encapsulated in the RADIUS format. The EAP frames are not modified or examined during encapsulation, and the authentication server must support EAP within the native frame format. When the switch receives frames from the authentication server, the server's frame header is removed, leaving the EAP frame, which is then encapsulated for Ethernet and sent to the client.

The devices that can act as intermediaries include the Catalyst 3550 multilayer switch, Catalyst 2950 switch, or a wireless access point. These devices must be running software that supports the RADIUS client and 802.1X.

Further Reading
http://goo.gl/xDjLL0

MAC authentication bypass

The best and most secure solution to vulnerability at the access edge is to use the intelligence of the network. One access control technique that Cisco provides is called MAC Authentication Bypass (MAB). MAB uses the MAC address of a device to determine what kind of network access to provide. MAB enables port-based access control using the MAC address of the endpoint. A MAB-enabled port can be dynamically enabled or disabled based on the MAC address of the device that connects to it.

Prior to MAB, the endpoint's identity is unknown and all traffic is blocked. The switch examines a single packet to learn and authenticate the source MAC address. After MAB succeeds, the endpoint's identity is known and all traffic from that endpoint is allowed. The switch performs source MAC address filtering to help ensure that only the MAB-authenticated endpoint is allowed to send traffic.

By default, a MAB-enabled port allows only a single endpoint per port. Any additional MAC addresses seen on the port will cause a security violation. Multi-domain authentication was specifically designed to address the requirements of IP telephony. When multi-domain authentication is configured, two endpoints are allowed on the port: one in the voice VLAN and one in the data VLAN. Either, both, or none of the endpoints can be authenticated with MAB. Additional MAC addresses will trigger a security violation.

Further Reading
http://goo.gl/c7uUuD
http://goo.gl/8G9WFF

Exam Essentials

- A traffic storm occurs when packets flood the LAN, creating excessive traffic and degrading network performance. The traffic storm control feature prevents LAN ports from being disrupted by a broadcast, multicast, or unicast traffic storm on physical interfaces

- A private VLAN partitions the Layer 2 broadcast domain of a VLAN into sub-domains, allowing you to isolate the ports on the switch from each other. A sub-domain consists of a primary VLAN and one or more secondary VLANs
- To filter incoming or outgoing IPv6 traffic on an interface, use the ipv6 traffic-filter command in interface configuration mode
- The IPv6 RA Guard feature provides support for allowing the network administrator to block or reject unwanted or rogue router advertisement (RA) guard messages that arrive at the network device platform
- IPv6 Neighbor Discovery (ND) inspection learns and secures bindings for stateless auto-configuration addresses in Layer 2 neighbor tables
- IPv6 source guard is an interface feature between the populated binding table and data traffic filtering. This feature enables the device to deny traffic when it is originated from an address that is not stored in the binding table
- MAB uses the MAC address of a device to determine what kind of network access to provide. MAB enables port-based access control using the MAC address of the endpoint. A MAB-enabled port can be dynamically enabled or disabled based on the MAC address of the device that connects to it
- By default, a MAB-enabled port allows only a single endpoint per port. Any additional MAC addresses seen on the port will cause a security violation
- When multi-domain authentication is configured, two endpoints are allowed on the port: one in the voice VLAN and one in the data VLAN
- EAPOL, STP and CDP traffic are not subjected to 802.1X access controls i.e. before traffic for these protocols will still pass even before an authentication takes place
- MAC ACLs are supported only in the inbound direction and can be applied to a VLAN or a physical interface
- Inside to outside NAT takes place after routing, whereas outside to inside NAT happens before routing
- The PVLAN edge (protected port) is a feature that has only local significance to the switch (unlike Private Vlans), and there is no isolation provided between two.
- IPv6 address glean is the foundation for many other IPv6 features that depend on an accurate binding table. It inspects ND and DHCP messages.

Chapter 17: Device Security

This chapter covers the following exam topics from Cisco's official 400-101 (v5) written exam curriculum.

- Implement and troubleshoot IOS AAA using local database
- Implement and troubleshoot device access control (VTY/AUX/Console, SNMP, management plane protection, password encryption)
- Implement and troubleshoot control plane policing
- Device security using IOS AAA with TACACS+ and RADIUS (AAA, local privilege authorization fallback)

Chapter 17: Device Security

Implement and troubleshoot IOS AAA using local database

The Local AAA Server feature allows you to configure your router so that user authentication and authorization attributes currently available on AAA servers are available locally on the router. The attributes can be added to existing framework, such as the local user database or subscriber profile. The local AAA server provides access to the complete dictionary of Cisco IOS supported attributes.

You can configure your router so that AAA authentication and authorization attributes currently available on AAA servers are made available on existing Cisco IOS devices. The attributes can be added to existing framework, such as the local user database or subscriber profile. For example, an attribute list can now be added to an existing username, providing the ability for the local user database to act as a local AAA server. For situations in which the local username list is relatively small, this flexibility allows you to provide complete user authentication or authorization locally within the Cisco IOS software without having a AAA server. This ability can allow you to maintain your user database locally or provide a failover local mechanism without having to sacrifice policy options when defining local users.

A subscriber profile allows domain-based clients to have policy applied at the end-user service level. This flexibility allows common policy to be set for all users under a domain in one place and applied there whether or not user authorization is done locally.

Further Reading

http://goo.gl/aaTqf5

Implement and troubleshoot device access control

Lines (VTY, AUX, Console)

The use of password protection to control or restrict access to the command line interface (CLI) of your router is one of the fundamental elements of an overall security plan. Protecting the router from unauthorized remote access, typically Telnet, is the most common security that needs configuring, but protecting the router from unauthorized local access cannot be overlooked.

The VTY lines are the Virtual Terminal lines of the router, used solely to control inbound Telnet connections. They are virtual, in the sense that they are a function of software - there is no hardware associated with them. They appear in the configuration as line vty 0 4.
Each of these types of lines can be configured with password protection. Lines can be configured to use one password for all users, or for user-specific passwords. User-specific passwords can be configured locally on the router, or you can use an authentication server to provide authentication.

To specify a password on a line, use the password command in line configuration mode. To enable password checking at login, use the login command in line configuration mode.

While transport preferred none provides the same output, it also disables auto telnet for the defined host that are configured with the ip host command. This is unlike the no logging preferred command, which stops it for undefined hosts and lets it work for the defined ones.

In this example, passwords are configured for users attempting to connect to the router on the VTY lines using Telnet.

From the privileged EXEC (or "enable") prompt, enter configuration mode and enter username/password combinations, one for each user for whom you want to allow access to the router:

1. router#configure termina

Enter configuration commands, one per line. End with CNTL/Z.
2. router(config)#username russ password montecito
3. router(config)#username cindy password belgium
4. router(config)#username mike password rottweiler

Switch to line configuration mode, using the following commands. Notice that the prompt changes to reflect the current mode.
5. router(config)#line vty 0 4
6. router(config-line)#

Configure password checking at login.
7. router(config-line)#login local

8. Exit configuration mode.

You will see "% Error in authentication" error message as you attempt to enter "enable" or privileged mode if you are using local database for authentication without setting an enable password.

Further Reading

http://goo.gl/4ICTlk
http://goo.gl/0mfGTv

SNMP

SNMP is an application-layer protocol that provides a message format for communication between SNMP managers and agents. SNMP provides a standardized framework and a common language used for the monitoring and management of devices in a network.

The SNMP framework has three components:

- An SNMP manager
- An SNMP agent
- A MIB

The SNMP manager is the system used to control and monitor the activities of network hosts using SNMP. The most common managing system is called a Network Management System (NMS). The term NMS can be applied to either a dedicated device used for network management, or the applications used on such a device. A variety of network management applications are available for use with SNMP. These features range from simple command-line applications to feature-rich graphical user interfaces (such as the CiscoWorks2000 line of products).

The SNMP agent is the software component within the managed device that maintains the data for the device and reports these data, as needed, to managing systems. The agent and MIB reside on the routing device (router, access server, or switch). To enable the SNMP agent on a Cisco routing device, you must define the relationship between the manager and the agent.

The Management Information Base (MIB) is a virtual information storage area for network management information, which consists of collections of managed objects. Within the MIB there are collections of related objects, defined in MIB modules.

The SNMP agent contains MIB variables whose values the SNMP manager can request or change through Get or Set operations. A manager can get a value from an agent or store a value into that agent. The agent gathers data from the MIB, the repository for information about device parameters and network data. The agent can also respond to manager requests to Get or Set data.

Further Reading

http://goo.gl/WjvDT3

Management plane protection

The Management Plane Protection (MPP) feature in Cisco IOS provides the capability to restrict the interfaces on which network management packets are allowed to enter a device. The MPP feature allows a network operator to designate one or more router interfaces as management interfaces.

Device management traffic is permitted to enter a device only through these management interfaces. After MPP is enabled, no interfaces except designated management interfaces will accept network management traffic destined to the device. Restricting management packets to designated interfaces provides greater control over management of a device, providing more security for that device. Other benefits include improved performance for data packets on non management interfaces, support for network scalability, need for fewer access control lists (ACLs) to restrict access to a device, and management packet floods on switching and routing interfaces are prevented from reaching the CPU.

Further Reading

http://goo.gl/w1vvxh

Password encryption

The enable password command is not recommended since password is stored in cleartext. Use the enable secret command instead for better security. Enable secrets are hashed using the MD5 algorithm. As far as anyone at Cisco knows, it is impossible to recover an enable secret based on the contents of a configuration file (other than by obvious dictionary attacks).

Almost all passwords and other authentication strings in Cisco IOS configuration files are encrypted using the weak, reversible scheme used for user passwords.
To determine which scheme has been used to encrypt a specific password, check the digit preceding the encrypted string in the configuration file. If that digit is a 7, the password has been encrypted using the weak algorithm. If the digit is a 5, the password has been hashed using the stronger MD5 algorithm.

For example, in the configuration command:

enable secret 5 1iUjJ$cDZ03KKGh7mHfX2RSbDqP.

The enable secret has been hashed with MD5, whereas in the command:

username abc password 7 07362E590E1B1C041B1E124C0A2F2E206832752E1A01134D

The password has been encrypted using the weak reversible algorithm.

Because protocol analyzers can examine packets (and read passwords), you can increase access security by configuring the Cisco IOS software to encrypt passwords. Encryption prevents the password from being readable in the configuration file.

To configure the Cisco IOS software to encrypt passwords, use the following command in global
configuration mode:

Router(config)# service password-encryption

The actual encryption process occurs when the current configuration is written or when a password is configured. Password encryption is applied to all passwords, including authentication key passwords, the privileged command password, console and virtual terminal line access passwords, and BGP neighbor passwords. The service password-encryption command is primarily useful for keeping unauthorized individuals from viewing your password in your configuration file.

Further Reading

http://goo.gl/qIiIER

Implement and troubleshoot control plane policing

Control Plane Policing (CoPP) is a Cisco IOS-wide feature designed to allow users to manage the flow of traffic handled by the route processor of their network devices. CoPP is designed to prevent unnecessary traffic from overwhelming the route processor that, if left unabated, could affect system performance. Route processor resource exhaustion, in this case, refers to all resources associated with the punt path and route processor(s) such as Cisco IOS process memory and buffers, and ingress packet queues.

More than just control plane packets can punt and affect the route processor and system resources. Management plane traffic, as well as certain data plane exceptions IP packets and some services plane packets, may also require the use of route processor resources. Even so, it is common practice to identify the resources associated with the punt path and route processor(s) as the Control Plane. The feature in Cisco IOS is CoPP.

CoPP protects the route processor on network devices by treating route processor resources as a separate entity with its own ingress interface (and in some implementations, egress also). Because of this behavior, a CoPP policy can be developed and applied only to those packets within the control plane. Unlike interface ACLs, for example, no effort is wasted investigating data plane (transit) packets that will never reach the control plane. This action has a significant simplifying implication on the construction of policies for CoPP.

CoPP is implemented using the Cisco IOS Modular QoS CLI (MQC), a highly flexible framework that allows users to create and attach traffic polices to interfaces The Cisco Modular QoS CLI (MQC) mechanisms are used by CoPP to define the classification and policing descriptions for its policies. In this way, in addition to the limited permit and deny actions associated with simple ACLs, specific packets may be permitted but rate-limited when using the MQC structure. For example, you may wish to permit certain ICMP packet types, but rate limit them so that the route processor is not adversely impacted. This action adds tremendously to the capabilities and flexibility of developing and deploying a useable CoPP policy.

CoPP doesn't encompass SMTP and RPC protocols.

Further Reading

http://goo.gl/swi8DE

Describe device security using IOS AAA with TACACS+ and RADIUS

AAA with TACACS+ and RADIUS

RADIUS is an access server that uses AAA protocol and combines authentication and authorization. It is a system of distributed security that secures remote access to networks and network services against unauthorized access. TACACS+ provides session encryption and can provide CLI authorization by user groups.

RADIUS comprises of three components:
- A protocol with a frame format that utilizes User Datagram Protocol (UDP)/IP
- A server
- A client

RADIUS uses UDP while TACACS+ uses TCP. TCP offers several advantages over UDP. TCP offers a connection-oriented transport, while UDP offers best-effort delivery. RADIUS requires additional programmable variables such as retransmit attempts and time-outs to compensate for best-effort transport, but it lacks the level of built-in support that a TCP transport offers:

- TCP usage provides a separate acknowledgment that a request has been received, within (approximately) a network round-trip time (RTT), regardless of how loaded and slow the backend authentication mechanism (a TCP acknowledgment) might be.
- TCP provides immediate indication of a crashed, or not running, server by a reset (RST). You can determine when a server crashes and returns to service if you use long-lived TCP connections. UDP cannot tell the difference between a server that is down, a slow server, and a non-existent server.
- Using TCP keepalives, server crashes can be detected out-of-band with actual requests. Connections to multiple servers can be maintained simultaneously, and you only need to send messages to the ones that are known to be up and running.
- TCP is more scalable and adapts to growing, as well as congested, networks.

Local privilege authorization fallback

The local database can act as a fallback method for several functions. This behavior is designed to help prevent accidental lockout. For users who need fallback support, it is recommended that their usernames and passwords in the local database match their usernames and passwords in the AAA servers. This provides transparent fallback support. Because the user cannot determine whether a AAA server or the local database is providing the service, using usernames and passwords on AAA servers that are different than the usernames and passwords in the local database means that the user cannot be certain which username and password should be given.

The local database supports the following fallback functions:
- Console and enable password authentication—When you use the aaa authentication console command, you can add the LOCAL keyword after the AAA server group tag. If the servers in the group all are unavailable, the security appliance uses the local database to authenticate administrative access. This can include enable password authentication, too.
- Command authorization—When you use the aaa authorization command command, you can add the LOCAL keyword after the AAA server group tag. If the TACACS+ servers in the group all are unavailable, the local database is used to authorize commands based on privilege levels.
- VPN authentication and authorization—VPN authentication and authorization are supported to enable remote access to the security appliance if AAA servers that normally support these VPN services are unavailable. The authentication-server-group

command, available in tunnel-group general attributes mode, lets you specify the LOCAL keyword when you are configuring attributes of a tunnel group. When VPN client of an administrator specifies a tunnel group configured to fallback to the local database, the VPN tunnel can be established even if the AAA server group is unavailable, provided that the local database is configured with the necessary attributes.

Exam Essentials

- The Local AAA Server feature allows you to configure your router so that user authentication and authorization attributes currently available on AAA servers are available locally on the router
- While transport preferred none provides the same output, it also disables auto telnet for the defined host that are configured with the ip host command. This is unlike the no logging preferred command, which stops it for undefined hosts and lets it work for the defined ones
- You will see "% Error in authentication" error message as you attempt to enter "enable" or privileged mode if you are using local database for authentication without setting an enable password.
- The enable password command is not recommended since password is stored in cleartext. Use the enable secret command instead for better security
- RADIUS is an access server that uses AAA protocol and combines authentication and authorization. It is a system of distributed security that secures remote access to networks and network services against unauthorized access. TACACS+ provides session encryption and can provide CLI authorization by user groups
- The local database can act as a fallback method for several functions. This behavior is designed to help prevent accidental lockout. For users who need fallback support, it is recommended that their usernames and passwords in the local database match their usernames and passwords in the AAA servers
- A router can be configured to authenticate for its enable password against a AAA server
- AAA local database allows for command authorization and network access authentication

Chapter 18: Network Security

This chapter covers the following exam topics from Cisco's official 400-101 (v5) written exam curriculum.

- Implement and troubleshoot switch security features (VACL, PACL, stormcontrol, DHCP snooping, IP source-guard, dynamic ARP inspection, port-security, private VLAN)
- Implement and troubleshoot router security features (IPv4 access control lists, standard/extended, time-based, IPv6 traffic filter, uRPF)
- Implement and troubleshoot IPv6 first hop security (RA guard, DHCP guard, binding table, device tracking, ND inspection/snooping, source guard, PACL)
- 802.1x (802.1x, EAP, RADIUS, MAC authentication bypass)

Chapter 18: Network Security

Implement and troubleshoot switch security features

VACL, PACL

VLAN ACLs (VACLs) can provide access control for all packets that are bridged within a VLAN or that are routed into or out of a VLAN or a WAN interface for VACL capture. Unlike Cisco IOS ACLs that are applied on routed packets only, VACLs apply to all packets and can be applied to any VLAN or WAN interface. VACLs are processed in the ACL TCAM hardware. VACLs ignore any Cisco IOS ACL fields that are not supported in hardware.

You can configure VACLs for IP and MAC-layer traffic. VACLs applied to WAN interfaces support only IP traffic for VACL capture. If a VACL is configured for a packet type, and a packet of that type does not match the VACL, the default action is to deny the packet.

The port ACL (PACL) feature provides the ability to perform access control on specific Layer 2 ports. A Layer 2 port is a physical LAN or trunk port that belongs to a VLAN. Port ACLs are applied only on the ingress traffic. The port ACL feature is supported only in hardware (port ACLs are not applied to any packets routed in software). They apply to both voice and data VLANs.

When you create a port ACL, an entry is created in the ACL TCAM. You can use the show tcam counts command to see how much TCAM space is available. The PACL feature does not affect Layer 2 control packets received on the port.

You can use the access-group mode command to change the way that PACLs interact with other ACLs.

PACLs use the following modes:

Prefer port mode—If a PACL is configured on a Layer 2 interface, the PACL takes effect and overwrites the effect of other ACLs (Cisco IOS ACL and VACL). If no PACL feature is configured on the Layer 2 interface, other features applicable to the interface are merged and are applied on the interface.
Merge mode—In this mode, the PACL, VACL, and Cisco IOS ACLs are merged in the ingress direction following the logical serial. This is the default access group mode.

You configure the access-group mode command on each interface. The default is merge mode.

Further Reading

http://goo.gl/l1YMZD

Stormcontrol

A traffic storm occurs when packets flood the LAN, creating excessive traffic and degrading network performance. The traffic storm control feature prevents LAN ports from being disrupted by a broadcast, multicast, or unicast traffic storm on physical interfaces. Traffic storm control (also called traffic suppression) monitors incoming traffic levels over a 1-second traffic storm control interval, and during the interval it compares the traffic level with the traffic storm control level that you configure. The traffic storm control level is a percentage of the total available bandwidth of the port. Each port has a single traffic storm control level that is used for all types of traffic (broadcast, multicast, and unicast).

Traffic storm control monitors the level of each traffic type for which you enable traffic storm control in 1-second traffic storm control intervals.

DHCP snooping

DHCP snooping is a security feature that acts like a firewall between untrusted hosts and trusted DHCP servers. The DHCP snooping feature performs the following activities:

- Validates DHCP messages received from untrusted sources and filters out invalid messages.
- Rate-limits DHCP traffic from trusted and untrusted sources.
- Builds and maintains the DHCP snooping binding database, which contains information about untrusted hosts with leased IP addresses.
- Utilizes the DHCP snooping binding database to validate subsequent requests from untrusted hosts.
- Other security features, such as dynamic ARP inspection (DAI), also use information stored in the DHCP snooping binding database.

DHCP snooping is enabled on a per-VLAN basis. By default, the feature is inactive on all VLANs. You can enable the feature on a single VLAN or a range of VLANs. The DHCP snooping feature is implemented in software on the route processor (RP). Therefore, all DHCP messages for enabled VLANs are intercepted in the Policy Feature Card (PFC) and directed to the RP for processing.

IP source-guard

IP source guard provides source IP address filtering on a Layer 2 port to prevent a malicious host from impersonating a legitimate host by assuming the legitimate host's IP address. The feature uses dynamic DHCP snooping and static IP source binding to match IP addresses to hosts on untrusted Layer 2 access ports.

Initially, all IP traffic on the protected port is blocked except for DHCP packets. After a client receives an IP address from the DHCP server, or after static IP source binding is configured by the administrator, all traffic with that IP source address is permitted from that client. Traffic from other hosts is denied. This filtering limits a host's ability to attack the network by claiming a neighbor host's IP address. IP source guard is a port-based feature that automatically creates an implicit port access control list (PACL).

Further Reading

http://goo.gl/QJPgaJ

Dynamic ARP inspection

ARP spoofing attacks and ARP cache poisoning can occur because ARP allows a gratuitous reply from a host even if an ARP request was not received. After the attack, all traffic from the device under attack flows through the attacker's computer and then to the router, switch, or host.

An ARP spoofing attack can target hosts, switches, and routers connected to your Layer 2 network by poisoning the ARP caches of systems connected to the subnet and by intercepting traffic intended for other hosts on the subnet

Hosts A, B, and C are connected to the switch on interfaces A, B and C, all of which are on the same subnet. Their IP and MAC addresses are shown in parentheses; for example, Host A uses IP address IA and MAC address MA. When Host A needs to communicate to Host B at the IP layer, it broadcasts an ARP request for the MAC address associated with IP address IB. When the switch and Host B receive the ARP request, they populate their ARP caches with an ARP binding for a host with the IP address IA and a MAC address MA; for example, IP address IA is bound to MAC address MA. When Host B responds, the switch and Host A populate their ARP caches with a binding for a host with the IP address IB and the MAC address MB.

Host C can poison the ARP caches of the switch for Host A, and Host B by broadcasting forged ARP responses with bindings for a host with an IP address of IA (or IB) and a MAC address of MC. Hosts with poisoned ARP caches use the MAC address MC as the destination MAC address for traffic intended for IA or IB. This means that Host C intercepts that traffic. Because Host C knows the true MAC addresses associated with IA and IB, it can forward the intercepted traffic to those hosts by using the correct MAC address as the destination. Host C has inserted itself into the traffic stream from Host A to Host B, which is the topology of the classic man-in-the middle attack.

Port-security

You can use port security with dynamically learned and static MAC addresses to restrict a port's ingress traffic by limiting the MAC addresses that are allowed to send traffic into the port. When you assign secure MAC addresses to a secure port, the port does not forward ingress traffic that has source addresses outside the group of defined addresses. If you limit the number of secure MAC addresses to one and assign a single secure MAC address, the device attached to that port has the full bandwidth of the port.

A security violation occurs in either of these situations:
- When the maximum number of secure MAC addresses is reached on a secure port and the source MAC address of the ingress traffic is different from any of the identified secure MAC addresses, port security applies the configured violation mode.
- If traffic with a secure MAC address that is configured or learned on one secure port attempts to access another secure port in the same VLAN, applies the configured violation mode.

Private VLAN

A private VLAN partitions the Layer 2 broadcast domain of a VLAN into sub-domains, allowing you to isolate the ports on the switch from each other. A sub-domain consists of a primary VLAN and one or more secondary VLANs.

All VLANs in a private VLAN domain share the same primary VLAN. The secondary VLAN ID differentiates one sub-domain from another. The secondary VLANs may either be isolated VLANs or community VLANs. A host on an isolated VLAN can only communicate with the associated promiscuous port in its primary VLAN. Hosts on community VLANs can communicate among themselves and with their associated promiscuous port but not with ports in other community VLANs.

Implement and troubleshoot router security features

IPv4 access control lists (standard, extended, time-based)

Cisco provides basic traffic filtering capabilities with access control lists (also referred to as access lists). Access lists can be configured for all routed network protocols (IP, AppleTalk, and so on) to filter the packets of those protocols as the packets pass through a router.

Access lists filter network traffic by controlling whether routed packets are forwarded or blocked at the router's interfaces. Your router examines each packet to determine whether to forward or drop the packet, on the basis of the criteria you specified within the access lists. Access list criteria could be the source address of the traffic, the destination address of the traffic, the upper-layer protocol, or other information. Note that sophisticated users can sometimes successfully evade or fool basic access lists because no authentication is required.

Standard ACLs are the oldest type of ACL. Standard ACLs control traffic by the comparison of the source address of the IP packets to the addresses configured in the ACL.

This is the command syntax format of a standard ACL.
access-list access-list-number {permit|deny} {host|source source-wildcard|any}

A source/source-wildcard setting of 0.0.0.0/255.255.255.255 can be specified as any. The wildcard can be omitted if it is all zeros. Therefore, host 10.1.1.2 0.0.0.0 is the same as host 10.1.1.2. After the ACL is defined, it must be applied to the interface (inbound or outbound). In early software releases, out was the default when a keyword out or in was not specified. The direction must be specified in later software releases.

interface <interface>
ip access-group number {in|out}

This is an example of the use of a standard ACL in order to block all traffic except that from source 10.1.1.x.

interface Ethernet0/0
ip address 10.1.1.1 255.255.255.0
ip access-group 1 in
access-list 1 permit 10.1.1.0 0.0.0.255

Zone-Based Policy Firewall (also known as Zone-Policy Firewall, or ZFW) changes the firewall configuration from the older interface-based model to a more flexible, more easily understood zone-based model. Interfaces are assigned to zones, and inspection policy is applied to traffic moving between the zones. Inter-zone policies offer considerable flexibility and granularity, so different inspection policies can be applied to multiple host groups connected to the same router interface.

When ZBF is enabled on an IOS router, any traffic to the self zone (that is, traffic destined to the router's management plane) is allowed by default in the IOS 15.x train of code. If you have created a policy for any zone (such as 'inside' or 'outside') to the self zone (out-to-self policy) or the reverse (self-to-out policy), you must explicitly define permissible traffic in the policies attached to these zones. Use the inspect or pass action in order to define the permissible traffic.

Zone-Based Firewall as DHCP Client with Pass Action for UDP Traffic Configuration

This example configuration utilizes the pass action set instead of the inspect action in the policy-map for all UDP traffic to or from the router.

```
zone security outside
zone security inside

interface Ethernet0/1
zone-member security outside
interface Ethernet0/2
zone-member security inside

class-map type inspect match-all dhcp
match protocol udp

policy-map type inspect out-to-self
class type inspect dhcp
 pass
class class-default
 drop
policy-map type inspect self-to-out
class type inspect dhcp
 pass
class class-default
 drop

zone-pair security out-to-self source outside destination self
zone-pair security self-to-out source self destination outside
```

Zone-Based Firewall with Pass Action for DHCP Traffic Configuration

This example configuration shows how to prevent all UDP traffic from a zone into your router's self zone except for DHCP packets. Use an access-list with specific ports in order to allow just DHCP traffic; in this example, UDP port 67 and UDP port 68 are specified to be matched. A class-map that references the access-list has the pass action applied.

```
access-list extended 111
10 permit udp any any eq 67

access-list extended 112
10 permit udp any any eq 68

class-map type inspect match-any self-to-out
match access-group 111
class-map type inspect match-any out-to-self
match access-group 112

zone security outside
zone security inside

interface Ethernet0/1
zone-member security outside
interface Ethernet0/2
zone-member security inside

policy-map type inspect out-to-self
class type inspect out-to-self
 pass
class class-default
 drop
policy-map type inspect self-to-out
class type inspect self-to-out
 pass
class class-default
 drop

zone-pair security out-to-self source outside destination self
zone-pair security self-to-out source self destination outside
```

Further Reading

http://goo.gl/TwuLVY

IPv6 traffic filter

To filter incoming or outgoing IPv6 traffic on an interface, use the ipv6 traffic-filter command in interface configuration mode. To disable the filtering of IPv6 traffic on an interface, use the no form of this command.

ipv6 traffic-filter access-list-name {in | out}
no ipv6 traffic-filter access-list-name

Further Reading

http://goo.gl/v7dzXe

Unicast reverse path forwarding

Network administrators can use Unicast Reverse Path Forwarding (Unicast RPF) to help limit the malicious traffic on an enterprise network. This security feature works by enabling a router to verify the reachability of the source address in packets being forwarded. This capability can limit the appearance of spoofed addresses on a network. If the source IP address is not valid, the packet is discarded. Unicast RPF works in one of three different modes: strict mode, loose mode, or VRF mode. Unicast RPF requires CEF to be enabled.

When administrators use Unicast RPF in strict mode, the packet must be received on the interface that the router would use to forward the return packet. Unicast RPF configured in strict mode may drop legitimate traffic that is received on an interface that was not the router's choice for sending return traffic. Dropping this legitimate traffic could occur when asymmetric routing paths are present in the network.

When administrators use Unicast RPF in loose mode, the source address must appear in the routing table. Administrators can change this behavior using the allow-default option, which allows the use of the default route in the source verification process. Additionally, a packet that contains a source address for which the return route points to the Null 0 interface will be dropped. An access list may also be specified that permits or denies certain source addresses in Unicast RPF loose mode.

Care must be taken to ensure that the appropriate Unicast RPF mode (loose or strict) is configured during the deployment of this feature because it can drop legitimate traffic. Although asymmetric traffic flows may be of concern when deploying this feature, Unicast RPF loose mode is a scalable option for networks that contain asymmetric routing paths.

Implement and troubleshoot IPv6 first hop security

RA guard

The IPv6 RA Guard feature provides support for allowing the network administrator to block or reject unwanted or rogue router advertisement (RA) guard messages that arrive at the network device platform. RAs are used by devices to announce themselves on the link. The IPv6 RA Guard feature analyzes these RAs and filters out RAs that are sent by unauthorized devices. In host mode, all RA and router redirect messages are disallowed on the port. The RA guard feature compares configuration information on the Layer 2 (L2) device with the information found in the received RA frame. Once the L2 device has validated the content of the RA frame and router redirect frame against the configuration, it forwards the RA to its unicast or multicast destination. If the RA frame content is not validated, the RA is dropped. You can use show ipv6 snooping command to get details of both RA guard and ND inspection features.

Further Reading
http://goo.gl/776y5S

DHCP guard

The DHCPv6 Guard feature blocks reply and advertisement messages that come from unauthorized DHCP servers and relay agents. Packets are classified into one of the three DHCP type messages. All client messages are always switched regardless of device role. DHCP server messages are only processed further if the device role is set to server. Further processing of server messages includes DHCP server advertisements (for source validation and server preference) and DHCP server replies (for permitted prefixes).

If the device is configured as a DHCP server, all the messages need to be switched, regardless of the device role configuration.

Further Reading
http://goo.gl/uyCyAx

Binding table

A database table of IPv6 neighbors connected to the device is created from information sources such as NDP snooping. This database, or binding table, is used by various IPv6 guard features to validate the link-layer address (LLA), the IPv4 or IPv6 address, and the prefix binding of the neighbors to prevent spoofing and redirect attacks.

The IPv6 first-hop security binding table recovery mechanism enables the binding table to recover in the event of a device reboot. The recovery mechanism will block any data traffic sourced from an unknown source, that is a source not already specified in the binding table and previously learnt via NDP or Dynamic Host Configuration Protocol (DHCP) gleaning. The IPv6 First-Hop Security Binding Table Recovery Mechanism feature recovers the missing binding table entries when the resolution for a destination address fails in the destination guard. Upon a failure, a binding table entry is recovered by querying the DHCP server or the destination host depending on the configuration.

Further Reading
http://goo.gl/CkmbLH

Device tracking

The IPv6 Device Tracking feature provides IPv6 host liveness tracking so that a neighbor table can be immediately updated when an IPv6 host disappears. The feature tracks the liveness of the neighbors connected through the Layer 2 device on a regular basis in order to revoke network access privileges as they become inactive.

Further Reading
http://goo.gl/Fg1jWP

ND inspection/snooping

IPv6 Neighbor Discovery (ND) inspection learns and secures bindings for stateless auto-configuration addresses in Layer 2 neighbor tables. IPv6 ND inspection analyzes neighbor discovery messages in order to build a trusted binding table database, and IPv6 neighbor discovery messages that do not have valid bindings are dropped. A neighbor discovery message is considered trustworthy if its IPv6-to-MAC mapping is verifiable.

This feature mitigates some of the inherent vulnerabilities for the neighbor discovery mechanism, such as attacks on duplicate address detection (DAD), address resolution, device discovery, and the neighbor cache.

Further Reading
http://goo.gl/IQyw9k

Source guard

IPv6 source guard is an interface feature between the populated binding table and data traffic filtering. This feature enables the device to deny traffic when it is originated from an address that is not stored in the binding table. IPv6 source guard does not inspect ND or DHCP packets; rather, it works in conjunction with IPv6 neighbor discovery (ND) inspection or IPv6 address glean, both of which detect existing addresses on the link and store them into the binding table.

IPv6 source guard is an interface between the populated binding table and data traffic filtering, and the binding table must be populated with IPv6 prefixes for IPv6 source guard to work.

IPv6 source guard can deny traffic from unknown sources or unallocated addresses, such as traffic from sources not assigned by a DHCP server. When traffic is denied, the IPv6 address glean feature is notified so that it can try to recover the traffic by querying the DHCP server or by using IPv6 ND. The data-glean function prevents the device and end user from getting deadlocked, whereupon a valid address fails to be stored into the binding table, there is no recovery path, and the end user is unable to connect.

Further Reading
http://goo.gl/6YGjus

PACL

The IPv6 PACL feature provides the ability to provide access control (permit or deny) on Layer 2 switch ports for IPv6 traffic. IPv6 PACLs are similar to IPv4 PACLs, which provide access control on Layer 2 switch ports for IPv4 traffic. They are supported only in the ingress direction and in hardware. A PACL can filter ingress traffic on Layer 2 interfaces based on Layer 3 and Layer 4 header information or non-IP Layer 2 information.

Further Reading
http://goo.gl/H3Y1GD

Describe 802.1x

The IEEE 802.1X standard defines a client-server-based access control and authentication protocol that restricts unauthorized devices from connecting to a LAN through publicly accessible ports. The authentication server authenticates each client connected to a switch port before making available any services offered by the switch or the LAN. Until the client is authenticated, 802.1X access control allows only Extensible Authentication Protocol over LAN

(EAPOL) traffic through the port to which the client is connected. After authentication is successful, normal traffic can pass through the port.

Further Reading
http://goo.gl/LE4d55

802.1x, EAP, RADIUS

With 802.1X port-based authentication, the devices in the network have specific roles.

Client—the device (workstation) that requests access to the LAN and switch services and responds to the requests from the switch. The workstation must be running 802.1X-compliant client software such as that offered in the Microsoft Windows XP operating system. (The client is the supplicant in the IEEE 802.1X specification.)

Authentication server—performs the actual authentication of the client. The authentication server validates the identity of the client and notifies the switch whether or not the client is authorized to access the LAN and switch services. Because the switch acts as the proxy, the authentication service is transparent to the client. In this release, the Remote Authentication Dial-In User Service (RADIUS) security system with Extensible Authentication Protocol (EAP) extensions is the only supported authentication server; it is available in Cisco Secure Access Control Server version 3.0. RADIUS operates in a client/server model in which secure authentication information is exchanged between the RADIUS server and one or more RADIUS clients.

Switch (edge switch or wireless access point)—controls the physical access to the network based on the authentication status of the client. The switch acts as an intermediary or proxy between the client and the authentication server, requesting identity information from the client, verifying that information with the authentication server, and relaying a response to the client. The switch includes the RADIUS client, which is responsible for encapsulating and decapsulating the Extensible Authentication Protocol (EAP) frames and interacting with the authentication server.

When the switch receives EAPOL frames and relays them to the authentication server, the Ethernet header is stripped and the remaining EAP frame is re-encapsulated in the RADIUS format. The EAP frames are not modified or examined during encapsulation, and the authentication server must support EAP within the native frame format. When the switch receives frames from the authentication server, the server's frame header is removed, leaving the EAP frame, which is then encapsulated for Ethernet and sent to the client.

The devices that can act as intermediaries include the Catalyst 3550 multilayer switch, Catalyst 2950 switch, or a wireless access point. These devices must be running software that supports the RADIUS client and 802.1X.

Further Reading
http://goo.gl/xDjLL0

MAC authentication bypass

The best and most secure solution to vulnerability at the access edge is to use the intelligence of the network. One access control technique that Cisco provides is called MAC Authentication Bypass (MAB). MAB uses the MAC address of a device to determine what kind of network access to provide. MAB enables port-based access control using the MAC address of the endpoint. A MAB-enabled port can be dynamically enabled or disabled based on the MAC address of the device that connects to it.

Prior to MAB, the endpoint's identity is unknown and all traffic is blocked. The switch examines a single packet to learn and authenticate the source MAC address. After MAB succeeds, the endpoint's identity is known and all traffic from that endpoint is allowed. The switch performs source MAC address filtering to help ensure that only the MAB-authenticated endpoint is allowed to send traffic.

By default, a MAB-enabled port allows only a single endpoint per port. Any additional MAC addresses seen on the port will cause a security violation. Multi-domain authentication was specifically designed to address the requirements of IP telephony. When multi-domain authentication is configured, two endpoints are allowed on the port: one in the voice VLAN and one in the data VLAN. Either, both, or none of the endpoints can be authenticated with MAB. Additional MAC addresses will trigger a security violation.

Further Reading
http://goo.gl/c7uUuD
http://goo.gl/8G9WFF

Exam Essentials

- A traffic storm occurs when packets flood the LAN, creating excessive traffic and degrading network performance. The traffic storm control feature prevents LAN ports from being disrupted by a broadcast, multicast, or unicast traffic storm on physical interfaces

- A private VLAN partitions the Layer 2 broadcast domain of a VLAN into sub-domains, allowing you to isolate the ports on the switch from each other. A sub-domain consists of a primary VLAN and one or more secondary VLANs
- To filter incoming or outgoing IPv6 traffic on an interface, use the ipv6 traffic-filter command in interface configuration mode
- The IPv6 RA Guard feature provides support for allowing the network administrator to block or reject unwanted or rogue router advertisement (RA) guard messages that arrive at the network device platform
- IPv6 Neighbor Discovery (ND) inspection learns and secures bindings for stateless auto-configuration addresses in Layer 2 neighbor tables
- IPv6 source guard is an interface feature between the populated binding table and data traffic filtering. This feature enables the device to deny traffic when it is originated from an address that is not stored in the binding table
- MAB uses the MAC address of a device to determine what kind of network access to provide. MAB enables port-based access control using the MAC address of the endpoint. A MAB-enabled port can be dynamically enabled or disabled based on the MAC address of the device that connects to it
- By default, a MAB-enabled port allows only a single endpoint per port. Any additional MAC addresses seen on the port will cause a security violation
- When multi-domain authentication is configured, two endpoints are allowed on the port: one in the voice VLAN and one in the data VLAN
- EAPOL, STP and CDP traffic are not subjected to 802.1X access controls i.e. before traffic for these protocols will still pass even before an authentication takes place
- MAC ACLs are supported only in the inbound direction and can be applied to a VLAN or a physical interface
- Inside to outside NAT takes place after routing, whereas outside to inside NAT happens before routing
- The PVLAN edge (protected port) is a feature that has only local significance to the switch (unlike Private Vlans), and there is no isolation provided between two.
- IPv6 address glean is the foundation for many other IPv6 features that depend on an accurate binding table. It inspects ND and DHCP messages.

Part 6 Infrastructure Services

Chapter 19: System management
Chapter 20: Quality of Service
Chapter 21: Network Services
Chapter 22: Network Optimization

Chapter 19: System Management

This chapter covers the following exam topics from Cisco's official 400-101 (v5) written exam curriculum.

- Implement and troubleshoot device management (Console/VTY, telnet, HTTP, HTTPS, SSH, SCP, FTP, TFTP)
- Implement and troubleshoot SNMP (v2c, v3)
- Implement and troubleshoot logging (local logging, syslog, debug, conditional debug, timestamp)

Chapter 19: System Management

Implement and troubleshoot device management

Console and VTY

The console port on the router is an EIA/TIA-232 asynchronous, serial connection with no flow control and an RJ-45 connector. The console port is used to access the router and is located on the front panel of the Route Processor (RP).

Telnet, HTTP, HTTPS, SSH, SCP

You can use the SSH server to enable an SSH client to make a secure, encrypted connection to a Cisco IOS device. SSH uses strong encryption for authentication. The SSH server in the Cisco IOS software can interoperate with publicly and commercially available SSH clients. There are three steps that need to be taken to enable SSH, i.e. generate a crypto key, configure a domain name, and configure VTY line(s) to use transport SSH (using transport input command).

The user authentication mechanisms supported for SSH are RADIUS, TACACS+, and the use of locally stored usernames and passwords. The behavior of SCP is similar to that of remote copy (rcp), which comes from the Berkeley r-tools suite, except that SCP relies on SSH for security. In addition, SCP requires that authentication, authorization, and accounting (AAA) authorization be configured so the router can determine whether the user has the correct privilege level.

The HTTP 1.1 Web Server and Client feature provides a consistent interface for users and applications by implementing support for HTTP 1.1 in Cisco IOS software-based devices. When combined with the HTTPS feature, the HTTP 1.1 Web Server and Client feature provides a complete, secure solution for HTTP services between Cisco devices.

FTP, TFTP

You can configure a router to serve as a RARP or TFTP server to reduce costs and time delays in your network while allowing you to use your router for its regular functions.

Typically, a router that is configured as a TFTP server provides other routers with system image or router configuration files from its Flash memory. You can also configure the router to respond to other types of service requests, such as requests.

To enable TFTP server operation, use the following commands, beginning in privileged EXEC mode:

Router(config)# tftp-server flash [partition-number:]filename1[alias filename2] [access-list-number]

You configure a router to transfer files between systems on the network using the File Transfer Protocol (FTP). With the Cisco IOS implementation of FTP, you can set the following FTP characteristics:

- Passive-mode FTP
- User name
- Password
- IP address

Implement and troubleshoot SNMP

SNMP v2c, v3

SNMP is an application-layer protocol that provides a message format for communication between managers and agents. The SNMP system consists of an SNMP manager, an SNMP agent, and a MIB. The SNMP manager can be part of a network management system (NMS) such as CiscoWorks. The agent and MIB reside on the switch. To configure SNMP on the switch, you define the relationship between the manager and the agent.

The SNMP agent contains MIB variables whose values the SNMP manager can request or change. A manager can get a value from an agent or store a value into the agent. The agent gathers data from the MIB, the repository for information about device parameters and network data. The agent can also respond to a manager's requests to get or set data.

An agent can send unsolicited traps to the manager. Traps are messages alerting the SNMP manager to a condition on the network. Traps can mean improper user authentication, restarts, link status (up or down), MAC address tracking, closing of a TCP connection, loss of connection to a neighbor, or other significant events.

SNMP v1—The Simple Network Management Protocol, a Full Internet Standard, defined in RFC 1157.

SNMP v2C replaces the Party-based Administrative and Security Framework of SNMP
v2Classic with the community-string-based Administrative Framework of SNMP v2C while
retaining the bulk retrieval and improved error handling of SNMP v2Classic. It has these
features:

- SNMPv2—Version 2 of the Simple Network Management Protocol, a Draft Internet
  Standard, defined in RFCs 1902 through 1907.
- SNMPv2C—The community-string-based Administrative Framework for SNMPv2, an
  Experimental Internet Protocol defined in RFC 1901.
- SNMPv3—Version 3 of the SNMP is an interoperable standards-based protocol
  defined in RFCs 2273 to 2275.

SNMPv3 provides secure access to devices by authenticating and encrypting packets over
the network and includes these security features:

- Message integrity—ensuring that a packet was not tampered with in transit
- Authentication—determining that the message is from a valid source
- Encryption—mixing the contents of a package to prevent it from being read by an
  unauthorized source.

Implement and troubleshoot logging

Local logging, syslog, debug, conditional debug

Cisco router's or switch's log messages can be handled in five different ways:

1. Console logging: By default, the router sends all log messages to its console port.
   Users that are physically connected to the router console port can view these
   messages.

2. Terminal logging: It is similar to console logging, but it displays log messages to the
   router's VTY lines instead. This is not enabled by default.

3. Buffered logging: This type of logging uses router's RAM for storing log messages.
   buffer has a fixed size to ensure that the log will not deplete valuable system memory.
   The router accomplishes this by deleting old messages from the buffer as new
   messages are added.

4. Syslog Server logging : The router can use syslog to forward log messages to external
   syslog servers for storage. This type of logging is not enabled by default.

5. SNMP trap logging: The router is able to use SNMP traps to send log messages to an
   external SNMP server.

Further Reading

http://goo.gl/VLZvW3

Timestamp

System log messages can contain up to 80 characters and a percent sign (%), which follows the optional sequence number or time-stamp information, if configured. Messages appear in this format:

Seq no:timestamp: %facility-severity-MNEMONIC:description

The part of the message preceding the percent sign depends on the setting of the service sequence-numbers, service timestamps log datetime, service timestamps log datetime [localtime] [msec] [show-timezone], or service timestamps log uptime global configuration command.

Exam Essentials

- The console port on the router is an EIA/TIA-232 asynchronous, serial connection with no flow control and an RJ-45 connector
- SNMP is an application-layer protocol that provides a message format for communication between managers and agents
- By default, the router sends all log messages to its console port. Hence only the users that are physically connected or using a terminal server to connect to the router console port can view these messages
- The last four bits of the register are called the boot field. If the last digit of the config register is 2, the router examines NVRAM for boot system commands
- The activation character is the character that starts a terminal session when it is typed
- On Cisco IOS, SNMPv1 is the default version
- All logged messages by default are sent to console port

Chapter 20: Quality of Service

This chapter covers the following exam topics from Cisco's official 400-101 (v5) written exam curriculum.

- Implement and troubleshoot end-to-end QoS (COS/DSCP mapping)
- Implement, optimize and troubleshoot QoS using MQC (classification, NBAR, IPP, DSCP, CoS, ECN, policing, shaping, congestion management/queuing, H-QoS, sub-rate ethernet link, congestion avoidance/WRED)
- Layer 2 QoS (queuing, scheduling, classification, marking)

Chapter 20: Quality of Service

Implement and troubleshoot end-to-end QoS

CoS and DSCP mapping

Differentiated Services (DiffServ) is a model in which traffic is treated by intermediate systems with relative priorities based on the type of services (ToS) field. DiffServ increases the number of definable priority levels by reallocating bits of an IP packet for priority marking.

The DiffServ architecture defines the DiffServ (DS) field, which supersedes the ToS field in IPv4 to make per-hop behavior (PHB) decisions about packet classification and traffic conditioning functions, such as metering, marking, shaping, and policing.

The RFCs do not dictate the way to implement PHBs; this is the responsibility of the vendor. Cisco implements queuing techniques that can base their PHB on the IP precedence or DSCP value in the IP header of a packet. Based on DSCP or IP precedence, traffic can be put into a particular service class. Packets within a service class are treated the same way. AF43 (100110) and AF11 (001010) are the highest and lowest priority classes respectively that can be configured using DSCP encoding.

The six most significant bits of the DiffServ field is called as the DSCP. The last two Currently Unused (CU) bits in the DiffServ field were not defined within the DiffServ field architecture; these are now used as Explicit Congestion Notification (ECN) bits. Routers at the edge of the network classify packets and mark them with either the IP Precedence or DSCP value in a DiffServ network. Other network devices in the core that support DiffServ use the DSCP value in the IP header to select a PHB behavior for the packet and provide the appropriate QoS treatment. COS 3 and 4 are mapped to DSCP 24 and 32 respectively.

The DSCP can be set to a desired value at the edge of the network in order to make it easy for core devices to classify the packet as shown in the Packet Classification section and provide a suitable level of service. Class-Based Packet Marking can be used to set the DSCP value as shown here:

```
policy-map pack-multimedia-5M
!--- Creates a policy map named pack-multimedia-5M.
 class management

!--- Specifies the policy to be created for the
!--- traffic classified by class management.
```

```
        bandwidth 50
            set ip dscp 8

!--- Sets the DSCP value of the packets matching
!--- class management to 8.

    class C1
            priority 1248
            set ip dscp 40
    class voice-signalling
            bandwidth 120
            set ip dscp 24
```

Further Reading

http://goo.gl/Wr0xt0

Implement, optimize and troubleshoot QoS using MQC

Classification

Packet classification involves using a traffic descriptor to categorize a packet within a specific group and making the packet accessible for QoS handling in the network. Using packet classification, you can partition network traffic into multiple priority levels or a class of service (CoS).

You can use either access lists (ACLs) or the match command in the modular QoS CLI to match on DSCP values.

```
Router(config)# access-list 101 permit ip any any ?
dscp       Match packets with given dscp value
fragments  Check non-initial fragments
log        Log matches against this entry
log-input  Log matches against this entry, including input interface
precedence Match packets with given precedence value
time-range Specify a time-range
tos        Match packets with given TOS value
```

When you specify the ip dscp value in the class-map command, you have these:
```
Router(config)# class-map match-all ABC
Router(config-cmap)# match ip dscp ?
```

```
<0-63>   Differentiated services codepoint value
af11     Match packets with AF11 dscp (001010)
af12     Match packets with AF12 dscp (001100)
af13     Match packets with AF13 dscp (001110)
af21     Match packets with AF21 dscp (010010)
af22     Match packets with AF22 dscp (010100)
af23     Match packets with AF23 dscp (010110)
af31     Match packets with AF31 dscp (011010)
af32     Match packets with AF32 dscp (011100)
af33     Match packets with AF33 dscp (011110)
af41     Match packets with AF41 dscp (100010)
af42     Match packets with AF42 dscp (100100)
af43     Match packets with AF43 dscp (100110)
cs1      Match packets with CS1(precedence 1) dscp (001000)
cs2      Match packets with CS2(precedence 2) dscp (010000)
cs3      Match packets with CS3(precedence 3) dscp (011000)
cs4      Match packets with CS4(precedence 4) dscp (100000)
cs5      Match packets with CS5(precedence 5) dscp (101000)
cs6      Match packets with CS6(precedence 6) dscp (110000)
cs7      Match packets with CS7(precedence 7) dscp (111000)
default  Match packets with default dscp (000000)
ef       Match packets with EF dscp (101110)
```

Network based application recognition (NBAR)

NBAR is a classification engine that recognizes and classifies a wide variety of protocols and applications, including web-based and other difficult-to-classify applications and protocols that use dynamic TCP/UDP port assignments.

When NBAR recognizes and classifies a protocol or an application, the network can be configured to apply the appropriate QoS for that application or traffic with that protocol. The QoS is applied using the MQC.

NBAR introduces several classification features that identify applications and protocols from Layer 4 through Layer 7. These classification features are as follows:

- Statically assigned TCP and UDP port numbers.
- Non-TCP and non-UDP IP protocols.
- Dynamically assigned TCP and UDP port numbers. This kind of classification requires stateful inspection, that is, the ability to inspect a protocol across multiple packets during packet classification.

- Subport classification or classification based on deep packet inspection, that is, classification for inspecting packets.

NBAR includes the Protocol Pack feature that provides an easy way to load protocols and helps NBAR recognize additional protocols for network traffic classification. A protocol pack is set a of protocols developed and packed together. A new protocol pack can be loaded on the device to replace the default IOS protocol pack that is already present in the device.

Policing, shaping

Traffic policing propagates bursts. When the traffic rate reaches the configured maximum rate, excess traffic is dropped (or remarked). The result is an output rate that appears as a saw-tooth with crests and troughs. In contrast to policing, traffic shaping retains excess packets in a queue and then schedules the excess for later transmission over increments of time. The result of traffic shaping is a smoothed packet output rate.

Shaping implies the existence of a queue and of sufficient memory to buffer delayed packets, while policing does not. Queuing is an outbound concept; packets going out an interface get queued and can be shaped. Only policing can be applied to inbound traffic on an interface. Ensure that you have sufficient memory when enabling shaping. In addition, shaping requires a scheduling function for later transmission of any delayed packets. The scheduling function allows you to organize the shaping queue into different queues. Examples of scheduling functions are Class Based Weighted Fair Queuing (CBWFQ) and Low Latency Queuing (LLQ). Shaped round robin queues that carry higher weights get serviced first.

Further Reading

http://goo.gl/Z72Dho

Congestion management (queuing)

Congestion management features allow you to control congestion by determining the order in which packets are sent out an interface based on priorities assigned to those packets. Congestion management entails the creation of queues, assignment of packets to those queues based on the classification of the packet, and scheduling of the packets in a queue for transmission. The congestion management QoS feature offers four types of queuing protocols, each of which allows you to specify creation of a different number of queues, affording greater or lesser degrees of differentiation of traffic, and to specify the order in which that traffic is sent.

During periods with light traffic, that is, when no congestion exists, packets are sent out the interface as soon as they arrive. During periods of transmit congestion at the outgoing interface, packets arrive faster than the interface can send them. If you use congestion management features, packets accumulating at an interface are queued until the interface is free to send them; they are then scheduled for transmission according to their assigned priority and the queuing mechanism configured for the interface. The router determines the order of packet transmission by controlling which packets are placed in which queue and how queues are serviced with respect to each other.

There four types of queuing, which constitute the congestion management QoS features:
- FIFO (first-in, first-out). FIFO entails no concept of priority or classes of traffic. With FIFO, transmission of packets out the interface occurs in the order the packets arrive.
- Weighted fair queuing (WFQ). WFQ offers dynamic, fair queuing that divides bandwidth across queues of traffic based on weights. (WFQ ensures that all traffic is treated fairly, given its weight.) To understand how WFQ works, consider the queue for a series of File Transfer Protocol (FTP) packets as a queue for the collective and the queue for discrete interactive traffic packets as a queue for the individual. Given the weight of the queues, WFQ ensures that for all FTP packets sent as a collective an equal number of individual interactive traffic packets are sent.)

Given this handling, WFQ ensures satisfactory response time to critical applications, such as interactive, transaction-based applications, that are intolerant of performance degradation. For serial interfaces at E1 (2.048 Mbps) and below, flow-based WFQ is used by default. When no other queuing strategies are configured, all other interfaces use FIFO by default.

There are four types of WFQ:
- Flow-based WFQ (WFQ)
- Distributed WFQ (DWFQ)
- Class-based WFQ (CBWFQ)
- Distributed class-based WFQ (DCBWFQ)
- Custom queuing (CQ). With CQ, bandwidth is allocated proportionally for each different class of traffic. CQ allows you to specify the number of bytes or packets to be drawn from the queue, which is especially useful on slow interfaces.
- Priority queuing (PQ). With PQ, packets belonging to one priority class of traffic are sent before all lower priority traffic to ensure timely delivery of those packets.

HQoS, sub-rate ethernet link

The QoS Hierarchical Queuing Framework (HQF) feature enables you to manage quality of service (QoS) at three different levels--the physical interface level, the logical interface level, and the class level of scheduling for applying QoS queuing and shaping mechanisms by using the modular QoS command-line interface (MQC) to provide a granular and flexible overall QoS architecture.

You can apply class-based queuing to any traffic class in the parent or child level of a hierarchical policy and obtain service levels for different sessions or subscribers.
In the example shown below, the traffic belonging to class parent-c2 has more scheduling time than class parent-c1:

```
policy-map child
 class child-c1
  bandwidth 400
 class child-c2
  bandwidth 400
policy-map parent
 class parent-c1
  bandwidth 1000
  service-policy child
 class parent-c2
  bandwidth 2000
  service-policy child
```

Congestion avoidance (WRED)

Congestion avoidance techniques monitor network traffic loads in an effort to anticipate and avoid congestion at common network bottlenecks. Congestion avoidance is achieved through packet dropping. Among the more commonly used congestion avoidance mechanisms is Random Early Detection (RED), which is optimum for high-speed transit networks. Cisco IOS QoS includes an implementation of RED that, when configured, controls when the router drops packets. If you do not configure Weighted Random Early Detection (WRED), the router uses the cruder default packet drop mechanism called tail drop. WRED avoids the globalization problems that occur when tail drop is used as the congestion avoidance mechanism on the router. Global synchronization occurs as waves of congestion crest only to be followed by troughs during which the transmission link is not fully utilized. Global synchronization of TCP hosts, for example, can occur because packets are dropped all at once. Global synchronization manifests when multiple TCP hosts reduce their transmission rates in response to packet dropping (thus reducing performance), then increase their transmission rates once again when the congestion is reduced.

- Tail drop. This is the default congestion avoidance behavior when WRED is not configured and can lead to global synchronization behavior.

- WRED and distributed WRED (DWRED)—both of which are the Cisco implementations of RED—combine the capabilities of the RED algorithm with the IP Precedence feature.

There are a few variations of WRED:
- Flow-based WRED. Flow-based WRED extends WRED to provide greater fairness to all flows on an interface in regard to how packets are dropped.
- DiffServ Compliant WRED. DiffServ Compliant WRED extends WRED to support Differentiated Services (DiffServ) and Assured Forwarding (AF) Per Hop Behavior (PHB). This feature enables customers to implement AF PHB by coloring packets according to differentiated services code point (DSCP) values and then assigning preferential drop probabilities to those packets.

Further Reading

http://goo.gl/E1fFAZ

Describe layer 2 QoS

QoS implementation is based on the DiffServ architecture, an emerging standard from the Internet Engineering Task Force (IETF). This architecture specifies that each packet is classified upon entry into the network. The classification is carried in the IP packet header, using 6 bits from the deprecated IP type of service (TOS) field to carry the classification (class) information. Classification can also be carried in the Layer 2 frame. These special bits in the Layer 2 frame or a Layer 3 packet are described here.

Prioritization values in Layer 2 frames:
- Layer 2 Inter-Switch Link (ISL) frame headers have a 1-byte User field that carries an IEEE 802.1p class of service (CoS) value in the three least-significant bits. On interfaces configured as Layer 2 ISL trunks, all traffic is in ISL frames.
- Layer 2 802.1Q frame headers have a 2-byte Tag Control Information field that carries the CoS value in the three most-significant bits, which are called the User Priority bits. On interfaces configured as Layer 2 802.1Q trunks, all traffic is in 802.1Q frames except for traffic in the native VLAN. Other frame types cannot carry Layer 2 CoS values. Layer 2 CoS values range from 0 for low priority to 7 for high priority.

Further Reading

http://goo.gl/Zf6J8m

Queuing, scheduling

Traffic queuing is the ordering of packets and applies to both input and output of data. Device modules can support multiple queues, which you can use to control the sequencing of packets in different traffic classes. You can also set weighted random early detection (WRED) and tail-drop thresholds. The device drops packets only when the configured thresholds are exceeded.

Traffic scheduling is the methodical output of packets at a desired frequency to accomplish a consistent flow of traffic. You can apply traffic scheduling to different traffic classes to weight the traffic by priority.

The queuing and scheduling processes allow you to control the bandwidth that is allocated to the traffic classes, so that you achieve the desired trade-off between throughput and latency for your network.

Exam Essentials

- NBAR is a classification engine that recognizes and classifies a wide variety of protocols and applications, including web-based and other difficult-to-classify applications and protocols that use dynamic TCP/UDP port assignments
- Examples of scheduling functions are Class Based Weighted Fair Queuing (CBWFQ) and Low Latency Queuing (LLQ). Shaped round robin queues that carry higher weights get serviced first
- Tail drop is the default congestion avoidance behavior when WRED is not configured and can lead to global synchronization behavior
- The queuing and scheduling processes allow you to control the bandwidth that is allocated to the traffic classes, so that you achieve the desired trade-off between throughput and latency for your network
- It is a best practice to explicitly tag the native VLAN and it can be done by using the "switchport trunk native vlan [vlanid]" command
- Switches come with pre-defined sizes of port buffers, i.e. increasing the buffer size is not possible without replacing either the chassis or the given ethernet module

Chapter 21: Network Services

This chapter covers the following exam topics from Cisco's official 400-101 (v5) written exam curriculum.

- Implement and troubleshoot first hop redundancy protocol (HSRP, GLBP, VRRP, redundancy using IPv6 RS/RA)
- Implement and troubleshoot network timing protocol (NTP master, client, v3, v4, authentication)
- Implement and troubleshoot IPv4 and IPv6 DHCP (DHCP client/service/relay, DHCP options, DHCP protocol operations, SLAAC/DHCPv6 interaction, stateful/stateless DHCPv6, DHCPv6 prefix delegation)
- Implement and troubleshoot IPv4 network address translation (static NAT, dynamic NAT, policy-based NAT, PAT, NAT ALG)
- IPv6 NAT (NAT64, NPTv6)

Chapter 21: Network Services

Implement and troubleshoot first-hop redundancy protocols

HSRP, GLBP, VRRP

HSRP, GLBP, and VRRP are examples of First Hop Redundancy Protocols (FHRP).

HSRP is the Cisco standard method of providing high network availability by providing first-hop redundancy for IP hosts on an IEEE 802.3 LAN configured with a default gateway IP address. HSRP routes IP traffic without relying on the availability of any single router. It enables a set of router interfaces to work together to present the appearance of a single virtual router or default gateway to the hosts on a LAN. When HSRP is configured on a network or segment, it provides a virtual Media Access Control (MAC) address and an IP address that is shared among a group of configured routers. HSRP allows two or more HSRP-configured routers to use the MAC address and IP network address of a virtual router. The virtual router does not exist; it represents the common target for routers that are configured to provide backup to each other. One of the routers is selected to be the active router and another to be the standby router, which assumes control of the group MAC address and IP address should the designated active router fail.

With HSRPv1, the virtual router's MAC address is 0000.0c07.ACxx whereas with HSRPv2, the virtual MAC address is 0000.0C9F.Fxxx, in both cases xxx denotes the HSRP group. HSRPv6 uses UDP 2029 and virtual MAC addresses starting from 0005.73a0.0000 to 0005.73a0.0fff.

VRRP is an election protocol that dynamically assigns responsibility for one or more virtual routers to the VRRP routers on a LAN, allowing several routers on a multi-access link to use the same virtual IP address. A VRRP router is configured to run VRRP in conjunction with one or more other routers attached to a LAN. In a VRRP configuration, one router is elected as the virtual router master, and the other routers act as backups in case it fails. It can be configured along with HSRP.

GLBP provides automatic router backup for IP hosts configured with a single default gateway on a LAN. Multiple first-hop routers on the LAN combine to offer a single virtual first-hop IP router while sharing the IP packet forwarding load. Other routers on the LAN act as redundant GLBP routers that become active if any of the existing forwarding routers fail. GLBP provides load balancing over multiple routers by using a single virtual IP address and multiple virtual MAC addresses. Each host is configured with the same virtual IP address, and all routers in the virtual router group forward packets.

Further Reading
http://goo.gl/0u20iD

Redundancy using IPv6 RS/RA

IPv6 routing protocols ensure router-to-router resilience and failover. However, in situations in which the path between a host and the first-hop router fails, or the first-hop router itself fails, first hop redundancy protocols (FHRPs) ensure host-to-router resilience and failover.

The Gateway Load Balancing Protocol (GLBP) FHRP protects data traffic from a failed router or circuit, while allowing packet load sharing between a group of redundant routers. The Hot Standby Router Protocol (HSRP) protects data traffic in case of a gateway failure.

The Gateway Load Balancing Protocol feature provides automatic router backup for IPv6 hosts configured with a single default gateway on an IEEE 802.3 LAN. Multiple first hop routers on the LAN combine to offer a single virtual first-hop IPv6 router while sharing the IPv6 packet forwarding load. GLBP performs a similar function for the user as HSRP. HSRP allows multiple routers to participate in a virtual router group configured with a virtual IPv6 address. One member is elected to be the active router to forward packets sent to the virtual IPv6 address for the group. The other routers in the group are redundant until the active router fails. These standby routers have unused bandwidth that the protocol is not using. Although multiple virtual router groups can be configured for the same set of routers, the hosts must be configured for different default gateways, which results in an extra administrative burden. The advantage of GLBP is that it additionally provides load balancing over multiple routers (gateways) using a single virtual IPv6 address and multiple virtual MAC addresses. The forwarding load is shared among all routers in a GLBP group rather than being handled by a single router while the other routers stand idle. Each host is configured with the same virtual IPv6 address, and all routers in the virtual router group participate in forwarding packets.

Further Reading
http://goo.gl/C0KelA

Implement and troubleshoot network time protocol

NTP is designed to synchronize the time on a network of machines. NTP runs over the User Datagram Protocol (UDP), using port 123 as both the source and destination, which in turn runs over IP. NTP Version 3 is used to synchronize timekeeping among a set of distributed time servers and clients. A set of nodes on a network are identified and configured with NTP and the nodes form a synchronization subnet, sometimes referred to as an overlay network. While multiple masters (primary servers) may exist, there is no requirement for an election protocol.

An NTP network usually gets its time from an authoritative time source, such as a radio clock or an atomic clock attached to a time server. NTP then distributes this time across the network. An NTP client makes a transaction with its server over its polling interval (from 64 to 1024 seconds) which dynamically changes over time depending on the network conditions between the NTP server and the client. The other situation occurs when the router communicates to a bad NTP server (for example, NTP server with large dispersion); the router also increases the poll interval. No more than one NTP transaction per minute is needed to synchronize two machines. It is not possible to adjust the NTP poll interval on a router.

NTP uses the concept of a stratum to describe how many NTP hops away a machine is from an authoritative time source. For example, a stratum 1 time server has a radio or atomic clock directly attached to it. It then sends its time to a stratum 2 time server through NTP, and so on. A machine running NTP automatically chooses the machine with the lowest stratum number that it is configured to communicate with using NTP as its time source.

This strategy effectively builds a self-organizing tree of NTP speakers. NTP performs well over the non-deterministic path lengths of packet-switched networks, because it makes robust estimates of the following three key variables in the relationship between a client and a time server.

- Network delay
- Dispersion of time packet exchanges—A measure of maximum clock error between the two hosts.
- Clock offset—The correction applied to a client's clock to synchronize it.

NTP avoids synchronizing to a machine whose time may not be accurate in two ways. First of all, NTP never synchronizes to a machine that is not synchronized itself. Secondly, NTP compares the time reported by several machines, and will not synchronize to a machine whose time is significantly different than the others, even if its stratum is lower.

The communications between machines running NTP (associations) are usually statically configured. Each machine is given the IP address of all machines with which it should form associations. Accurate timekeeping is made possible by exchanging NTP messages between each pair of machines with an association. However, in a LAN environment, NTP can be configured to use IP broadcast messages instead. This alternative reduces configuration complexity because each machine can be configured to send or receive broadcast messages. However, the accuracy of timekeeping is marginally reduced because the information flow is one-way only.

The time kept on a machine is a critical resource and it is strongly recommend that you use the security features of NTP to avoid the accidental or malicious setting of incorrect time. The two security features available are an access list-based restriction scheme and an encrypted authentication mechanism.

Further Reading

http://goo.gl/sTmssX

NTP Authentication

You can configure the device to authenticate the time sources to which the local clock is synchronized. When you enable NTP authentication, the device synchronizes to a time source only if the source carries one of the authentication keys specified by the ntp trusted-key command. The device drops any packets that fail the authentication check and prevents them from updating the local clock. NTP authentication is disabled by default.

Implement and troubleshoot IPv4 and IPv6 DHCP

DHCP client, IOS DHCP server, DHCP relay

The Cisco IOS DHCP Server feature is a full DHCP Server implementation that assigns and manages IP addresses from specified address pools within the router to DHCP clients. If the Cisco IOS DHCP Server cannot satisfy a DHCP request from its own database, it can forward the request to one or more secondary DHCP Servers defined by the network administrator.

The Cisco IOS DHCP client now enables you to obtain an IP address from a DHCP Server dynamically using the DHCP protocol as specified in RFC 2131. The Cisco IOS DHCP client offers the following benefits:
- Reduces time to configure and deploy
- Reduces the number of configuration errors
- Enables customers to centrally control the IP address assigned to a Cisco IOS router

A DHCP relay agent is any host that forwards DHCP packets between clients and servers. Relay agents are used to forward requests and replies between clients and servers when they are not on the same physical subnet. Relay agent forwarding is distinct from the normal forwarding of an IP router, where IP datagrams are switched between networks somewhat transparently. Relay agents receive DHCP messages and then generate a new DHCP message to send out on another interface.

The Cisco IOS DHCP relay agent supports the use of unnumbered interfaces. The DHCP relay agent automatically adds a static host route specifying the unnumbered interface as the outbound interface.

The DHCPv6 client function can be enabled on individual IPv6-enabled interfaces.
The DHCPv6 client can request and accept those configuration parameters that do not require a server to maintain any dynamic state for individual clients, such as DNS server addresses and domain search list options. The DHCPv6 client can also request the delegation of prefixes. The prefixes acquired from a delegating router will be stored in a local IPv6 general prefix pool. The prefixes in the general prefix pool can then be referred to from other applications; for example, the general prefix pool can be used to number router downstream interfaces.

The DHCPv6 server function can be enabled on individual IPv6-enabled interfaces.
The DHCPv6 server can provide those configuration parameters that do not require the server to maintain any dynamic state for individual clients, such as DNS server addresses and domain search list options. The DHCPv6 server may be configured to perform prefix delegation.
All the configuration parameters for clients are independently configured into DHCPv6 configuration pools, which are stored in NVRAM. A configuration pool can be associated with a particular DHCPv6 server on an interface when it is started. Prefixes to be delegated to clients may be specified either as a list of pre-assigned prefixes for a particular client or as IPv6 local prefix pools that are also stored in NVRAM. The list of manually configured prefixes or IPv6 local prefix pools can be referenced and used by DHCPv6 configuration pools.
The DHCPv6 server maintains an automatic binding table in memory to track the assignment of some configuration parameters, such as prefixes between the server and its clients. The automatic bindings can be stored permanently in the database agent, which can be, for example, a remote TFTP server or local NVRAM file system.

A DHCPv6 relay agent, which may reside on the client's link, is used to relay messages between the client and the server. The DHCPv6 relay agent operation is transparent to the client. A DHCPv6 client locates a DHCPv6 server using a reserved, link-scoped multicast address. For direct communication between the DHCPv6 client and the DHCPv6 server, both of them must be attached to the same link. However, in some situations where ease of management, economy, or scalability is a concern, it is desirable to allow a DHCPv6 client to send a message to a DHCPv6 server that is not connected to the same link.

The DHCPv6 server sends its replies to the source address of relayed messages. Normally, a DHCPv6 relay uses the address of the server-facing interface used to send messages as the source. However, in some networks, it may be desirable to configure a more stable address (such as a loopback interface) and have the relay use that interface as the source address of relayed messages. The DHCPv6 Relay Source Configuration feature provides this capability.

Further Reading

http://goo.gl/LxGdFg
http://goo.gl/WG2Y7Z

DHCP options

Cisco routers running Cisco IOS software include Dynamic Host Configuration Protocol (DHCP) server and relay agent software. The Cisco IOS DHCP server is a full DHCP server implementation that assigns and manages IP addresses from specified address pools within the router to DHCP clients. The DHCP server can be configured to assign additional parameters such as the IP address of the domain name system (DNS) server and the default router.

There can be various types of DHCP IPv6 server options.

- Refresh options
- NISP or NISP+ related options
- SIP or SNTP
- Stateless server options

DHCP protocol operations

The DHCP protocol employs a connectionless service model, using the User Datagram Protocol (UDP). It is implemented with two UDP port numbers for its operations which are the same as for the BOOTP protocol. UDP port number 67 is the destination port of a server, and UDP port number 68 is used by the client. DHCP operations fall into four phases: server discovery, IP lease offer, IP request, and IP lease acknowledgment. These stages are often abbreviated as DORA for discovery, offer, request, and acknowledgment. The DHCP protocol operation begins with clients broadcasting a request. If the client and server are on different subnets, a DHCP Helper or DHCP Relay Agent may be used. Clients requesting renewal of an existing lease may communicate directly via UDP unicast, since the client already has an established IP address at that point.

Further Reading

http://goo.gl/ARZXIj

SLAAC/DHCPv6 interaction

Stateless DHCPv6 is a combination of "stateless Address Autoconfiguration" and "Dynamic Host Configuration Protocol for IPv6" and is specified by RFC 3736. When using stateless-DHCPv6, a device will use Stateless Address Auto-Configuration (SLAAC) to assign one or more IPv6 addresses to an interface, while it utilizes DHCPv6 to receive "additional parameters" which may not be available through SLAAC. For example, additional parameters could include information such as DNS or NTP server addresses, and are provided in a stateless manner by DHCPv6. Using stateless DHCPv6 means that the DHCPv6 server does not need to keep track of any state of assigned IPv6 addresses, and there is no need for state refreshment as result. On network media supporting a large number of hosts associated to a single DHCPv6 server, this could mean a significant reduction in DHCPv6 messages due to the reduced need for address state refreshments.

Stateless Address Autoconfiguration (SLAAC) is one of the most convenient methods to assign Internet addresses to IPv6 nodes. This method does not require any human intervention at all from an IPv6 user. If one wants to use IPv6 SLAAC on an IPv6 node, it is important that this IPv6 node is connected to a network with at least one IPv6 router connected. This router is configured by the network administrator and sends out Router Advertisement announcements onto the link. These announcements can allow the on-link connected IPv6 nodes to configure themselves with IPv6 address and routing parameters without further human intervention.

DHCPv6 prefix delegation

When DHCPv6 server has the Prefix Delegation feature enabled, it acts as a delegating router. The delegating router automates the process of assigning prefixes to the requesting router (that is, the DHCP client). Once the server has delegated prefixes to the client, the interface that is connected to the local area network (LAN) of the requesting router has an IPv6 address using the received prefix block. The requesting router then announces this address in the Router Advertisement messages. The client routers (that is, the routers in the local network) can use the autoconfig option to pull the global IP address from the advertised Router Advertisement messages by the DHCP client.

```
ipv6 unicast-routing
ipv6 dhcp pool dhcpv6

!--- The DHCP pool is named "dhcpv6."

prefix-delegation pool cciein8weeks lifetime 1800 600
```

```
!--- The prefix delegation pool name is "cciein8weeks".
!
dns-server 2001:DB8:3000:3000::42
domain-name example.com
!
interface Serial0/0
 no ip address
 ipv6 address 2010:AB8:0:1::1/64
 ipv6 enable
 ipv6 dhcp server dhcpv6
 clock rate 2000000
!
ipv6 local pool cciein8weeks 2001:DB8:1200::/40 48

!--- The prefix pool named cciein8weeks has a prefix of length
!--- /40 from which it will delegate (sub)prefixes of length /48.
```

Further Reading

http://goo.gl/au7JIC

Implement and troubleshoot IPv4 network address translation

Static NAT, dynamic NAT, policy-based NAT, PAT

You can implement address translation as dynamic NAT, Port Address Translation (PAT), static NAT, static PAT, or as a mix of these types. You can also configure rules to bypass NAT; for example, to enable NAT control when you do not want to perform NAT (e.g. IPSec VPN IP subnets). The following translation types are available:

- Dynamic NAT—Dynamic NAT translates a group of real addresses to a pool of mapped addresses that are routable on the destination network.
- PAT—PAT translates multiple real address to a single mapped IP address.
- Static NAT—Static NAT creates a fixed translation of real addresses to mapped addresses. With dynamic NAT and PAT, each host uses a different address or port for each subsequent translation.
- Static PAT—Static PAT is the same as static NAT, except that it enables you to specify the protocol and port for the real and mapped addresses

Further Reading

http://goo.gl/eB6W6z

NAT ALG

Network Address Translation (NAT) performs translation service on any TCP/UDP traffic that does not carry source and/or destination IP addresses in the application data stream (ie: http, TFTP, telnet, NTP, NFS, rlogin, rsh, rcp).

Specific protocols that do embed IP address information within the payload require support of an application level gateway (ALG). NAT performs translation service on any TCP/UDP traffic that does not carry the source and destination IP addresses in the application data stream. These protocols include HTTP, TFTP, telnet, Network Time Protocol (NTP), Network File System (NFS), remote login (rlogin), remote shell (rsh) protocol, and remote copy (rcp). Specific protocols that do embed IP the address information within the payload require support of an ALG.

NAT with an ALG will translate packets from applications that do not use H.323, as long as the applications use port 1720.

Further Reading

http://goo.gl/QlRVfy
http://goo.gl/JQXgzz

Describe IPv6 network address translation

NAT64

Network Address Translation IPv6 to IPv4, or NAT64, technology facilitates communication between IPv6-only and IPv4-only hosts and networks (whether in a transit, an access, or an edge network). This solution allows both enterprises and ISPs to accelerate IPv6 adoption while simultaneously handling IPv4 address depletion. The DNS64 and NAT64 functions are completely separated, which is essential to the superiority of NAT64 over NAT-PT.

All viable translation scenarios are supported by NAT64, and therefore NAT64 is becoming the most sought translation technology.

- AFT using NAT64 technology can be achieved by either stateless or stateful means:
- Stateless NAT64, defined in RFC 6145, is a translation mechanism for algorithmically mapping IPv6 addresses to IPv4 addresses, and IPv4 addresses to IPv6 addresses.

Like NAT44, it does not maintain any bindings or session state while performing translation, and it supports both IPv6-initiated and IPv4-initiated communications.
- Stateful NAT64, defined in RFC 6146, is a stateful translation mechanism for translating IPv6 addresses to IPv4 addresses, and IPv4 addresses to IPv6 addresses. Like NAT44, it is called stateful because it creates or modifies bindings or session state while performing translation. It supports both IPv6-initiated and IPv4-initiated communications using static or manual mappings.

Further Reading

http://goo.gl/bJKpLh

NPTv6

NPTv6 is simply rewriting IPv6 prefixes. If your current IPv6 prefix is 2001:db8:cafe::/48 then using NPTv6 it would allow you to change it to 2001:db8:fea7::/48 - that is it. It is a one for one prefix rewrite - you can't overload it, have mismatching prefix allocations sizes, re-write ports or anything else. Importantly, it doesn't touch anything other than the prefix. Your network/host portion remains intact with no changes.

Further Reading

http://goo.gl/UtLSe5

Exam Essentials

- HSRP, GLBP, and VRRP are examples of First Hop Redundancy Protocols (FHRP)
- GLBP provides load balancing over multiple routers by using a single virtual IP address and multiple virtual MAC addresses. Each host is configured with the same virtual IP address, and all routers in the virtual router group forward packets
- A machine running NTP automatically chooses the machine with the lowest stratum number that it is configured to communicate with using NTP as its time source
- Stateless DHCPv6 is a combination of "stateless Address Autoconfiguration" and "Dynamic Host Configuration Protocol for IPv6" and is specified by RFC 3736
- Stateless Address Autoconfiguration (SLAAC) is one of the most convenient methods to assign Internet addresses to IPv6 nodes
- Network Address Translation (NAT) performs translation service on any TCP/UDP traffic that does not carry source and/or destination IP addresses in the application data stream (ie: http, TFTP, telnet, NTP, NFS, rlogin, rsh, rcp)

Chapter 22: Network Optimization

This chapter covers the following exam topics from Cisco's official 400-101 (v5) written exam curriculum.

- Implement and troubleshoot IP SLA (ICMP, UDP, Jitter, VoIP)
- Implement and troubleshoot object tracking (tracking object, tracking list, tracking interfaces/routes)
- Implement and troubleshoot NetFlow (v5, v9, local retrieval, export)
- Implement and troubleshoot embedded event manager (EEM policy using applet)
- Performance routing (basic load balancing, voice optimization)

Chapter 22: Network Optimization

Implement and troubleshoot IP SLA

ICMP, UDP, Jitter, VoIP

The IP SLAs ICMP jitter operation supports the following statistical measurements:

- Jitter (source-to-destination and destination-to-source)
- Latency (source-to-destination and destination-to-source)
- Round-trip time latency
- Packet loss
- Successive packet loss
- Out-of-sequence packets (source-to-destination, destination-to-source, and round-trip)
- Late packets

IP SLAs ICMP jitter uses a two ICMP timestamp messages, an ICMP Timestamp Request (Type 13) and an ICMP Timestamp Reply (Type 14), to provide jitter, packet loss, and latency. IP SLAs ICMP jitter operations differ from IP SLAs ICMP echo operations in that ICMP echo uses ICMP Echo request and reply (ping). Devices that are fully compliant with ICMP must be able to respond to the time stamp messages without requiring an IP SLA responder at the destination.

The IP Service Level Agreements (SLAs) UDP jitter operation diagnoses network suitability for real-time traffic applications such as VoIP, video over IP, or real-time conferencing.

However, the IP SLAs UDP jitter operation does more than just monitor jitter. As the UDP jitter operation includes data returned by the IP SLAs UDP operation, the UDP jitter operation can be used as a multipurpose data gathering operation. The packets that IP SLAs generate carry packet-sending and receiving sequence information, and sending and receiving time stamps from the source and the operational target.

- Based on this information, UDP jitter operations are capable of measuring the following:
- Per-direction jitter (source to destination and destination to source)
- Per-direction packet loss
- Per-direction delay (one-way delay)
- Round-trip delay (average round-trip time)

As paths for sending and receiving data may be different (asymmetric), the per-direction data allows you to more readily identify where congestion or other problems are occurring in the network. IP SLA responder, on a target device, is not required for any probes.

The UDP jitter operation functions by generating synthetic (simulated) UDP traffic. Asymmetric probes support custom-defined packet sizes per direction with which different packet sizes can be sent in request packets (from the source device to the destination device) and in response packets (from the destination device to the source device).

The IP SLAs operations function by generating synthetic (simulated) network traffic. A single IP SLAs operation (for example, IP SLAs operation 10) repeats at a given frequency for the lifetime of the operation. IP SLA requires schedule to be configured before it can be functional and out of default pending state.

Further Reading

http://goo.gl/01BUPl

Implement and troubleshoot tracking object

Tracking object, tracking list

The object tracking feature allows you to create a tracked object that multiple clients can use to modify the client behavior when a tracked object changes. Several clients (such as EEM) register their interest with the tracking process, track the same object, and take different actions when the object state changes.

Clients include the following features:
- Embedded Event Manager (EEM)
- Gateway Load Balancing Protocol (GLBP)
- Hot Standby Redundancy Protocol (HSRP)
- Virtual port channel (vPC)
- Virtual Router Redundancy Protocol (VRRP)

Further Reading

http://goo.gl/zc6vlG

Tracking different entities (e.g. interfaces, routes, IPSLA, and such)

An object track list allows you to track the combined states of multiple objects. Object track lists support the following capabilities:
- Boolean "and" function—Each object defined within the track list must be in an up state so that the track list object can become up.
- Boolean "or" function—At least one object defined within the track list must be in an up state so that the tracked object can become up.

- Threshold percentage—The percentage of up objects in the tracked list must be greater than the configured up threshold for the tracked list to be in the up state. If the percentage of down objects in the tracked list is above the configured track list down threshold, the tracked list is marked as down.
- Threshold weight—Assign a weight value to each object in the tracked list, and a weight threshold for the track list. If the combined weights of all up objects exceeds the track list weight up threshold, the track list is in an up state. If the combined weights of all the down objects exceeds the track list weight down threshold, the track list is in the down state.

track ip route command enables tracking of an IP prefix in the routing table. Entire set of attributes that can be tracked are as follows:

track object-number {interface interface-id {line-protocol | ip routing} | ip route ip-address/prefix-length {metric threshold | reachability} | list{boolean {and | or}} | {threshold {weight | percentage}}}

HSRP, VRRP and GLBP can act as client protocols to use enhanced object tracking.

Implement and troubleshoot Netflow

Netflow v5, v9

Netflow is a feature that was introduced on Cisco routers that give the ability to collect IP network traffic as it enters or exits an interface. By analyzing the data that is provided by Netflow a network administrator can determine things such as the source and destination of the traffic, class of service, and the cause of congestion. Netflow consists of three components: Flow Caching, Flow Collector, and Data Analyzer.

A network flow can be defined in many ways. Cisco standard NetFlow version 5 defines a flow as a unidirectional sequence of packets that all share the following 7 values:
1. Ingress interface (SNMP ifIndex, can change upon reload)
2. Source IP address
3. Destination IP address
4. IP protocol
5. Source port for UDP or TCP, 0 for other protocols
6. Destination port for UDP or TCP, type and code for ICMP, or 0 for other protocols
7. IP Type of Service

Table 22-1, describes various NetFlow versions and their description

Version #	Description

v1	First implementation, now obsolete, and restricted to IPv4 (without IP mask and AS Numbers).
v2	Cisco internal version, never released.
v3	Cisco internal version, never released.
v4	Cisco internal version, never released.
v5	Most common version, available (as of 2009) on many routers from different brands, but restricted to IPv4 flows.
v6	No longer supported by Cisco.
v7	Like version 5 with a source router field. Used on Cisco Catalyst switches.
v8	Several aggregation form, but only for information that is already present in version 5 records
v9	Templated-based, available on most routers. Mostly used to report flows like IPv6, MPLS, or even plain IPv4 with BGP next-hop.
v10	aka IPFIX, IETF Standardized NetFlow 9 with several extensions like Enterprise-defined fields types, and variable length fields.

The traditional show command for NetFlow is show ip cache flow also available are two forms of top talker commands. If the show ip cache flow command output shows same SrcIf (source interface) and DstIf (destination interface), that would be indicative of a routing loop.

Further Reading

http://goo.gl/In2r3j

Export (configuration only)

Expired flows are grouped into "NetFlow export" datagrams for export from the NetFlow-enabled device. NetFlow export datagrams can consist of up to 30 flow records for Version 5 or Version 9 flow export. The NetFlow functionality is configured on a per-interface basis. To configure NetFlow export capabilities, you need to specify the IP address and application port number of the Cisco NetFlow or third-party flow collector. The flow collector is a device that provides NetFlow export data filtering and aggregation capabilities.

ip flow-export destination {ip-address | hostname} udp-port

It specifies the IP address, or hostname of the NetFlow collector, and the UDP port the NetFlow collector is listening on.

Further Reading
http://goo.gl/pz8udZ

Implement and troubleshoot embedded event manager

EEM policy using applet

An EEM applet is a concise method for defining event screening criteria and the actions to be taken when that event occurs. In applet configuration mode, three types of configuration statements are supported. The event commands are used to specify the event criteria to trigger the applet to run, the action commands are used to specify an action to perform when the EEM applet is triggered, and the set command is used to set the value of an EEM applet variable. Currently only the _exit_status variable is supported for the set command when you use the sync option. Only one event configuration command is allowed within an applet configuration. When applet configuration mode is exited and no event command is present, a warning is displayed stating that no event is associated with this applet. If no event is specified, this applet is not considered registered. When no action is associated with this applet, events are still triggered but no actions are performed. Multiple action configuration commands are allowed within an applet configuration. Use the show event manager policy registered command to display a list of registered applets.

Before modifying an EEM applet, be aware that the existing applet is not replaced until you exit applet configuration mode. While you are in applet configuration mode modifying the applet, the existing applet may be executing. It is safe to modify the applet without unregistering it. When you exit applet configuration mode, the old applet is unregistered and the new version is registered.

The action configuration commands are uniquely identified using the label argument, which can be any string value. Actions are sorted in ascending alphanumeric key sequence using the label argument as the sort key, and they are run using this sequence. The Embedded Event Manager schedules and runs policies on the basis of an event specification that is contained within the policy itself. When applet configuration mode is exited, EEM examines the event and action commands that are entered and registers the applet to be run when a specified event occurs.

event manager applet applet-name

Above command registers the applet with the EEM and takes you to applet configuration mode for configuration of event criteria when there is a matching syslog message. The applet-name can be any case-sensitive alphanumeric string up to 29 characters. There are two possible actions after an event is detected by EEM, i.e. send an SNMP trap or simply reload the router.

Further Reading
http://goo.gl/0dzSXH

Identify performance routing (PfR)
PfR has three monitoring modes of operations, namely

- Active mode: uses IP SLA probes
- Passive mode: uses NetFlow
- Fast mode: uses IP SLA probes (based on FRR feature)

No explicit NetFlow or IP SLAs configuration is required; support for NetFlow and IP SLAs is enabled and configured automatically by the master controller. You can use both active and passive monitoring methods for each traffic class. The master controller uses both passive and active monitoring by default. All traffic classes are passively monitored using integrated NetFlow functions, whereas the OOP traffic classes are actively monitored using IP SLA functions.

Passive monitoring metrics include the following:
- Delay: Cisco PfR measures the average delay of TCP flows for a given prefix or traffic class. Delay is the measurement of the round-trip response time (RTT) between the transmission of a TCP synchronization message and receipt of the TCP acknowledgement.
- Packet loss: Cisco PfR measures packet loss by tracking TCP sequence numbers for each TCP flow; it tracks the highest TCP sequence number. If it receives a subsequent packet with a lower sequence number, PfR increments the packet-loss counter. Packet loss is measured in packets per million.
- Reachability: Cisco PfR measures reachability by tracking TCP synchronization messages that have been sent repeatedly without receiving a TCP acknowledgement.
- Throughput: Cisco PfR measures throughput by measuring the total number of bytes and packets for each interesting traffic class or prefix for a given interval of time.

Active monitoring metrics include the following:
- Delay: Cisco PfR measures the average delay of TCP, User Datagram Protocol (UDP), and Internet Control Message Protocol (ICMP) flows for a given traffic class or prefix.
- Reachability: Cisco PfR measures reachability by tracking TCP synchronization messages that have been sent repeatedly without a received TCP acknowledgement.

- Jitter: Cisco PfR measures jitter, or interpacket delay variance, by sending multiple packets to a target address and a specified target port number and measuring the delay interval between packets arriving at the destination.
- MOS: MOS is a standards-based method of measuring voice quality.

Further Reading

http://goo.gl/pbsG9r

Basic load balancing

Cisco PfR is essentially application routing based on network performance. It automatically detects path degradation and responds to avoid continued degradation. In many cases for a multi-homed enterprise, the traffic on an initial path is routed through another egress path that can meet the application performance requirements. This routing is different from classic routing, because classic routing looks only at reachability and does not look into the required traffic service needs, such as low loss or low delay. In addition, Cisco PfR allows a multi-homed enterprise to use all available WAN or Internet links. It can track throughput, link usage, and link cost, and automatically determine the best load balancing to optimize throughput, load, and cost-and network operators define the Cisco PfR policies that implement these adaptive routing techniques.

Cisco PfR policies can be based on the following parameters:
- WAN out-bound performance (traffic exiting from an enterprise): Delay, loss, reachability, throughput, jitter, and MOS
- WAN in-bound performance (traffic arriving into an enterprise): Delay, loss, reachability, and throughput
- WAN and Internet path parameters: Reachability, throughput, load, and link usage cost

Cisco Performance Routing consists of two distinct elements: border routers and a master controller. The border routers connect enterprises to the WAN; the master controller is a software entity supported by Cisco IOS Software on a router platform. Border routers gather traffic and path information and send this information to a master controller, which places all received information into a database. The master controller is configured with the requested service policies, so it is aware of everything that happens at the network edge and can automatically detect and take action when certain parameters are out-of-policy (OOP). Delay, jitter, and packet loss are used to determine the best exit path by the PfR engine.

Further Reading

http://goo.gl/BTI5AZ

http://goo.gl/v7Mzqf

Voice optimization

Voice packets traveling through an IP network are no different from data packets. In the plain old telephone system (POTS), voice traffic travels over circuit-switched networks with predetermined paths and each phone call is given a dedicated connection for the duration of the call. Voice traffic using POTS has no resource contention issues, but voice traffic over an IP network has to contend with factors such as delay, jitter, and packet loss, which can affect the quality of the phone call.

Delay

Delay (also referred as latency) for voice packets is defined as the delay between when the packet was sent from the source device and when it arrived at a destination device. Delay can be measured as one-way delay or round-trip delay. The largest contributor to latency is caused by network transmission delay. Round-trip delay affects the dynamics of conversation and is used in Mean Opinion Score (MOS) calculations. One-way delay is used for diagnosing network problems. A caller may notice a delay of 200 milliseconds and try to speak just as the other person is replying because of packet delay. The telephone industry standard specified in ITU-T G.114 recommends the maximum desired one-way delay be no more than 150 milliseconds. Beyond a one-way delay of 150 milliseconds, voice quality is affected. With a round-trip delay of 300 milliseconds or more, users may experience annoying talk-over effects.

Jitter

Jitter means inter-packet delay variance. When multiple packets are sent consecutively from source to destination, for example, 10 ms apart, and if the network is behaving ideally, the destination should be receiving them 10 ms apart. But if there are delays in the network (like queuing, arriving through alternate routes, and so on) the arrival delay between packets might be greater than or less than 10 ms. Using this example, a positive jitter value indicates that the packets arrived more than 10 ms apart. If the packets arrive 12 ms apart, then positive jitter is 2 ms; if the packets arrive 8 ms apart, then negative jitter is 2 ms. For delay-sensitive networks like VoIP, positive jitter values are undesirable, and a jitter value of 0 is ideal.

Packet Loss

Packet loss can occur due an interface failing, a packet being routed to the wrong destination, or congestion in the network. Packet loss for voice traffic leads to the degradation of service in which a caller hears the voice sound with breaks. Although average packet loss is low, voice quality may be affected by a short series of lost packets.

Mean Opinion Score (MOS)

With all the factors affecting voice quality, many people ask how voice quality can be measured. Standards bodies like the ITU have derived two important recommendations: P.800 (MOS) and P.861 (Perceptual Speech Quality Measurement [PSQM]). P.800 is concerned with defining a method to derive a Mean Opinion Score of voice quality. MOS scores range between 1 representing the worst voice quality, and 5 representing the best voice quality. A MOS of 4 is considered "toll-quality" voice.

PfR voice traffic optimization provides support for outbound optimization of voice traffic on the basis of the voice performance metrics, delay, packet loss, jitter, and MOS. Delay, packet loss, jitter and MOS are important quantitative quality metrics for voice traffic, and these voice metrics are measured using PfR active probes. The IP SLA jitter probe is integrated with PfR to measure jitter (source to destination) and the MOS score in addition to measuring delay and packet loss. The jitter probe requires a responder on the remote side just like the UDP Echo probe. Integration of the IP SLA jitter probe type in PfR enhances the ability of PfR to optimize voice traffic. PfR policies can be configured to set the threshold and priority values for the voice performance metrics: delay, packet loss, jitter, and MOS.

Configuring a PfR policy to measure jitter involves configuring only the threshold value and not relative changes (used by other PfR features) because for voice traffic, relative jitter changes have no meaning. For example, jitter changes from 5 milliseconds to 25 milliseconds are just as bad in terms of voice quality as jitter changes from 15 milliseconds to 25 milliseconds. If the short-term average (measuring the last 5 probes) jitter is higher than the jitter threshold, the prefix is considered out-of-policy due to jitter. PfR then probes all exits, and the exit with the least jitter is selected as the best exit.

MOS policy works in a different way. There is no meaning to average MOS values, but there is meaning to the number of times that the MOS value is below the MOS threshold. For example, if the MOS threshold is set to 3.85 and if 3 out of 10 MOS measurements are below the 3.85 MOS threshold, the MOS-low-count is 30 percent. In the output of the show commands the field, ActPMOS, shows the number of actively monitored MOS packets with a percentage below threshold. If some of the MOS measurements are only slightly below the threshold, with percentage rounding, an ActPMOS value of zero may be displayed. When PfR runs a policy configured to measure MOS, both the MOS threshold value and the MOS-low-count percentage are considered. A prefix is considered out-of-policy if the short term (average over the last 5 probes) MOS-low-count percentage is greater than the configured MOS-low-count percentage. PfR then probes all exits, and the exit with the highest MOS value is selected as the best exit.

Further Reading

http://goo.gl/a1Kv2A

Exam Essentials

- The object tracking feature allows you to create a tracked object that multiple clients can use to modify the client behavior when a tracked object changes. Several clients (such as EEM) register their interest with the tracking process, track the same object, and take different actions when the object state changes
- track ip route command enables tracking of an IP prefix in the routing table
- NetFlow v9 is template based, available on most routers. Mostly used to report flows like IPv6, MPLS, or even plain IPv4 with BGP next-hop
- The traditional show command for NetFlow is show ip cache flow also available are two forms of top talker commands. If this command output shows same SrcIf (source interface) and DstIf (destination interface), that would be indicative of a routing loop
- An EEM applet is a concise method for defining event screening criteria and the actions to be taken when that event occurs
- PfR has three monitoring modes of operations, namely
    - Active mode: uses IP SLA probes
    - Passive mode: uses NetFlow
    - Fast mode: uses IP SLA probes (based on FRR feature)
- Delay, jitter, and packet loss are used to determine the best exit path by the PfR engine
- Event register keyword and body are must have components of an EEM policy
- If no primary PfR group links are available, the traffic classes are routed through the best link from the fallback group
- NetFlow provides network resource utilization accounting
- PfR provides direct route control over routes learned via static, BGP and EIGRP protoco

CPSIA information can be obtained at www.ICGtesting.com
Printed in the USA
LVOW10s0519121215
466395LV00030B/1516/P